UFO PROPHECY

VISIONS FROM THE TOWN HAUNTED BY FLYING SAUCERS

50TH ANNIVERSARY COLLECTORS EDITION

ALL NEW MATERIAL!

Additional Contributions By:
Janina Shuttlewood
Kevin Goodman
Steve Dewey
Steve Wills
Timothy Green Beckley
Sean Casteel
Tim R. Swartz

Arthur Shuttlewood

UFO PROPHECY

VISIONS FROM THE TOWN HAUNTED

BY FLYING SAUCERS

50TH ANNIVERSARY COLLECTORS EDITION

ALL NEW MATERIAL

Arthur Shuttlewood

With Additional Material By Janina Shuttlewood, Kevin Goodman, Steve Dewey, Timothy Green Beckley, Sean Casteel, Tim R. Swartz

INNER LIGHT/GLOBAL COMMUNICATIONS

UFO PROPHECY - VISIONS FROM THE TOWN HAUNTED BY FLYING SAUCERS

50TH ANNIVERSARY COLLECTORS EDITION

By Arthur Shuttlewood

With Additional Material By Janina Shuttlewood, Kevin Goodman, Steve Dewey, Timothy Green Beckley, Sean Casteel, Tim R. Swartz

Copyright © 2016 - Timothy Green Beckley DBA Inner Light/ Global Communications,

All Rights Reserved

Nonfiction - Printed in the United States of America

No part of this book may be reproduced, stored in retrieval system or transmitted in any form or by any means, electronic, mechanical, photocopying, recording, without express permission of the publisher.

Timothy Green Beckley: Editorial Director, Carol Rodriguez: Publishers Assistant,

Editor and Layout: Tim R. Swartz, Sean Casteel: Associate Editor,

William Kern: Editorial Assistant

For free catalog write:

Global Communications

P.O. Box 753

New Brunswick, NJ 08903

Free Subscription to Conspiracy Journal E-Mail Newsletter:

www.conspiracyjournal.com

Email: mrufo8@hotmail.com

UFO PROPHECY

CONTENTS

Arthur Shuttlewood 7

Arthur Shuttlewood and the Thing 11

Investigating the Warminster "Thing" And The Beat Goes On!..........15

The House of Lords UFO Group, Warminster's Thing, and the Loch Ness Monster Connection 19

How a Series of UFO Encounters Changed the Life of Radio DJ Bryce Bond 37

The Sound and Fury of The Thing 45

UFO Prophecy By Arthur Shuttlewood 56

UFO PROPHECY

Above: UFO over Warminster rooftop.

Below: Arthur Shuttlewood with Astronomer Sir Patrick Moore looking for UFOs above Chapel Hill.

UFO PROPHECY

Arthur Shuttlewood

By Kevin Goodman and Steve Dewey

IN the 1960s, Warminster, in Wiltshire, became a hot-spot for ufologists. Night after night, UFOs were seen gamboling in the local skies. The phenomena around Warminster, known locally as the Thing, had begun late in 1964 as unexplained sounds, but by mid-1965 had given way to classic Lights-in-the-Sky. Warminster quickly attracted big-hitters from the ufological fraternity, such as Gordon Creighton and John Cleary-Baker. But the one man at the centre of it all was local journalist, Arthur Shuttlewood.

Shuttlewood was born in Chelmsford, Essex, in 1920, and died in Warminster in 1996. He had moved to Warminster in 1940 and worked as a reporter, first for the Wiltshire Times, then for The Warminster Journal, from the early 1950s. By the time the Thing started flying around Warminster, Shuttlewood was 44, and had been writing for the Journal for many years. He is still, as Bob Rickard noted, remembered with respect and affection. [1]

Before becoming a journalist, Shuttlewood had been a member of the Grenadier Guards and the Air Ministry Constabulary, and had been a councilor on Warminster Urban District Council. While Shuttlewood might be remembered at the Journal with respect, at least one journalist I have talked to, who knew Shuttlewood when he worked at the Wiltshire Times - Shuttlewood's first job as a journalist - remembers that Shuttlewood even then embroidered his reports of local events for dramatic effect.

Shuttlewood always proclaimed his hard-headedness and cynicism, stating "I am not easily fooled. I dare not be. I have built my reputation as a journalist on the bedrock of integrity."[2] However, once he had been converted to a belief in UFOs as evidence of extraterrestrials, he quite consciously proselytized this belief. By the time of his first book, **The Warminster Mystery**, he obviously believes that the Things are alien spacecraft. Given that his position as a journalist gave him access to most of the witnesses of the Thing, he became the primary source of information about the Thing. Shuttlewood was also the first to hear any strange stories. The fact that so many strange occurrences were being reported in Warminster would have made sure of its place in ufological history. It is a moot point whether Shuttlewood's own conversion to the cause fanned the flames, yet it is a theme returned to again and again in UFO books that discuss the Warminster phenomenon. For example, **The UFO Encyclopedia** notes that "for around a decade [Warminster] was to remain the British centre of Ufology, largely due to the diligent efforts of a local devotee, Arthur Shuttlewood."[3] There is no doubt that, as he became a skywatcher himself, he began to generate stories. However, it also cannot be forgotten that, for many months, Shuttlewood was just a reporter of the phenomenon.

That the phenomenon became centered on one man can be seen from books and interviews of the period. When UFO investigators or reporters came to Warminster, the person to whom they were inevitably directed was Arthur Shuttlewood. Shuttlewood's charm won over many journalists, and even skeptical ufologists such as John Rimmer of Magonia. Everybody who met Shuttlewood, it seems, was struck by his sincerity, dedication and rustic charm. These simple virtues, along with his intimate knowledge of, and contact with, the Thing and its pilots, gave him a charisma that appealed to many ufologists. However, even in the 1960s, when interest in the Thing first peaked, skeptics began to suspect that Shuttlewood blurred the boundary between reality and fiction. The Merseyside UFO Research Group (MUFORG), in particular, were deeply skeptical of Warminster's almost nightly displays of UFO activity. Nonetheless, John Rimmer thought it unlikely that Shuttlewood deliberately created the Thing phenomenon, nor did he believe that Shuttlewood deliberately exaggerated the sightings he reported in his books. For Rimmer, Shuttlewood was simply a skilled reporter, doing what came naturally.

However, Shuttlewood did deliberately exaggerate his stories. Shuttlewood's first book, **The Warminster Mystery**, revisits many of the stories first reported in the *Warminster Journal*. The stories related in the Journal are nowhere near as hysterical as their later retellings in Shuttlewood's book. Shuttlewood was undoubtedly reworking his material to make it more dramatic, more appealing to ufologists – it is deliberately exaggerated. The stories in his books are also related uncritically, as are the theories and explanations that he received from correspondents. Even as late as 1982 Shuttlewood was still as uncritical as ever. Ian Mrzyglod, in the magazine *The Probe Report*, discusses photographs of a UFO that had been described by Shuttlewood, in the magazine *Magic Saucer*, as "perfect UFO discs, definite and beyond doubt."

Mrzyglod had the good sense to ask Shuttlewood for a copy of these photographs. When he received the prints, Mrzyglod immediately recognized the "UFOs" as flaws in the development process. Shuttlewood was shown the prints, and Mrzyglod was surprised to find that this was the first time Shuttlewood had seen them – Shuttlewood's comments to *Magic Saucer* had been made without seeing the prints. Despite this, he still asked Mrzyglod for enlargements to be made, as Shuttlewood hoped to interest some color magazines or the *Daily Mirror* in the photographs. The enlargements were duly made, which only confirmed that the 'UFOs' had been development flaws. Shuttlewood himself reluctantly agreed that this was indeed the case; the Daily Mirror had returned Shuttlewood's copies of the enlargements, also agreeing with Mrzyglod's verdict.

Eventually, Shuttlewood became a guru for the ufological fraternity that frequented Warminster; not only because of his charisma, but also through his position as the favored intermediary, and his increasing comfort in the language of the mystic and the visionary. Did Shuttlewood become a guru by simply being the right man, in the right place, at the right time? Partly. While there is no doubt that Shuttlewood played only a small part in the genesis of the Thing - and here, the part of ufologists such as Gordon Creighton should be recognized - we must also accept that his central position in the Warminster phenomenon was aided by his charisma, his own beliefs, and his willful exaggerations.

[1] Bob Rickard, obituary in Fortean Times Number 96, March 1997, p. 42.

[2] Arthur Shuttlewood, Warnings From Flying Friends, p. 38.

[3] John Spencer, The UFO Encyclopaedia

UFO PROPHECY

ARTHUR SHUTTLEWOOD AND THE THING
A Brief Retrospect By His Granddaughter – Janina Shuttlewood

IN 2015, a small Wilshire market town in the UK celebrated events which occurred more than fifty years ago now. A series of strange, unexplainable, sounds first barraged the town and culminated in an astonishing UFO flap which reached fever pitch around the August bank holiday in 1965, when the city council of Warminster, England organized an extraordinary meeting to allay fears that the town wasn't actually being invaded by flying saucers.

The story of Warminster's Thing had grown by leaps and bounds, and news of its arrival had spread throughout Europe and eventually around the world.

Although no firm conclusions or advice was offered to the good townspeople of Warminster, the phenomena continued unabated with sightings being made all the way through to the very end of the 1970s…and there are still some reported to this day!

One man who took an early interest into the goings on in the town was local news reporter Arthur Shuttlewood who also happened to be my grandfather.

He soon picked up on the strange tales of the odd audible anomalies and started reporting on them in the pages of the town's newspaper, *The Warminster Journal*.

Many months passed with reports of the peculiar noise still appearing in the press – stories of roof tiles being lifted then slammed back into place. And of an unknown force that was said to have killed birds dead in flight. The sound also rendered pets sick. It was said to be a dreadfully awful noise!

Then the sound became ambiguous no longer, as now a visible manifestation could be attached to the mystery as elliptical, sphere or cigar-shaped objects hung about in the sky around the town.

UFO PROPHECY

My grandfather soon became a firm believer in The Thing as it became known following his own sightings from his window in the Portway region of the municipality.

My grandfather soon became an avid skywatcher. He set up his own team of observers and headed up the hills which surrounded the town to watch for UFOs on a regular basis. Cradle and Starr Hill became the most popular points to watch the sky for unexplained phenomena.

Numerous sightings were made by the group and by many UFO enthusiasts from around the country and the world. They flocked to join Arthur to learn about past events and to keep their eyes open for anything odd streaking across the heavens. Sometimes as many as fifty or sixty people gathered at a time. They were seldom disappointed.

My grandfather had become an unofficial ambassador for all things UFOlogical in Warminster and had now started writing books on the subject. In 1968 he saw his first work published. *The Warminster Mystery* was well received and is now considered a classic within its genre.

He went on to write another five titles on the subject. One of the books, **Warning From Flying Friends** was published eventually in the United States as **UFO Prophecy** by Timothy Green Beckley, who is commemorating the half century of UFO activity that has taken place near Stonehenge with an updated version of the text. I am told the original was well received.

Although on rereading many of these UFO books today, they seem very much "of their day," they still give a unique insight on the thought process on the UFO phenomena viewed at the time.

I was asked last year by Steve Wills, a local UFO researcher who lives in the town, if I and other members of the family would present an award in my grandfather's name at the 50th Anniversary Warminster UFO Conference. We made the presentation to Dot Street and Brenda Butler, who were the first to be be given "The Arthur Shuttlewood Award For Outstanding Services To UFOlogy," for their trailblazing initial investigation into the events of late 1980 that took place in Rendlesham Forest.

I do believe that this was a fitting tribute to my grandfather who would have been honored to be remembered for his UFO interest and writings fifty years on.

Janina Shuttlewood - May 2016

Above: Janina Shuttlewood

Below: Arthur Shuttlewood relaxing after a busy evening of skywatching.
Photo courtesy John Hanson.

UFO PROPHECY

INVESTIGATING THE WARMINSTER "THING" AND THE BEAT GOES ON!

RECENTLY my co-host Tim Swartz and I were pleased to have British UFO investigator Steve Wills on our podcast, *Exploring The Bizarre,* to discuss the continuing UFO saga regarding the most prolonged UFO wave in European UFOlogical history. And while the sightings have certainly died down from their peak in the 1960s and 70s, these sleek, fast moving objects do pop up from time to time and are even recorded digitally for the world wide web to see, as witness the four pictures of UFOs over Warminster that were just added to Steve Willis' Facebook page.

Wills reminded us that it all began as best as can be ascertained on Christmas day 1964, when Mrs. Mildred Head was woken at her home at 1:25AM. "Our ceiling," she reported "came alive with strange sounds that lashed at our roof." The sounds began as if twigs or leaves were being drawn across her roof, and then changed to a noise she described as being like giant hailstones. Plucking up courage, she got out of bed and looked out of the window, where the night was dry and clear. Mrs. Head also noted a strange humming sound, which grew louder and then faded away, except for "a faint whisper." Later that day on the way to church a woman was thrown to the ground as the sound like a 1000 bees filled the air. The Warminster "Thing" was thus born, and for over a period of more than a decade, a multitude of the curious and the deadly serious gathered from across Europe and the world in this town of 10,000 in the British countryside, not far from Stonehenge, to report incredible objects zipping across and hovering in the sky. The first crop circles appeared here. Several individuals reported missing time. And contacts and abductions were said to be going forth on a regular basis. Clocks and watches owned and worn by people in the town were said to have stopped at the same time on at least one occasion

Steve Wills is a UFO researcher and investigator from Warminster whose interest in the town's unusual aerial activity dates back to the early eighties, developing after reading his father's collection of UFO magazines. His dad also had a number of UFO books which included *The Warminster Mystery* by Arthur Shuttlewood, a book that detailed astonishing UFO sighting accounts in Steve's own home town.

UFO PROPHECY

Last year saw the 50 year anniversary of the first appearance of The Thing in and around Warminster. Steve along with 1970s skywatchers Colin Rees and Kevin Goodman put on a very well received conference rekindling interest in the UFOlogical history of the town. Steve told us on *Exploring The Bizarre* that while the main body of witnesses are passing on, there were several in attendance who remembered the odd activity overhead.

Indeed, the once frenzied UFO activity has lessened; however, our special on air guest illuminated our listeners that there are still sightings being reported. As well, he also informed them about journalist Arthur Shuttlewood's involvement in the mystery and how the town actually has its own X-files to this very day.

Little known is the fact that I had a sighting in Warminster in the early 1980s and actually attempted to communicate with an unknown object in the sky over the Warminster countryside. I described this incident in detail on the same program with Steve Wills.

Currently, Wills is helping as a contributor on a forthcoming special edition of *Haunted Skies*, an acclaimed series of UFO books written by retired police officer John Hanson and his partner Dawn Holloway.

Steve remains very active in the field and promises to continue his research and writing, and to keep everyone informed on any further UFO activity in Warminster.

Maybe "They" will return in mass soon, and this time we might be more equipped to deal with their arrival!

Tim Beckley
May, 2016

Steve Wills on Facebook

https://www.facebook.com/steve.wills.14?fref=ts

Attack On Warminster – The Thing Redux On YouTube

https://www.youtube.com/watch?v=cTvyfoPO-lo

Warminster Community on Facebook

https://www.facebook.com/UFO-Warminster-174632342638283/?fref=ts

Kevin Goodman – UFO Conference Organizer

https://www.facebook.com/kevin.goodman.96?fref=ts

Above: Steve Wills is more than comfortable roaming around Stonehenge not far from the UFO activity in Warminster.

Below: Look up into the sky -- its a bird, its a plane it's the Thing in its most recent UFO "attack."

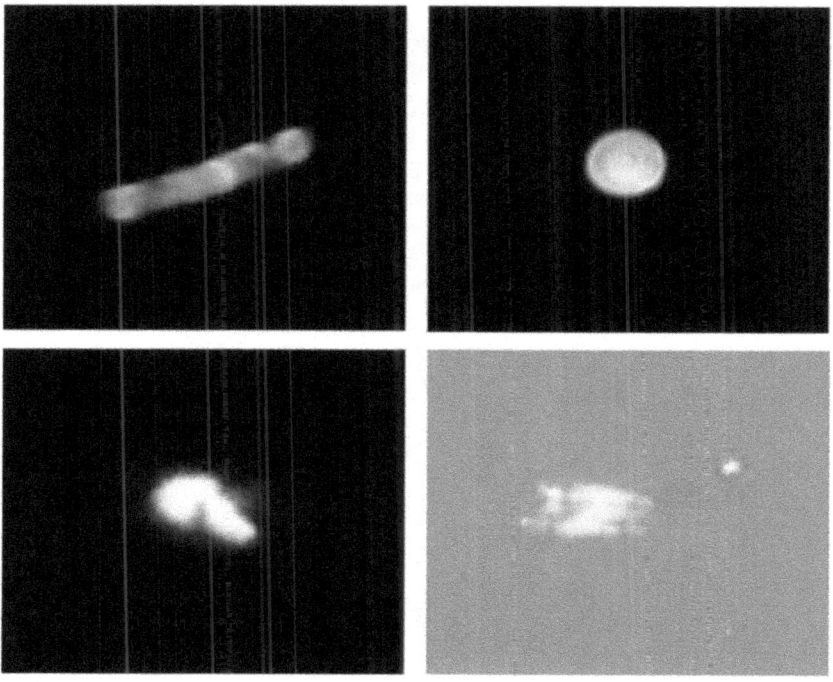

UFO PROPHECY

THE HOUSE OF LORDS UFO GROUP, WARMINSTER'S THING, AND THE LOCH NESS CONNECTION

THE INCREDIBLE BRITISH SOJOURN OF TIMOTHY GREEN BECKLEY

IT was in 1981 that I traveled to the UK at the request of my good friend, the late Earl of Clancarty, Brinsley Le Poer Trench, who had arranged for me to speak at the House of Lords in front of a special group organized to get to the bottom of the UFO mystery and to press for "full disclosure," long before the phrase was part of UFO terminology. The group, consisting of roughly one hundred members of both houses of Parliament, included Lord Hill Norton, the former Defense Minister who had taken a combative interest in the subject of our unidentified visitors. Norton and I had a brief chat about Nikola Tesla, whom the Ret. Admiral of the British fleet held dear to his heart because of the possibility of alternative energy sources being sparked by other-worldly life forms.

REALITY OF THE BEASTS

I will, indeed, never forget my trip to the British Isles to speak before members of the House of Lords nor my subsequent journey throughout the countryside where I had an exciting UFO experience just a stone's throw from the legendary monolith Stonehenge.

It's been approximately three decades, and my friend who invited me, Brinsley Le Poer Trench, has removed himself from his mortal coil. As many will recognize, Brinsley was the author of such books as **The Sky People**, about the visitation by extraterrestrials to our planet in ancient times (presumably from Mars). His well-written thesis was widely read and discussed before Eric Von Daniken's popular **Chariots of the Gods?** was published. Brinsley — aka the Earl – was, as mentioned, an actual hereditary member of the House of Lords who had championed the reality of the UFO phenomenon for years and attempted to get the Crown and the MOD to release their massive files on the subject. This was long before the MOD did eventually open their archives on aerial phenomenon some thirty or more years later.

From time to time, members of the House of Lords had heatedly debated the legitimacy of the subject. Brinsley had invited various researchers from all over the world to help him get his point across that UFOs were a subject of "high concern." Those who had previously spoken before the group included the UK's own Timothy Good, Hungarian-born researcher Colman Von Kevicky, and Italy's Roberto Pinotti. The Earl had requested that I travel "across the pond" to reveal what I "knew" about a subject that has fascinated so many for so many years.

Though our "appeal" was not made in front of the full Lord's body, I did get a chance to pitch my findings before members of both the House of Lords and the House of Commons who more or less took Brinsley's "side," though there were admittedly some skeptical members among the rank-and-file of this group, unofficial as it was. I must say I was prepared to take my lumps from those who thought Brinsley and I were promoting the "silly season" too early in the year.

Before delivering my presentation, Brinsley had me join with members of the House of Lords. As we all marched together into the main hall, the Lords began taking their seats on the floor below while I was ushered to a seat in the main gallery. It was, to say the least, an exciting day in my career as an author and journalist. Looking around, I couldn't help but be impressed. The ornamentation on the banisters, the stairwells and the chambers were tremendous. I realized that there was centuries of history before me.

One of the things I immediately noticed was the number of wooden carvings of unicorns and dragons to be found above the entranceway and along the many railings. It seems odd, I thought at the time, that such mythical creatures would have found a home among such stately gentlemen, many of whom did not even have a taste for UFOs, much less creatures who supposedly only live in our fantasies and our dreams.

Soon I was to find out I was entirely wrong! In fact, as I traveled throughout England, I discovered figures of unicorns and dragons carved on the sides of churches and old architectural structures....as if they had actually existed at one time or another and were ready to fly off their perches again.

Some fourteen hundred years ago, Saint Columba supposedly saw a fearsome dragon in Loch Ness. There were similar stories throughout the sixteenth and seventeenth centuries that seem to be more than "fairy tales."

While in the U.K. I was introduced to the work of the late F.W. Holiday, a researcher who made a lifelong career out of attempting to prove that dragon-like creatures existed in

UFO PROPHECY

Despite the fact that he has been deceased for sometime, Brinsley Le Poer Trench's works still remain popular. Above is a recent U.S. expanded edition of his Sky People book which was the first popular work on Ancient Astronauts.

Trench was the 8th Earl of Clancarty. Here he in his London apartment with his huge UFO collection in his 4th floor library.

the various Scottish and Irish lakes, and that carvings of "flying discs" were often directly associated with such dragons and serpents.

And as it turns out, other researchers have put their reputation on the line that dragons and unicorns not only may have once walked the earth, but there is still a chance that they could be wandering around very much unabated even to this very day.

But more on that after a cup of tea perhaps – complete with saucer of course!

TIME DISTORTION AND STOPPED WATCHES

Most titillating to me was journalist Arthur Shuttlewood's conviction that the perplexing timepiece-stopping phenomena, rampant in England at the time, was a direct result of UFO activity (maybe with a little help from Uri Geller who was appearing on the telly during that same period with his watch starting commands). Without a doubt this is one of the strangest UFO-related effects we must contend with in our dealing with the Warminster events. On the night of September 9, 1969, a dozen residents of Potten End (a town suburb) had the singular and disturbing experience of having their timepieces remain motionless for about an hour. All the stories seem to coincide, although there was no direct relationship between the witnesses, nor did they know of anyone outside their own dwelling having the same experience.

One of those who found himself faced with such a situation was Norman Gilbert, an engineer who said, "I set my watch as usual and placed it on the nightstand before retiring. Upon awakening the next morning and seeing that it was still early, I dozed again, thinking I still had yet an hour more of sleep coming to me before getting ready for work. Arriving at my job, at what I thought was 7:00 AM; I was jokingly browbeaten by my fellow employees for being late." Gilbert then discovered that his watch was an hour slow.

Similarly, Mr. E.W. Rayment, a Potten End builder, had the unusual experience of having both his watch and bedside clock lose one hour on the same night. Another one of those who had the puzzling experience was Mr. John Booth of Dunbar Cottage. He described how his wife Kathleen's watch had stopped altogether on that same Saturday night. "We fiddled about with it for around an hour trying to get it to go again, but without success."

The following morning, Booth observed that the watch had started to work again without anyone touching it, and his wife has had no trouble with it since. Each watch-stopping individual could offer no explanation why watches stopped on Saturday night and precisely at 8:00 PM. They were thoroughly convinced that it was not due to lack of winding.

Above: Intuitive artist Carol Ann Rodriguez gives her impression of a gigantic "cross-like" object said to have been seen on several occasions over Cradle Hill.

Below: Approaching UFO observation point. Photo by Steve Wills

UFO PROPHECY

A spokesman for the Science Research Council based at the Ministry of Defense, Navy Department's observatory at Hurstmonceux, near Eastbourne, said: "Nothing like this has ever been reported before."

Furthermore, hometown journalist turned UFO investigator Shuttlewood was told that at the instant the watches and clocks stopped working, a number of Berkhamsted people heard "odd humming sounds" and saw a peculiar shape in the sky – which experts determined to be an extraterrestrial ship.

Shuttlewood himself was involved in an episode where he had a 45-minute time disorientation while atop Cradle Hill watching a pair of UFOs through binoculars. The incident, which transpired in November of 1970, had Shuttlewood – who described in detail his multitude of experiences with flying saucers over this tiny English town in the Summer Issue of *Saga's UFO Report* – observing celestial multi-hued lights that resembled a string of burning beads. Shuttlewood immediately noted the time on the luminous hands of his wrist watch, marking down the time of the sighting as 11:31 PM. At this point he attempted to signal one of the UFOs, which had descended to a point approximately 30 feet from where he stood. As the beam of this flash pierced the solemn darkness, he was able to distinguish the metallic gray outline of the ship's hull, straddled on top by a spherical dome.

"At this point, something odd and unworldly happened to me," Shuttlewood recalled. "To be honest, I cannot recall with any degree of clarity what transpired next. In short, I cannot remember if the object disappeared or if it continued to hover, or if indeed I walked away from Cradle Hill at all. What I do know is that an awful numbing sensation affected my limbs. I shut my dazzled eyes and felt desperately tired all of a sudden. The next thing I knew – I don't know how I got there – I was standing by a wooden fence at the bottom of Cradle Hill. Glancing at my watch, I was horror-struck. The time was now 12:35 AM. Despite the fact that it was a deadly-cold night and I was well wrapped against the bitter winter chill, my body was bathed in sweat. Moreover, tears were cascading down my face, and I could taste the salt in my mouth."

Shuttlewood says that he was upset because "my son was to have picked me up in my car at midnight at a nearby rendezvous point." Reaching the waiting auto, Shuttlewood apologized for being 40 minutes late. The editor's son, looking at his watch, remarked "You're not late, you're bang on time."

At this point, Shuttlewood realized that he had been the pawn of a bizarre time-distortion game. Checking his timepiece once again, he discovered that time had once more jostled, this time backward. It was now 12:07!

UFO PROPHECY

As odd as it may seem, scientific research has actually been conducted at laboratories throughout the world to penetrate the mystery of the perplexing time distortion. They have used as their "guinea pig" a direct link to the sky intelligences by the name of Uri Geller. This amazing Israeli-born psychic has astounded the world by being able to bend metal and teleport objects. Among his other skills is the uncanny gift of manipulating the hands of a wristwatch backward and forward. Geller boldly states that he is the earthly representative of extraterrestrials aboard spaceships hovering in our atmosphere.

Why is this manipulation of time taking place? Geller says that the forces behind these effects are trying to warn the world about some impending catastrophe, and since they operate on another vibrational level and from another dimension, this is the only means they have at their disposal.

Explaining further, Geller related that, to the UFOnauts, time is NOT proportioned the same as it is here. In other words, where they exist – in another time-space continuum – the passing of time is in no way related to what it is here on Earth. What the "moment" is to us might be construed as an hour to them. But back to the most intriguing Warminister UFO quandary and my own whacky involvement that put me knee deep in the middle of this perplexing puzzle.

COMMUNICATING WITH THE "SPACE BROTHERS"

I arrived in Warminster and had lunch at one of the best Indian restaurants I have ever set foot in – and believe me I have eaten in hundreds all over the world. Seated around the table were my buddy Arthur and his sky-watch companion, a retired RAF pilot named Bob Strong. While we munched on a nan appetizer, Strong showed me several scrapbooks filled with literally dozens of photos showing UFO craft of all shapes and sizes, from "railroad cars," to huge, bat-like objects. Unfortunately, Strong sadly admitted that many of his best pictures had gone "missing" as they had been borrowed by the curious who wanted to copy them but had never returned them as they promised to do. Thus was lost an important part of UFO history that can never be replaced, as well as essential evidence proving the Warminster mystery was not a hoax or based upon faulty eyesight or mushroom inducing hallucinations.

That night, I journeyed with my newfound compatriots to Cradle Hill, a few miles from the center of town, where we gathered with a couple from Scotland who had come on their own having read about the town's ethereal intruders. They did so without knowing that they would soon be joined by the two gentlemen who had literally put Warminster's Thing on the landscape, and a traveling "thrill seeker" from across the pond.

UFO PROPHECY

At first we saw nothing unusual but were fascinated by several meteors streaking across our line of vision. All that was to change around 10 PM, when we spotted something unusual fairly high up that seemed to just be hovering or loitering about. To what intended purpose, if any, we had no way of knowing. Cueing us that this was no twinkling star or planet, Shuttlewood went to the trunk of his car and retrieved his trusty high powered flashlight. He told us he had used this same heavy-duty torch upon numerous occasions to signal to what he assured us were his Space Brother friends. Arthur then pointed it at the object in the sky and flashed a beam of light several times in its direction. He then offered the flashlight to me, and I also flashed it at the object. None of us knew ship-to-shore or any kind of Morse code, so we just blinked the light on and off like we were playing a game of "close encounters."

The reaction was unexpected and tremendously positive. Every time we blinked at it, the UFO would appear to sort of swing back and forth, like a pendulum. It seemed to be looking down on us. Maybe it picked up our thoughts telepathically. I was told to keep a positive mind because that's what the Ultra-Terrestrials seemed to respond to the most.

Our sky-watch went on for another 20 minutes or so, and then it started to rain and clouds obscured our view. When we saw nothing more, we retired for the evening.

Had I made contact with a UFO over Warminister? To this day I still wonder. I will never know for sure, but it did seem as if the object was under intelligent control and was responding to our request to prove it was not just an ordinary object in the heavens. Another strange thing: We took several photos of Cradle Hill that night. When developed, one of them showed a strange phenomenon behind two of the witnesses — streaks or bolts of light which were not visible to the naked eye at the time, and for which I am mostly certain there is no "legitimate" explanation. There were no streetlamps or houses with porch lights nearby . . . only a vast open field where many a strange incident had taken place over a timeframe of several decades and which still ignited a fire in the hearts and minds of many seeking the truth about the UFOs seen over this locale.

Arthur Shuttlewood waxed nostalgic about the strange happenings in the town he called home.

"All these stories," he said, "no matter how bizarre they sound, are easily verifiable. All observers, whose names are on file, will attest to what has been reported here. Over a nine-year period I have faithfully recorded in over 35 notebooks each event I have personally witnessed or been told about. Admittedly, many of the incidents which have occurred around Warminster are incredible to our way of thinking, but we must keep in mind that they represent a truly alien pattern of behavior.

Above: The Dragon and the Disc by F.W. Holiday.

Below: Artist Tom Goff depicts a possible connection between UFO and the monster associated with Scotland's Loch Ness.

UFO PROPHECY

"As for the reasoning behind this mass 'invasion' of Warminster," he continued, "I feel strongly that Salisbury Plain is a 'window' to another dimension through which a superior race of beings can pass easily to our realm. From the ancient structures which still remain intact it is possible to assume that this location has, for the longest period of time, been of immense importance to whoever pilots flying saucers."

For historical purposes, we provide an audio link to a public interview made by Arthur Shuttlewood -- the man who put Warminster "on the map," – at the time of all the UFO hoopla in the area.

https://www.box.com/shared/4hki2zkhnk#/s/4hki2zkhnk/1/23529576/248084286/1

THE DRAGON AND DISCS OF THE LOCH

"I was going through the woods near Loch Ness, when I saw this cigar-shaped object for two or three minutes just above the trees. It had a rim going around it. It wasn't very big – perhaps the size of a large table. It was in daytime in March. I was alone working as an excavator. It landed about 50 yards away. I never saw it take off. Since I was in the forest, there were trees blocking my view, and I couldn't see it while it was on the ground."

A typical UFO sighting? Perhaps, but what makes it so unusual is the fact that it is one of a considerable number of reports which have come from the Scottish Highlands, all within a short distance of the world famous Loch Ness, home of the legendary water creature.

At first there wouldn't seem to be any connection between UFOs and the famed long-necked serpent. However, evidence has recently emerged that the two anomalies might indeed be associated in some peculiar paranormal way.

On an early 1980s expedition to Iverness, Scotland, I found the locals willing to talk about both riddles, be it in the sky or in amidst the murky waves.

"People around these parts may joke about the monster to outsiders, but they take the subject quite seriously," noted the knowledgeable Anthony Harmsworth, Curator of the Loch Ness Monster Exhibition located in Drumnadrochit, a tiny community nestled on the banks of Loch Ness. Tony Harmsworth has been tracking down stories of the 30-foot long creature for many years. He is convinced beyond a shadow of a doubt that something "unusual" DOES live in the loch.

As we sipped a cup of coffee in an out-of-the-way corner of the exhibition, Tony revealed that just before my visit there were at least four authentic sightings of the monster. "Currently (circa 1981), there is a group of British and American scientists stationed around the loch attempting to verify the presence of the monster with highly sophisticated sonar equipment. Targets have been picked up previously, and they are attempting to do a more detailed analysis of what the targets are doing."

And what does the loch's monster look like? According to Tony, "The most common description is of a creature with a large hump that is longer than it is high. Occasionally, people see a long neck that doesn't seem to have any particular shape or head on the end of it. The neck seems to end like a worm, although I don't hold to any theories that suggest that the animals (yes, there is more than one monster, he believes) might be an overgrown worm."

As I quickly discovered, according to local folklore, the Loch Ness Monster has been around for centuries.

"Fourteen hundred years ago, Saint Columba supposedly saw a fearsome beast in the loch. There were similar stories throughout the sixteenth and seventeenth centuries. Modern sightings began in 1933, when detailed records started to be kept," the loch's then curator revealed to me. He pointed out that many reliable individuals have seen the monster, including the former editor of the Inverness newspaper and several monks from an abbey situated right on the loch. The monster has been photographed and analyzed in still pictures as well as in motion picture films, that strongly suggest that something beyond the realm of the norm does reside in Loch Ness.

In fact, with the exception of UFOs, probably more has been written about the Loch Ness Monster than any other "offbeat" subject. Hundreds of magazine articles have been written. TV specials have been filmed, and *Variety* (the show business trade paper) once ran a full-page ad announcing a feature length motion picture on the subject, produced by none other than the late David Frost. It would seem that just about every man, woman and child over the age of six has at one time either read or heard about this remarkable scientific curiosity that continues to go unexplained. But what they probably haven't heard is that there are those who definitely believe that, through some set of bizarre circumstances, the Loch Ness Monster and UFOs are related.

The late F.W. Holiday made a lifelong career out of investigating the Loch Ness Monster. For many a summer, he worked round the clock at this beautiful locale, which is a 13-hour trip by train from London over lush Scottish landscape.

Holiday discovered early on that similar dragon-like creatures existed in the various Scottish and Irish lakes, and carvings of "flying discs" were often directly associated with such dragons or serpents. During his travels around the United Kingdom, Holiday came across etchings on the walls of churches that showed large serpents, complete with humps, and directly overhead the unmistakable image of a flying saucer.

Comparing notes, F.W. Holiday began to realize that a distinct similarity existed between monster sightings and UFO reports.

"When monster phenomena and UFO phenomena are compared point by point, a number of parallels emerge," he wrote in his book, ***The Dragon and the Disc***: "Both change shape and vary their color. White, yellow, red, brown, greenish and black monsters have been described to me by reliable eyewitnesses. I have myself seen yellow and black specimens. Both monsters and UFOs produce great excitement in domestic animals, e.g. dogs, and both sorts of phenomena are reported to move about at high speeds. Moreover, monsters on land appear never to leave any excreta or other traces one associates with ponderous animals. I have examined the surroundings of lakes in all parts of Britain and Ireland and spoken to hundreds of local people without hearing of a single discovery of this nature."

Holiday adds that the sonar returns which have "unquestionably been obtained from monsters are duplicated by the radar returns which have equally unquestionably been obtained from UFOs."

Though his theories are highly controversial, Holiday soberly suggests that both UFOs and sea serpents make up a sort of "netherworld." At times they can take on a physical appearance but are not made of flesh and blood. He furthermore contended that the chemical makeup of Loch Ness somehow attracted both monster and flying saucer. To Holiday's way of thinking, aerial phantoms and dragons have long had a pronounced effect on humankind and are the cornerstones of modern religion.

Without even being overly familiar with the literature in the field of UFOlogy, Holiday points out the sometimes uncanny frustrations that almost always seem to hamper attempts to get good, solid evidence proving that phenomena such as the Loch Ness Monster really exist. Such frustrations often happen when witnesses attempt to record and photograph the activity of unidentified flying objects.

Says Holiday: "In most cases, either a camera was not available to record what was observed, or, if it was available, circumstances frustrated the photographer. Almost everyone rejected such a notion because it introduced an element of irrationality. It also raised doubts about the true nature of dragons, which those who were anxious to press the claim for an unknown animal chose not to encourage. Normal animals do not behave in such an inexplicable way because they cannot; therefore you had to conclude that the peculiarities were due to chance."

UFO PROPHECY

Holiday didn't see this explanation as being a satisfactory one. In "The Dragon and the Disc," Holiday took note of the "psychological effects" on witnesses at Loch Ness. In one case, he quotes a letter from Dr. Kenneth MacLeod, M.D., Commissioner of Public Health, Cortland, New York, in which the doctor describes his sighting of the monster while driving near the loch in July 1968. Dr. MacLeod states that he was motoring with his father when suddenly "a gray-black object 15-20 feet long" caught his attention and began to speed "down the loch in the same direction as the car." In his letter to F.W. Holiday, Dr. MacLeod states: "It was curious that I did not even mention it to my father . . ." Yet, he later made a note about his observation in his diary.

Holiday also reportedly experienced similar "psychological reactions," as he called them. "After chasing a large, yellowish mass down Loch Ness in 1965 (it was being watched simultaneously by two witnesses on the opposite shore), I remember writing in the Loch Ness Bureau's report: 'It could have been a boat.' Yet manifestly it was not a boat, as I could see through my binoculars; nor did I believe it to be a boat. At the time, I put the aberration down to tiredness until I found it was not uncommon in witnesses."

ON THE SHORES OF THE LOCH

No one has kept an active log of UFO sightings made near Loch Ness, but such reports do exist. Taking up lodging for the evening in a bed-and-breakfast establishment operated by Peggy MacGennis, I was told firsthand about several fascinating UFO encounters. The incident quoted in the opening paragraph of this section of the article was related personally by a young man named Ronnie who had kept his sighting more or less secret up until my arrival in Drumnadrochit. After furnishing my publication "UFO Review" (now defunct) with the details of his own experience, the sincere excavator revealed the details of yet another sighting.

"There was one boy who left work one night at midnight," Ronnie recounted. "He was coming down the road when he saw this thing 30 feet above him. It followed him down the road, and when he got home he ran indoors and got his family to come outside and observe the strange thing in the sky."

According to Ronnie, the youth was shaken by his run-in with a UFO, and it took him a while to calm down. While he doesn't put much stock in there being a connection between the Loch Ness Monster and UFOs, Anthony Harmsworth of the Loch Ness Monster Exhibition has seen UFOs twice in his life. One was a bell-shaped craft that appeared in the sky 25 miles north of London, and the other sighting was very near Loch Ness.

UFO PROPHECY

"It was a green light and it was moving from north to south," Harmsworth said. "I watched it for a short while and then finally it disappeared over some hills."

The Loch Ness Monster and UFOs are both unexplainable in rational, scientific terms. Regardless of any possible connection, both mysteries deserve to be studied with an open mind. Just because they do not fit with our modern concepts of reality doesn't mean that they should be relegated to the scrapheap where many such puzzles have ended up throughout the history of mankind.

ALEISTER CROWLEY, THE BEAST OF BOLESKINE HOUSE

A longtime fan of the rock band Led Zeppelin, I already knew about the legends involving Boleskine House, a fortress-like estate overlooking Loch Ness once owned by the famed occultist and novelist Aleister Crowley, often dubbed "the beast" for his ability to consort with the elemental forces he apparently was able to conjure at will. The uninformed said Crowley was a Satanist and that his invisible forces were really demons. But anyone who has studied his life will know that, to Crowley, these spirits were not of a hellish origin, but were residents of another place who occasionally – when called upon – would cross over to this dimension to do the bidding of humans who were in tune with them through proper magickal ritual.

Well, it seems that Led Zeppelin's guitarist, Jimmy Page, had purchased Boleskine House because of its peaceful surroundings and closeness to Loch Ness, but that bad things had started happening in his life. Some say Crowley was responsible for bringing a "dark aura" over the place and had accidentally called up the monster through magick. Everyone I spoke with pretty much knew the place to be haunted.

I understand a man was beheaded outside the estate, and that his severed head could be heard rolling around the vast hallways at night while mysterious shadows filled the dimly lit rooms. A TV documentary aired on the BBC told how locals refuse to pass the house after dark and by some accounts there were various strange happenings connected with the place. For instance, a coachman who worked there became a tragic alcoholic, Crowley's housekeeper vanished and another workman tried to kill himself after going mad.

Furthermore, I can personally testify to Boleskine's spooky reputation.

I was staying near Boleskine, on the other side of the loch, as previously mentioned, at a very wonderful bed-and-breakfast owned by a delightful elderly lady who was tickled pink to have an American staying in her home that had spoken at the House of Lords. She was one of those Brits still into royalty and could say nothing bad about the Queen. Anyway,

UFO PROPHECY

Above: 1965 newspaper clipping from the Daily Mirror detailing the UFO flap in Warminster.

Below: Warminster in the mid-1960's.

she proceeded to introduce me to everyone who stopped by the house. She even called neighbors and friends on the phone to tell them this wacky gentleman was staying at her place who was interested in the monster and UFOs as well as local ghosts and legends.

In the middle of the afternoon, the milkman came to visit. He really didn't know Led Zep from a hole in the wall but he did have an interesting tale to tell. He said that every time he drove by "the rocker's place," his dog would literally claw its way under the seat of the milk truck and refuse to come out. It got to the point where he had to leave the dog at home because the seat was almost ripped up and there wasn't any other route he could take except going past Boleskine House.

Apparently, most deliveries are left at the gate because a lot of tradesmen in the area refuse to go up the long driveway to the eerie estate. Jimmy Page sold the house years ago and the current owners want travelers to respect their privacy.

So don't go there, because if the monster or Crowley's "demons" don't get you, the present dwellers might skin your hide. LOL!

A VERY ODD SYNCRONICITY

Some years later I found myself personally embroiled – in a sense – with the bizarre happenings at Boleskine House. While staying in the manor by the Loch, at the height of his interest in the occult and Aleister Crowley, Zep's Jimmy Page had agreed to do the soundtrack for an underground movie. "Lucifer Rising" was the brain child of avant-garde moviemaker, author and artist Kenneth Anger. He was "extreme" before Andy Warhol or other trendy cultural icons. His film shorts were cutting edge. He is perhaps best known for the book **Hollywood Babylon**, which told sexually titillating and scandalous tales of Hollywood stars and starlets. When initially released, **Hollywood Babylon** was as controversial and mind-blowing as you could get. Anger intrigued me and I always wanted to meet him. I got the opportunity in a very strange and clandestine way.

I was putting on one of my UFO/Conspiracy conferences years before anyone else decided that it was hip and maybe profitable. I had decided to promote fifty years of UFOs and contactees in the California desert in Palm Springs near Giant Rock, where such luminaries as George Adamski, Dan Fry and George Van Tassel had gathered throughout the 1950s and 60s to speak of their contacts with the illustrious Space Brothers. The weekend's keynote speaker was Hollywood director Robert Wise, the guiding force behind the mesmerizing film "The Day the Earth Stood Still." Near and dear to the hearts of many

UFO PROPHECY

sci-fi and UFO buffs, Wise did not consider himself to be a UFO believer but, knowing of my interest in film, he agreed to speak before my gathering.

It was to be a long weekend affair and vendors had started to set up early on Friday.

The conference was not really open to the public yet but people were starting to gather and walk up and down the rows of book and video vendors. At one point I noticed a small stack of letters had been left on one of the tables I was putting up. The stack was rubber banded as if the letters had just been picked up from the post office. I looked at the name typed on the top letter. It was addressed to KENNETH ANGER. I was taken aback…stunned. Could this be THE Kenneth Anger I had always wanted to meet?

I looked down the long corridor and saw a gentlemen walking alone, seemingly immensely interested in the vendors who were setting up. I walked up to him and asked if this was his mail and if he was the moviemaker Kenneth Anger? He said he was. I invited him to our banquet that evening where I was to introduce Robert Wise. I put both of the filmmakers – one a Hollywood giant and the other his equal in terms of underground cinema – at the same banquet table, and, as it turned out, it was my distinct pleasure to introduce these creative forces to each other.

My paranormal calling has been full of so-called "coincidences" and synchronizations, so much so that I have decided to write a book on how UFO/occult researchers have more "chance events" in their lives than your average person. I feel there is an intelligence behind a lot of these "you can't explain them" happenings, and that this intelligence is trying to speak to us in a sort of code which we have to decipher. Those wanting to hear a brief talk by Kenneth Anger need only go to this You Tube link:

https://www.youtube.com/watch?v=hV89WCXgFhI

Or type in his name and all sorts of counterculture listings will appear to you as if by magick.

And so I have, to the best of my ability, told of my extremely eventful trip to Britain and how it has affected me for decades. Certainly the sightings around Warminster – and perhaps even Loch Ness – have died down for the time being, but assuredly sightings at both locations will rise from the ashes like the great Phoenix. Coming up is the 50th anniversary of the start of the UFO wave in Warminster. Festivities are planned and organizer Kevin Goodman is no doubt already putting his energies into the mighty task at hand. It is only too bad that such men as Arthur Shuttlewood, Bob Strong and the 8th Earl of Clancarty are not around to join in the proceedings and subsequent sky-watches.

UFO PROPHECY

SUGGESTED READING – BOOKS BY TIMOTHY GREEN BECKLEY ON AMAZON INCLUDE:

Our Alien Planet: This Eerie Earth (co-authored by Sean Casteel)

UFOs – Wicked This Way Comes

Timothy Green Beckley's Strange Sage

Round Trip To Hell In A Flying Saucer

Beckley may be reached at MrUFO8@hotmail.com

Website: www.conspiracyjournal.com

UFO PROPHECY

HOW A SERIES OF UFO ENCOUNTERS CHANGED THE LIFE OF RADIO DJ BRYCE BOND

By Sean Casteel

THE story of how the new reprint of the late Bryce Bond's book *UFOs: Key To Inner Perfection* came about is almost as interesting as the book itself. It started in late 2014 when Inner Light/Global Communications CEO Timothy Green Beckley received an all-too-rare order for Bryce's book on the impact that UFO contact had had on his philosophical and metaphysical perceptions of himself and humanity in general.

In his introduction to the recent updated and expanced edition, Beckley writes of how he first met Bryce in the mid-1960s. At the time, Beckley, along with his partner in crime, the late Jim Moseley, was organizing small meetings for a flying saucer club in midtown Manhattan. Bryce was working as a deejay at New York radio station WTFM, where he eschewed rock and roll and played mainly standards like Frank Sinatra. Bryce had a mild interest in UFOs and would announce news of the flying saucer club meetings on the air free of charge.

During one of their brief conversations, with "Old Blue Eyes" crooning in the background, Bryce told Beckley he was going to England soon for a vacation. Bryce asked Beckley if he knew of any suggestions about what to do there, things that were off the beaten track and not just the usual "touristy" fare.

Beckley had just published a book by British journalist Arthur Shuttlewood called "UFO Prophecy" that dealt with an enormous wave of sightings then taking place in a small hamlet called Warminster, located on the Salisbury Plain a stone's throw from Stonehenge.

Eventually thousands of ordinary witnesses would observe "The Thing," which one of the more mysterious Warminster UFOs had been dubbed by the local press. Several celebrities also made their way to the top of Warminster landmark Cradle Hill to see what they might see, including Mick Jagger and David Bowie. The national media hopped on the Warminster UFO bandwagon for a while and produced a number of television documentaries, including this rare classic, which can be found archived on YouTube – https://www.youtube.com/watch?v=EInZ5rV4qZE

Beckley dashed off a letter of introduction for Bryce and air-mailed it to Shuttlewood.

"The next thing I heard," Beckley writes, "was that the two gentlemen had gotten along rather famously and that Bryce had become, in essence, Shuttlewood's sky-watching buddy. Word came back to me from several sources that Bryce had not only seen a UFO but that he had felt the psychic energies given off by standing inside a crop circle, one of the early ones at that, and that he had had several unexplainable experiences which are detailed throughout the pages of this book."

Bryce's experiences in Warminster over the years included several "missing time" episodes and he was also brought onboard a landed space pod for a brief sojourn among the crew members. As Shuttlewood told it, there was an incident in which Bryce was absent from the group of sky-watchers for a period of hours. But, upon his return, Bryce stated that he felt he'd been gone a much shorter time.

Beckley writes that such an experience might shake up almost anyone, but Bryce's response was one of elation, of suddenly being high on life. Almost immediately upon returning to New York, he quit his job at WTFM, saying he could no longer do anything as superficial as spin Frank Sinatra records. Bryce had to be free to help others and save humanity.

Bryce began to lecture at Beckley's New York School of Occult Arts and Sciences, became an instructor for Silva Mind Control and a well-known faith healer in the area.

"UFOs had changed his life," Beckley writes, "as they have for many other individuals – both positively and negatively. Sometime later, Bryce began working on a book he called 'Keys to Inner Perfection' which he asked me to publish and which I did. There was nothing really significant about UFOs in the book, but I felt that what Bryce had to say was important enough to print a small edition of 2,000 copies."

That first book is reprinted in the new Inner Light/Global Communications release. It reads like a sort of "alien-inspired" self-help book in which Bryce tries to teach the open-minded reader to realign one's consciousness with the cosmos. Which admittedly is not easy to do, even with help from the flying saucer occupants. He also preaches the always worthy sentiments of unselfishness and unconditional love for one's fellow man and the world in general.

UFO PROPHECY

"Unfortunately," Beckley writes, "Bryce Bond never lived to see his book published. He passed away less than a month before the cartons arrived at our warehouse from the printer. I was always sad about this fact as I knew Bryce had put his heart and soul into preparing this publication."

The book sold moderately well over the next couple of decades, but some of that small initial press run were consumed by bad weather and hungry rodents who had infested Beckley's warehouse. When Beckley received the aforementioned order with only the one copy on his shelves, he decided to return the customer's money and tell the person they were going to reissue the book. Beckley then handed the book over to William Kern, one of his graphics people, to have it scanned.

Then, as "luck" would have it, Beckley was going through his extensive files and came across a dusty black binder. He realized it was a partially-edited, typewritten manuscript by none other than Bryce on his experiences in the U.K. Beckley vaguely remembered that Bryce had given him the book around the time he had submitted the *Keys To Inner Perfection* manuscript and asked Beckley to publish it at a later date if he could. The pages were now brittle and had changed color from white to a brownish-yellow.

This newly discovered, detailed account of the UFO encounters that had led to *Keys To Inner Perfection* would add more depth and meaning to the reprinting project. It was now apparent that UFOs had impacted Bryce's life more than he had let on.

"Frankly," Beckley writes, "I can't help but believe that somehow Bryce was behind all this. As he looked down from some lofty place in space or a heavenly realm, I am sure he wanted others to discover the glory of his transformation experiences so they might experience their own. I think Bryce put me up to doing this because his complete story was never really told. I realized the work needed to be updated and a 'final' version published."

The "lost" manuscript is a gripping narrative of what happened to Bryce as he took his leap of faith and visited the paranormal-soaked world of the small British hamlet.

"Warminster, at this time of night," Bryce writes, "even for a Saturday, was somewhat deserted. Only a few people ambled along the narrow streets. I felt that I had eyes on me all the way. It was a most unusual feeling. The small narrow streets, with high brick walls, sky overcast, and the town strangely quiet — maybe a prelude to what I was about to experience that night! After walking a short distance through narrow archways and flower-lined paths, I was amazed how lovely it smelled and how clean it was. On the hill, some of the group had their telescopes set up on tripods; others had binoculars and cameras ready.

UFO PROPHECY

"The thing that really struck me was how friendly everyone was. A good portion are very curious, another percentage are thrill-seekers, and the remainder, well, they just enjoyed being there with this warm, loving group of spiritual individuals, sharing stories and conversations . . . UFOs have been here for eons of years. History is filled with reports of strange glowing craft, of landings and contactees. But due to negative programming regarding these ancients, and fear of the unknown being magnified out of all proportion from mouth to mouth, it spread right into modern times. Only in these times we blame television and motion pictures for doing the damage: creating near mass-panic in the mind, showing these UFOs as hostile, coming down from the heavens to devour, murder and rape — and to gobble us up!

"This travesty of beings who are thousands or even millions of years ahead of us in technology, intelligence and spiritual intent. . . . What the masses do not understand, they fear. When they fear, they shoot and run. There are numerous reports that UFOs were shot at, out of panic — even by the military. Put yourselves in their shoes and think: What would you do if you went to their planet, or dimension, or universe, or another period in time? We drove over to Starr Hill, another ancient burial ground area. This sector is where the Romans built upon, with a few of the remnants still in evidence. The location was down in a valley, wheat fields all around and high hills. The sky started to clear, filled with thousands of beautiful stars and still no UFOs . . .

"It was getting awfully late and still I had not interviewed Arthur Shuttlewood. My voice was getting weaker, my head clogged up due to the cool dampness. I got his attention and we crawled into one of the nearby cars to keep warm while I interviewed him. He was telling me that, only a few nights ago, three large entities about eight feet in height were seen down in a little hollow, to which he pointed. While in their presence, people felt a great warmth exuded from them; they were engulfed by it and the scent of roses and violets was very strong. All of a sudden, while Arthur was speaking, his conversation went to a peculiar light that just appeared in the field in front of us. He was somewhat blasé about the whole thing . . .

"Arthur then said quietly: 'I'm very glad you are here tonight, Bryce. There in front of us is a UFO. Notice the triangle shape and colored lights going around? That is a very good sign.' It then started to lift off in a weird pattern — then just disappeared. I was flabbergasted! It was so close. While describing that one on tape for American listeners, another one popped up about 25 degrees along the horizon. This one was very brilliant white, while the other was a blaze of colored lights. The intensity increased as it raised itself very slowly, did a little dance in the sky, then took off and disappeared. But before it did, Arthur jumped from the car, borrowed a flashlight from someone and sent Morse code to it.

UFO PROPHECY

Above: Bryce Bond, author of the book "UFOs - Key to Inner Perfection."
Photo by Phillis Brinkerhoff.

Below: Illustration of Bond's encounter with extraterrestrials while visiting Warminster. Art by Marc Brinkerhoff.

UFO PROPHECY

It in turn sent back the same signal that Arthur flashed out. Then it flew off. This was the highlight of my British trip: a close sighting; yet I honestly felt spiritually close to the lights in the field."

Bryce had begun interviewing other watchers as to what they witnessed when he suddenly felt called away once more.

"I turned off the recorder and made a mad dash out into the field, went into a light trance state and asked higher intelligence to make contact again. Leaving the group, I made my way down to the hollow, where two nights before three entities were seen. Again I went into a light trance state for what seemed to be a few minutes only . . . I was awakened by my friends, who thought I had gone. I must have been there for about an hour. I truly do not know what transpired while I was there or in trance. I told my friends I would return shortly and they went back to where the others were standing. I then made my way slowly back to the parked cars and people. Now here is a strange thing: the wheat in the field next to me as I walked back up the dirt road was about waist high . . .

"I walked along the road very close to the fence. Suddenly I heard a noise — like something crushing the wheat down. There was no breeze blowing that night. I looked over. The moon had just come out, shining very brightly — and there, before my eyes, a large depression was being formed. The wheat was being crushed down in a counterclockwise position. It too was shaped like a triangle and measured about twenty feet from point to point. I stood there a few moments and experienced a tremendous tingling sensation — the same sweet smell — being engulfed by warm air. Not fully understanding what had happened, I walked up the road to get Arthur, my host.

"Speaking of the field, Arthur pointed out some landing impressions in the section fronting the farm barn: a circle about thirty feet in circumference, with another depression spotted, but this one in a long cigar shape. All the depressions, recently made and noticed, were in a counterclockwise fashion. After all this, I was very happy and thankful. My mission had been a success."

Bryce never wavers in his belief that he has contacted something compassionate and loving in the fields near Warminster. Later in the new book, he writes, "None of us seemed to feel fear. Perhaps we didn't have time for fear, or perhaps it just didn't exist in this dimension of consciousness and contact. Perhaps these beings created a state of Samadhi, the experience of ultimate union with the source of creation, called God, higher consciousness, the Supreme; whatever the name, the feeling of total oneness is the same. Somehow we had been guided to this destination at this specific time to make contact with these extraterrestrial intelligences and to share in the extraordinary experience together."

UFO PROPHECY

This shared sensation of bliss – absent any sort of fear – is not always the case for UFO witnesses. Many sighting and abduction reports tend to be all about the terror of encountering a phenomenon that is nonhuman, supremely intelligent, and able to hold us helplessly spellbound even as it defies what we believe are the natural laws of space and time.

But the way in which Bryce and Shuttlewood and the rest of the group were having such a pleasant time of it is also not without precedent, as in the contactee accounts that began to proliferate in the 1950s. One recalls the Betty Andreasson Luca case, beginning in 1967, in which a New England housewife and other members of her family were regularly abducted over many years by what Betty continues to feel are benevolent aliens preparing the way for the Second Coming of Jesus.

Bryce quotes Arthur Shuttlewood thusly on the subject: "I think the UFO intelligence is essentially of God. But man must sink his ego before he can get the truth."

Beckley has also added the elegiac recollections of two of Bryce's old friends to **UFOs: Key To Inner Perfection**. One of those friends is Marc Brinkerhoff, who contributes a pencil drawing he made for Bryce depicting his late friend's face-to-face encounter with both a gray alien and a human-looking, female alien. The event had taken place during a later trip to Warminster by Bryce in 1974, and Marc provides a brief but relatively detailed account of the meeting between Bryce and the friendly UFO occupants.

Psychic Shawn Robbins writes about discovering Bryce's dedicated interest to UFOs one day when they were conversing about Jimmy Carter's famous sighting experience in 1969 as he was campaigning for the governorship of Georgia. Bryce opened up and told Shawn that he'd been in a kind of mental contact with UFOs for many years, but Shawn felt that he was trying to establish a psychic bond with the aliens through her as well. After all his years of encounters with the UFO occupants, Bryce somehow still felt like an "outsider" even as he struggled to communicate the reality of the alien presence to the people. Shawn believes that mission was accomplished by Bryce's books.

Bryce died in January 1992 at the age of 63 from a brain aneurism. He had been due to give a short lecture on metaphysics and healing at the United Nations that day, and when the always punctual and reliable Bryce didn't show up on time nor answer his phone, Marc decided it was time to call the police. Bryce was discovered collapsed in his home and taken to a New York City hospital, where he was kept on life support for several days. Marc claims to have had an out-of-the-body meeting with Bryce in which Bryce appeared youthful and vigorous but concerned about what was happening to his body. Shortly after this otherworldly encounter, Bryce was taken off life support and passed away.

UFO PROPHECY

Perhaps Timothy Green Beckley is right when he says the publication of *UFOs: Keys To Inner Perfection* may have been guided by Bryce Bond from some heavenly location. The various components of the new book have come together after the passage of many years and now form something like a completed puzzle. The final pieces were the newly discovered manuscript and the testimonies of those who knew and loved Bryce. One can only hope that, after meeting the aliens and preaching unconditional love, Bryce has found it for himself and is still able to lead others to it.

"UFO at speed over Warminster." Picture taken by ex-RAF bomber crewman and airborne fighter, Bob Strong, at 7:12 AM. on October 24, 1966.

UFO PROPHECY

THE SOUND AND FURY OF THE THING
By Tim R. Swartz

THE Warminster mystery is now known almost exclusively for the weird UFO flap that enveloped the area in the mid-1960s. However, what has been largely forgotten is that the so-called "Thing" of Warminster started out as an unusual noise that left residents of the area mystified about what they were hearing.

Allegedly, the Warminster Thing first made its presence known on Christmas morning, 1964, but there had been reports of strange occurrences in the area for several years prior to that date. Mrs. Mildred Head told reporter Arthur Shuttlewood that she had been awakened at 1:25AM with strange sounds lashing at her roof like twigs or leaves being drawn across it. This then changed into what Mrs. Head described as sounding like "giant hailstones."

Gathering up her courage, Mrs. Head ventured outside, only to find the night was dry and clear. She did note an odd humming sound from above that got louder but then faded as if something was flying away from her house. Sometime later that same morning, over thirty soldiers at Knook camp, about four miles from Warminster, were awakened by a loud noise. A sergeant told Shuttlewood that the sound was similar to that of a huge chimney being ripped from a roof and scattered in pieces across the whole of the camp. The guard was alerted, but nothing developed beyond the strange sound. The soldiers were surprised but unable to explain the sound.

The Christmas morning reports continued to come in when Mrs. Marjorie Bye was walking to the Holy Communion Service around 6:12AM. The air around her was suddenly filled with "menacing sound and vibrations" that seemed to come from overhead.

"Chilling in intensity and descending on her savagely. She was caught by a peculiar droning that held her in a steel-like grip."

UFO PROPHECY

Before she had reached the church wall "shockwaves" of violent force pounded at her head, neck and shoulders and numbed her. Helpless, she was pinned down by invisible fingers of sound.

"Wailing, whining, droning and frightening," Shuttlewood wrote, "Mrs. Bye was so shocked; she only reached the sanctuary of the church with difficulty."

In his book, **The Warminster Mystery**, Shuttlewood wrote that at the exact same time that Mrs. Bye was having her terrifying experience, Robert Rump, Warminster's head postmaster, heard noises almost identical to those described by Mrs. Bye. His house was not far from Christ Church and he described the noise as "a terrific clatter...as though the roof tiles were being rattled about and plucked off by some tremendous force. Next was a scrambling sound, as if the roof tiles were being loudly slammed back into place. I could hear an odd humming tone. It was most unusual."

The September-October issue of the APRO (Aerial Phenomena Research Organization) Bulletin noted that on the same morning, a nine-year-old girl by the name of Josie went outside around 6:12AM to comfort her dog that was cowering and whimpering in the backyard woodshed. After petting the dog, Josie headed back to the house, but before she reached the back door, there came a "weird crackling and a high whine" and she was "battered down" by something she could only hear, but not see.

"I felt what I thought was an ice cold sponge on the back of my neck," the girl reported. "My shoulders ached and my head was jerked forward and down. I struggled and screamed and managed to stumble into the house."

The unidentified noises continued on until at least June 1966, with over 49 people claiming to have heard them. Many people reported that the sounds also had peculiar, physical effects on them. Eric Payne had just such an encounter on the night of March 28, 1965. Payne was walking down a country road when he heard a sound he described as "the sound of the wind in telegraph wires."

The sound increased in intensity and he was pushed to the ground by "a tremendous racket like a gigantic tin can with huge nuts and bolts inside it, rattling over your head." Payne heard a shrill whining and buzzing which "nearly drove me mad." He reported that his "head was pushed from side to side and I might as well have left my arms and legs at home for all the use they were. I simply could not stop this tremendous downward pressure. I crawled round in the road for a bit and then sank to my knees on the grass verge."

Possibly the penultimate noise-event at Warminster happened on the evening of August 17, 1965. The houses on the Boreham Field housing estate were rocked by a huge explosion that was followed by a series of earthquake-like jolts that residents said they felt underfoot. Some said the blast was so great that they thought a gas main opposite of the houses had blown up. When David Pinnell heard the explosion, he rushed outside and saw "a monstrous orange flame in the sky...it was shaped like an electric light bulb...the light was so bright I could clearly see the nearby hills."

After the light faded, Pinnell saw what appeared to be a large ball of smoke with "a funny yellow core" that floated down from the hills, crackling and hissing whenever it touched grass or trees. The ball of smoke, along with its "fiery center," settled onto the road and slowly disappeared. Oddly, other than some broken windows, there was little damage caused by the incident.

Some researchers have tried to brush off what happened that evening as a meteor that exploded high up over Warminster. This explanation is as good as any other. After all, there have been similar meteoric events reported throughout history. Nevertheless, considering the other unexplained incidents involving strange noises around Warminster, it just seems a little too coincidental that an exploding fireball would take place during the same time period.

After UFOs began to be seen in the area starting around May, 1965, reports of the strange sounds became less and less. It may be that interest in the inexplicable noises had simply been appropriated by the growing UFO frenzy that soon overwhelmed Warminster, or that the sounds vanished as mysteriously as they had arrived. Even though reports of sounds that overtook and struck people down appeared to disappear, one interesting aspect of the Warminster mystery were the reports of "Invisible helicopters/aircraft" in the Warminster, Silbury Hill, Glastonbury, Avebury area.

Someone who goes by the name of "Firemoon" wrote on the Above Top Secret forum that they are still being heard as recently as 2006. "A mate of mine was on Silbury Hill as the dawn was breaking and clearly heard the engines of some aerial object yet saw absolutely nothing even though they were sure it flew over them on the top of the mound. The sky was crystal clear at the time. Another friend of mine told me their one and only 'UFO type experience' was at Glastonbury in 70-71 where, he and several friends swore they heard the engines of some object land in a field by the base of the Tor and yet there was nothing visual sighted at all."

A HIDEOUS NOISE

One detail that is often noted in association with UFO sightings is the fact that witnesses stress that the object(s) they saw was completely silent. This fact, however, is not a hard and fast rule, as many UFOs are accompanied with a wide variety of unusual sounds that are at times heard before the UFO is spotted.

The sounds reported in association with UFOs have been of three general types; (1) motor-like (2) explosive and (3) sonic booms. From the accounts of what the UFOs were doing at the time these sounds were heard, it could be that these three types correspond to (1) motive power, (2) partial vacuum created by sudden displacement, and (3) breaking the sound barrier, respectively.

Some cases are on record of UFOs having been seen at the same time that a "sky quake" or "sky explosion" occurred. One such case was reported in the New Zealand Evening Post, March 22, 1954. At 2:35PM Mr. P. S. Berkett, a farmer of Whangamoa, heard "zooming" noises and saw "a round, flat object of a whitish color" pass overhead. At the same time, strange vibrations and loud explosions were heard over a wide area.

Like those in Warminster who were unlucky enough to hear "The Thing," there are numerous accounts where UFOs have reportedly emitted deep, resonating, humming noises and vibrations that seem to exert some form of both physical and mental influence over the witnesses. Not only that, such encounters have also left eyewitnesses feeling extremely disorientated and sick.

Nick Redfern in his article *"The Sound of a UFO"* (http://mysteriousuniverse.org/2011/04/the-sound-of-a-ufo/) writes that on March 30 and 31, 1993, during a series of UFO sightings in the UK involving over a hundred witnesses, a triangular-shaped UFO was seen by the Meteorological Officer at RAF Shawbury. He described how it had moved slowly across the countryside towards the base, at a speed of no more than 30 or 40 mph. He saw the UFO fire a narrow beam of light (like a laser) at the ground and saw the light sweeping backwards and forwards across the field beyond the perimeter fence, as if it were looking for something. He heard an unpleasant low frequency humming sound coming from the craft and said he could feel as well as hear this - rather like standing in front of a bass speaker and was quite unpleasant."

The Cannock Chase area in England seems to be focal point for odd occurrences including loud and annoying UFOs. A strange aircraft was spotted around 9:00PM on March 24, 2015, moving slowly and loudly across the night sky over Cannock.

Hundreds of residents posted on social media after first hearing a loud drone, then spotting the massive object move slowly over their homes. One individual posted: "My house was rumbling, and I'm still shaking. It was slow and it was huge."

Another wrote: "It wasn't a fighter jet…way too big. It had three red lights, one at the rear, and one on each wing. Usually commercial planes have flashing lights but this just had three solid red lights. It flew directly over our house, made a sharp left turn and carried on."

The craft, which was described as being incredibly large, was so low that many thought it was a plane in trouble. Paranormal investigator Lee Brickley witnessed the same phenomenon and began blogging as the drama unfolded. He described the thunderous rumbling as like a World War Two bomber.

"Before anything could be seen with the naked eye, there was a deep and very loud droning," he said. "After around three minutes, the craft came into sight. It seemed incredibly large and astonishingly low in the sky with three red lights that were easily noticeable.

"The UFO travelled very slowly and many people thought it was about to crash."

Brickley claimed the growl of the engines could still be heard after the mystery machine disappeared.

Cannock journalist Hannah Hiles, who has worked for the *Sunday Mercury*, was also alerted by the thunderous noise.

"It was ever so loud and it went on for quite a while," she said. "It was much more prolonged than a military jet. It was very curious."

Another resident described the sound of jets followed by a loud whirr, akin to propellers.

Brickley checked online with flight tracking services and also contacted Birmingham Airport, but found that there were no scheduled airline flights in the area at that specific time.

Later that year, on September 16, a loud, pulsating bass noise booming in the skies above Greater Manchester left residents mystified. Confused people across the region reported hearing the rhythmic pulsing in Stockport, Rochdale and Middleton.

Like the original sounds heard over Warminster years before, even though no object was seen, the sounds over Manchester seemed to "move" across the sky.

Posting on Reddit, user SkoomaOverdose said it sounded like a "UFO." Under the heading "Weird, loud, pulsating bass noise in the sky…did anybody else hear this? It sounded like a UFO or something. I checked Twitter and only one other person posted that they heard it in Stockport which is the other side of Manchester to me. Anybody hear anything?"

UFO PROPHECY

In reply, user MrBrizola, who also heard the unusual sound, said: "Me and a friend both heard it while walking home around east Manchester and thought it was really odd. It lingered around for ages, sounding deeper as it got further away. Clear sky but couldn't see anything."

He went on to describe it as "low and rhythmically pulsating with no massive jumps in pitch" and said he heard it "over the space of about five solid minutes until it was too far away."

THE SENSATION OF SOUND

The deep, bass-like quality of the mysterious sounds, which are often felt as well as heard, was part of an interesting account as reported by Kim Shaffer of MUFON Tennessee. Shaffer wrote that the incident took place on Saturday, October 2, 2004, at 5:30AM in Bristol, Tennessee. The witness told Shaffer that he was driving home when he saw what looked to be at first a fire on a ridge top. However, as he continued to drive, he spotted the "fire" again, but much closer and moving towards him.

The witness stopped at an intersection and got out of his car. He began hearing a deep, throbbing hum, and then a triangle-shaped object suddenly emerged from the tree line and moved directly toward him. He estimated it to be around 300 feet in length with brilliant reddish orange domes filled with a violent, turbulent fire that illuminated the bottom.

As it glided overhead, the witness said that he felt his skin burning and the sound seemed to penetrate his body, making his hair stand on end. The giant object passed over and made a westward turn without banking and disappeared behind the trees. The sound slowly faded away, but the man said he could still feel the throbbing for a few seconds after the UFO vanished.

Shaffer reported that the next day the witness suffered from sensations of his back and face burning, a nosebleed and a metallic taste in his mouth. "He also noted that he brushed his hair and strands of it were coming out, unlike ever before," Shaffer said. "The witness was weak, lethargic and was filled with fear over the events of the previous day."

The deleterious effects of getting too close to a UFO has been closely studied, but it has been difficult to determine what part of the UFO encounter actually results in injury. Heat and radiation have long been favorites; however, science is beginning to recognize that certain acoustic frequencies can also be factored in when it comes to the damaging influence of UFOs.

UFO PROPHECY

Strange Noise At Warminster

SETTING off for church at 6.30 on Christmas morning, a Bradley Road, Warminster, housewife heard a crackling noise from the direction of Bell Hill. At first she thought it was a lorry spreading grit on the hill. But the noise grew louder, came *over* her head and passed on across Ludlow Close.

She will not let me use her name because she is afraid of being laughed at. The noise sounded like branches being pulled over gravel and there was a faint hum. It was quite loud but not above talking level. The sky was dark but brilliantly starlit and she could see nothing above her.

Explanations have included static electricity caused by wet power lines; natural static electricity caused in certain weather conditions; a satellite; — and Father Christmas taking off!

This shy lady would be glad to hear from anybody else who heard the noise or who could give some explanation. Her knees were knocking all the way to church!

Above: Article from the December 25, 1964 editon of the *Warminster Journal* detailing the strange sounds heard around Warminster.

Below: Photograph of UFO taken by John Macdonald on February 28, 2016 near the town of Rossie Ochil in Scotland. Macdonald said before he saw the UFO, he first heard noises that sounded like a thousand "hoovers."

UFO PROPHECY

Shirley Greenfield (pseudonym) can certainly attest to how a UFO can cause damage to the human body. On January 23, 1976, around 5:20PM, 17-year-old Greenfield was coming home from work and had gotten off the bus to her home in the Pennines ridges. It was almost dark and the streets were quiet as she walked to her house.

Greenfield's walk was interrupted when an object she described as looking like "an upturned pudding basin" appeared above her. The UFO was about 20 or 30 feet across and rotating like a spinning top. It had what seemed to be windows in its side that glowed with an eerie orange color.

The UFO slowly drifted down until it was no more than a few feet over the terrified girl's head. At the same time a physical pressure emerged from the object and forced Greenfield onto the ground. She tried to resist the downward force with her umbrella, but it did little good, and she felt that she was being crushed by an invisible wall.

At the same time, a low frequency sound enveloped the girl causing her teeth to painfully vibrate in resonance to the strange force. She said that her mouth was filled with a "metallic taste" and she feared her head was going to explode as the vibrations intensified.

Just as Greenfield thought she was about to die, the object appeared to rotate and flip before moving away over the nearby rooftops. The girl took the opportunity to push herself upward from the decreasing pressure and run away.

In the days that followed her frightening encounter, Greenfield's health deteriorated and her mouth had become sore. She also found a small burn mark on her arm, and her eyes had become red and swollen. Her muscles started to ache, and a purple rash formed on her neck and shoulders, the areas that had been most directly exposed to the UFO.

For her, the most disturbing thing was that her top fillings in her teeth had crumbled into powder and had fallen out. Some of the fillings in her lower mouth had become embedded in the gums and extensive dental work was needed to repair everything. Her dentist, who did not know of her UFO experience, told her that in all his years of work he had never come across a case like this one.

This incredible account continued and subsequent investigations uncovered missing time, a possible abduction revealed under hypnotic regression, and Men-In-Black involvement. Full details of Shirley Greenfield's amazing story can be found in Jenny Randles 1997 book ***The Truth Behind Men-In-Black.***

Greenfield's encounter with a UFO is very similar to the Warminster Thing incidents ten years earlier involving Mrs. Marjorie Bye, the nine-year-old girl named Josie and Eric Payne…all who had been battered to the ground by an invisible, vibrating force. The only difference is that Shirley Greenfield had seen a UFO that was apparently emitting a destructive acoustic force, while with the Warminster cases, no UFO was seen.

Sound can produce amazing effects and we are starting to realize the amazing potential that infra and ultrasound has for both constructive and destructive purposes. Experiments by the U.S. military and others indicate that infrasound can have profound psychological and physical effects on humans and other animals. Humans exposed to various frequencies of infrasound have reported disorientation, nausea, fear, panic, sorrow, loss of bowels, drowsiness, visual hallucinations, chills, high blood pressure, increased blood flow, internal respiratory problems, and even organ damage. The U.S. Navy reports that it is unsafe for humans to be exposed to infrasound at a level of 140 dB. It is reported that infrasound can rupture organs and make objects explode, and it is a matter of history that there has been research into sonic weapons.

Normally, humans hear sounds that are above 20 Hertz. Frequency is not to be confused with the intensity (more commonly, volume) of a sound, which is measured in decibels. Sounds with low frequencies cannot be heard, but our bodies can still sense them. If the intensity of a sound is high enough, in other words, if it's "loud" enough, your body will feel it. Think about how a car with a big sound system shakes because of the bass. You don't hear the music very well, but you can still feel the vibrations.

Studies show that infrasound between 7 and 19 Hertz can cause feelings of fear and panic in humans. Our eardrums pick up these sounds and transmit them to our brain without setting off our auditory sense. To study the effects of these sounds on human organs, researchers from the University of Hertfordshire conducted an experiment where they played music with and without tones of 17 Hertz frequency in the background. When the participants heard (or felt, rather) the music with the 17 Hertz tones, they felt nervous, anxious, and fearful. They also felt pressure on their chests and chills down their spine. These are the feelings that most people describe when they experience a paranormal event.

It is suggested by the researchers who conducted these experiments that infrasound (sound below 20 Hz of frequency) is present at supposedly haunted sites. Upon examining the frequencies present at advertised haunted houses, researchers detected several wavelengths of infrasound being emitted. They hypothesize that these frequencies caused feelings of panic and dread among visitors.

An important point concerning the sound emitted by UFOs is that the noise is often felt as much as heard. This "feeling" the noise indicates that a vibrational force of exactly the same frequency as the sound is at work. With intense sound pressures, low-frequency sound vibrations are felt as a shaking of the body, but high-frequency sound is not felt as a shaking, although it is painful to the ears. It could be then that people who are feeling the sound from a UFO are getting some form of direct input or effect from a pulsating or vibrating force field, rather than feeling vibrations just from the air.

It could be that a vibrational force from a UFO may be producing an external acoustic effect upon objects below the UFO, such as buildings, cars, even a human body. These acoustic forces can be both infra and ultrasonic, though ultrasonic waves usually require a medium through which to travel. In medicine, a clear jelly is applied as a go-between, connecting a sound transmitting apparatus and the body area to be treated. Infrasound doesn't need a medium to propagate, however, and its use can explain the feelings of unease and downright panic reported by many eyewitnesses to close UFO encounters.

It is clear that more study is needed in this field to get a better understanding of why UFOs exhibit certain characteristics and why/how they affect nearby physical objects, including humans. The recommendation is that until we know what is going on with UFOs, it is best to stay away from them. Ignoring this advice can lead to possible dangerous situations and probable injury.

Don't say you weren't warned.

UFO PROPHECY

DEDICATION

'Truth is the most precious Jewel in the whole Crown of Creation. Peace is the fairest Flower in the Universe, each petal beyond price. Love is the most valuable of Ornaments, which should adorn every Household, every Hearth and every Heart.'

With gratitude and affection, the Author dedicates this serious work on the most important subject he knows to People of this Earth and other Planets who are genuinely concerned for the continuing safety, welfare and evolutionary progress of everyone in a vast and ever-changing Universe that gives us our homes.

To my fellow researchers Bob and Sybil, two faithful and tireless observers during cold and lonely hours on Cradle Hill, my special thanks also. May our combined efforts not be in vain!

Arthur Shuttlewood.

17 Portway
Warminster

UFO PROPHECY

CONTENTS

		Page
	Dedication	56
	Foreword	58
1	*Magnetic Balance and Changing Polarity*	67
2	*Fireflies that Elude Scientific Appraisals*	79
3	*Trifling Pointers are Embryonic Clues*	93
4	*Visual Communication Possible with UFOs*	108
5	*Technical Secrets of Crashed UFO 'Hushed'*	122
6	*Flying Crosses and Excaliburs Nothing New!*	133
7	*Bizarre Changes of Form and Dimension*	146
8	*Possible Methods of Spacecraft Propulsion*	159
9	*UFOs not Bourgeois Journalist Fabrications*	169
10	*Reconstruction of Ancient Grid System?*	179
11	*Watch-Stopping, Space Scripts and Sounds*	191
12	*Interstellar Visitors Furtive and Secretive?*	201
13	*Constructed According to Cosmic Principles*	211
14	*Young Drug-Takers Groped and Grovelled*	223
15	*Progression from Elementary Life Patterns*	237
16	*'Earth Time is Desperately Short' Warning*	249
17	*A Reprimand for Inadequate Understanding*	263
18	*Anatomy of a Holocaust—and 'Dying Fish'*	274
19	*The Dawning of the Golden Age of Man*	282
20	*Interplanetary Existence 'Priceless Pearl'*	291
21	*What do Unique UFO Experiences Foretell?*	301
	Conclusions	311

UFO PROPHECY

Foreword

We may be poised on the threshold of momentous happenings at this present critical stage in the development and evolution of Man on Earth. It is therefore of paramount urgency to prepare ourselves, as sensibly as possible, for any sudden emergency arising in the near future.

Many portents, strange and bewildering, have already manifested in our skies since the year 1947, reflected by dynamic thought that ripples through the minds of a discerning portion of Humanity, and transfuses emotion into other hearts hitherto barren and unresponsive to finer aspects of Life and its Purpose.

These aerial phenomena could well prove warning forerunners of significant events whose world-wide impact will fully be felt in the course of the next few years. We live in an unsafe and unpredictable period fraught with hidden dangers. Crisis point might easily be reached much sooner than most people expect.

This is an ugly and war-torn age where the threat of physical extinction by misapplied and misused thermo-nuclear devices is a frightening possibility lurking around several hostile corners, waiting to pounce on the unprotected. Oil is often poured on troubled waters, tempers mount and opposing political doctrines of major world powers mouth glib phraseology to placate public anxiety after each experimental detonation.

If we dare assume that more progressive and enlightened societies flourish elsewhere in an enormous Universe, they must surely have learned at least one vital lesson in the Power Game: Working in harmony with Nature brings an end product of peace and plenty; whereas mastery gained by splitting the atom and harnessing solar energy is short-lived and ill-fated if employed in contradiction to wise designing influences of Nature, by recourse to destructive outlets for such powerful forces.

Accumulated evidence favours the undeniable existence of extra-terrestrials. One can reasonably deduce that they have advanced farther along highways of service and byways of usefulness by virtue of successfully surmounting dangers inherent in the penultimate type of technological phase now confronting our planet, perhaps millenia ago.

They are bound to be more than mildly concerned over the future of a planet arriving at a crossroad pockmarked with potential perils for the unwary and unaware. Hence their advent in celestial chariots into our native atmosphere at this crucial time. Yet there may be underlying reasons of even greater magnitude.

No rational person on Earth would reject the clear fact that fearful fuses awaiting ignition are supercharged with colossal menace to our current civilization, if detonated by the folly of tragic misunderstanding or precipitate action. Touchpapers lit by human agencies of ill-founded suspicion, fear and hostility could spread a consuming fire around the whole of the Earth's envelope and decimate all life.

There may be signposts and warning notices that we, in materialistic blindness, do not see or choose to ignore in complacent unwisdom. Man individually may still cherish ideals of happy family relationships, fairly high standards of conventional and ethical behaviour.

He may be a strong advocate of helping neighbours in adversity, clinging with commendable tenacity to statutes of brotherly love, which is genuine concern for all no matter what their skin colour, politics, creed, nationality or circumstances in life.

Structures of moral stability and spiritual balance, however, are gradually sinking into the mire of forgetfulness and neglect when one views Man collectively. Unfortunately, he is the same destructive animal who cunningly preaches peace while fostering hatred, suspicious and unrelenting even in face of the pitiful plight of starving children in undeveloped regions of his planet.

No single power or combination of powers can break this stranglehold on Humanity, thus overcoming the three main retrogressive influences in our world today—war, hunger and disease. Man has his priorities all wrong and is reverting to prehistoric measures stemming from unnatural fears and clashing ideologies.

Ancient Man was in the unforgivable habit of killing, but there was more excuse then for his actions, enforced because of sheer self-preservation against wild and primitive forces surrounding him. There is no excuse today! Wealth deposits and accumulations from his natural environs, his geological and mineralogical excavations, are squandered by Man today on blatantly bad causes at the expense

UFO PROPHECY

FOREWORD

of measures to further true progress of Humanity and humanitarian principles.

This is grievous truth we cannot dispute. Somewhere along the tortuous trail to adult thinking and behaviour, Man has lost his way and very purpose in life. His mind is clouded by cobwebs of misapprehension and doubt, by fears and phobias that should not clog enlightened minds seeking higher aspirations in the journey to reach the stars . . .

I hope this book may assist in redirecting faltering footsteps, groping minds, lost incentives to better living, back to sanity and life that should be a richly rewarding experience for all. Flying friends from other sectors of the Universe are surely trying to guide us at a worrying juncture in human affairs on a Planet of Strengthening.

Most strongly, I feel that we should offer them this chance of aiding us. We require wise guidance and direction nowadays. For the golden prospect of a Heaven on Earth we hope to earn when present troubles and tribulations draw to a welcome close, it is worth taking a speculative risk, a mild gamble which could easily come off with benefits to us in golden dividends of supreme happiness.

The conclusions I draw at the end of this work are my own. My skywatching team-mates, Bob Strong and Sybil Champion, may not necessarily concur with all that I write. However, they have supported me all the way in our physical and practical approach to the enigma our flying friends and their incredible machines constitute. If ever a third book develops from my pen, their own conclusions will appear.

If one accepts the feasibility of unidentified flying objects, then it can readily be seen that the system of propulsion which they employ, and their reasons for visiting us, seem to be more and more strongly linked. Here are a few preliminary thoughts for the scientific to mull over on the fascinating theme of 'What Makes Them Tick?'

For a long time it has been said, written, quoted and recorded that, of all the numerous testimonies of colour changes—so characteristic of UFOs—none indicates anything beyond something we can all associate as arising from electrical phenomena. This is fairly obvious to anyone closely studying these machines.

There are many cases, also on record, of television sets, radios, radar, other electrical appliances and compasses being seriously upset by UFOs. Indeed, it has been soberly suggested—and it is acceptable —that the great power failure in the United States of America a couple of years ago was caused by UFOs 'tripping' the switches over.

Therefore, it is apparent that celestial chariots show colour changes connected with electrical-magnetic phenomena. They are also known to affect adversely the appliances and apparatus we use in our homes and laboratories. Yet, in looking at the picture in broadest terms, what do we really know about the Earth, the planets of our Solar System, the Galaxy in which we live, and the immense Universe?

We know that the Earth has a central magnetic fluid or liquid core content. We are acquainted with the shape of the magnetic field of the Earth. Moreover, we also realise that there is a Universal magnetic field; and that this field is linked in with ours and those of the other planets. Our scientists have discovered a number of truths in this important sphere of research.

The Earth spins on a tilting axis. It is thought that such spinning in effect makes our planet behave like a gigantic dynamo, generating electromagnetic fields. Maintained within, and in a certain ratio balance, are the great filter belts, in two parts.

Held high above the Earth, these two belts—the Van Allen radiation girdles—actually protect us, and the surface of the Earth, from high energy radiation bombardment from Outer Space. Their preservation is vital to us all, as anyone with a modicum of scientific knowledge appreciates.

The particles which do manage to get through to us, such as the high energy particles from the Sun, cause considerable radio and other communicational disturbance. They also result in such strange flickering light patterns as we find in the Northern hemisphere. These are the famous Northern Lights.

In times of really bad influx of these high energy particles, it is not unknown for these 'flickering fan' lights to be seen a long way around the world—their visibility extending almost down to Southern France. There are the Southern Lights, too, not so frequently referred to in literature.

It is possible to draw maps of the magnetic field of the Earth in two dimensions. A chart of this is easily obtained from J. D. Potter and Sons, The Minories, London (Admiralty Charts), showing vast concentrations of swirling and straight lines of force.

These vary from time to time, although over a period of years their positions and concentrations are roughly the same. Much that has been observed in UFO phenomena has related to the concentrations

UFO PROPHECY

FOREWORD

of the magnetic lines of force of Earth; and many sightings in the States, both South and North America, have been closely networked with the main lines of force 'wiggling' their way up that large continent.

Warminster is a case in point... An article published in 'Nature' last year analyzed the changing directions of the magnetic lines of force over England during a year. It was significant that, whilst all the force lines altered in magnitude and direction, one concentration of force lines—although suffering a tortuous fluctuation and alteration during the year—certainly always passed through the Warminster area.

It may well be that, if the Earth generates its own gravitational and magnetic fields, it is capable of behaving like electric motors and generators. These can either be generators (producing current) or, if they are fed with current, they can be driven and thus become motors.

If, for example, the Van Allen radiation belts were interfered with, or there occurred a difference in the magnetic field from what is in truth a well maintained and balanced interplanetary electromagnetic-gravitational system, then the Earth could well be speeded up in rotation. This could correspond to the 'shortening' of 'time' as we know it.

In the event, it would put an enormous strain on an otherwise small, thin and highly vulnerable crust, cause giant cracks (particularly under the ocean beds), and result in such general upheaval, overall, that the Earth could well nigh disintegrate and be flung forcibly out of orbit.

Such a happening would be an exponential vicious circle. Faster turning speed might result in the generation of more electromagnetic-gravitational fields and greater imbalance, increased turning speed, etc. Alternatively, the planet could be slowed down. Result? No gravity, no magnetic field, etc. This is unlikely, however, and so of minor importance because of the improbability.

There is another factor and possible pressing reason for space visitors maintaining a close interest in us. It is probable from all that we learn on the Warminster UFO front alone (i.e., spinning, colours, etc.) that these craft operate on a minor system similar to a planet, in that they generate their own electromagnetic-gravitational fields and work on an imbalance system.

In brief, at rest they do not rotate. They rotate, under a controlled fashion, with a central liquid core, so as to generate their fields and thus move within the magnetic fields of Earth and space. If such is the case; the conflict of electromagnetic energy would explain the emission of light, and heat, plus sundry other electromagnetic effects which we so much associate with them.

Also, the disintegration of UFOs is explainable in terms of their unfortunately meeting 'pockets' of intense electromagnetic phenomena, swirls or three-dimensional whirlpools if you like. These would cause violent imbalance, far more spin—and sudden disintegration. Such contingencies cannot be unknown to spacecraft crews.

They would obviously need to use a three-dimensional graphical system for observation of pure energy concentration in space and here, around our planet. Often, it may well be that pockets of electro-magnetic energy can be the result of the exploitation by Man of his environment.

This is worth thinking over carefully, unless we treat all UFO occupants as hostile, which is a childish attitude judging from my own experiences. Our own mass suicide through unreasoning flirtation with imponderables in a nuclear age is the greater danger!

All these factors could lead to alteration of the electromagnetic-gravitational fields of Earth, cause interplanetary imbalance, shifting of poles, Solar System disturbances, and wreak havoc with physical intercommunication channels far beyond the limitations of our own planet.

They could create a great deal of trouble for interplanetary travellers who use these systems, which Nature herself employs, throughout the whole of the Universe. We would do well to ponder on these considerations at the present time. They are so vital—to us and to 'them.' Events of near future years should be noted and evaluated carefully. If our world is found to be changing, it must be for the better, eventually . . .

'Are UFOs still appearing over Warminster?' In answer to hosts of inquiring letters I have received since publication of my last book, '*The Warminster Mystery*,' the short and honest reply is: 'Yes.' Here is one fairly recent news story in the *Wiltshire Times and News* dated May 10th of this year, written by staff reporter Bob Randall and carrying the front page headline 'Blinding Light Swoops on Car,' for instance:

'The Warminster Thing has reappeared. Telecommunications engineer Mr. Trevor Marsh, of 10 The Close, Warminster, used to have an open mind about the Thing, but he says after it hovered over

UFO PROPHECY

FOREWORD

his car on the main Warminster to Bath road near Warminster on Monday night, last week, he has no doubts left.

'Trevor was driving home between 10.45 and 11 p.m. after visiting his girl friend when he saw a flashing light over Norridge Wood. He thought it was a helicopter's navigation light. But the light came towards the car, almost blinding him and creating static on his car radio.

'He slowed down to 10 m.p.h. because he was dazzled. As the light came right over the car, it was blotted out by a huge circular object underneath it. Trevor estimates the object was about three times as big as his Morris 1000 and about thirty feet above it.

'But it could have been bigger and higher, or smaller and lower. The object was blue-green at one end and red at the other. He was unable to tell what it was made of and unable to see any metallic shine or rivets.

'As soon as the light was masked and he could see properly again, Trevor drove into Warminster as fast as he could. "It gave me a right old breeze-up," he admitted later. "I was shaking all over.

"When I got into town I slowed down and looked back, but it had gone. There was no sound. I came along the road about the same time on Tuesday night. I went like hell, I can tell you, but I did not see anything this time."'

The lad reported his unnerving experience to his parents—then, on his father's advice, came to my house in Portway shortly before midnight. He was certainly shaken and bemused. At one point he feared that the UFO was going to strike the car, as it seemed to hover just over his bonnet and headlights.

A Red Indian prayer entreats: 'Great Spirit, help me never to judge another until I have walked in his moccasins for two weeks.' A good one for the serious investigator in any new field of research could be: 'Let not that happen which I wish, but that which is right.'

After intensive study of and close contact with the UFO mystery over a long period, I would personally plump for: 'O Lord, reform Thy world, beginning with me;' for I am ever deeply conscious of the tremendous responsibility borne by all who seek to inform in very truth on such a still-futuristic subject.

It is a particularly difficult task when, as is the case with Ufology, so many unknown factors have to be faced and evaluated, together with a number of incongruities and irrationalities that are an infuriating part of the UFO behaviour pattern.

UFO PROPHECY

One man living in the Warminster district whose views I highly respect is David C. Holton, of Sutton End, Crockerton. He brought many of the earlier mysteries to light in early 1965. Here is his highly original viewpoint with regard to UFO perplexities:

'Writers and critics who endeavour to explain the occurrences away by every conceivable explanation, from geological faults to hallucinations, have simply never heard all the facts. Their ardour arises from their materialistic outlook in which they would like to feel secure.

'But the steady stream of reliable testimony ranging from police patrols in Devon last year, who observed the famous flying crosses, to the recent experience of a motorist on the Bath Road at Warminster, show that energies of an occult nature not only exist but manifest themselves frequently.

'Etheric energy is the basic energy of the atom; it is the fundamental " substance " of " mind " and " matter "—there is no real difference between natural science and occult science here. The Warminster Thing and the flying crosses are no " nine-day wonder "—they will appear again and again as they have done for centuries past.

'To modern man they are an affront to his intelligence, because he does not understand the subtle relationship between mind and matter. The Warminster Thing is as mysterious to people today as television would have been in the time of Christ—the one is no more " supernatural " than the other.

'Our understanding of these fascinating matters can only be enhanced by continual research and observation,' he added, claiming that the entire mystery is explained in his manuscript 'Psychism and the Warminster Tumuli.' It contains accounts never before appearing in print, he says, describing events in the Warminster area in the last century and during 1964-65 which have a direct bearing on ' this collection of mysterious happenings.'

I have not read his manuscript, so cannot judge its worth, but anything which is conducive to making people think for themselves at this critical juncture in human affairs on Earth must serve a good purpose. My later conclusions in this book may coincide with his, or be oppositely inclined: mine are formed on evidence available to me in modern times.

We hope you will like the poetry and not consider it totally irrelevant. The majority of verses are by one of our observer friends, artist

UFO PROPHECY

FOREWORD

Pauline Roberts, of Southampton. She and her artist husband Gil are fairly regular companions of ours on Cradle Hill. The final two poems are by another stalwart, Veronica Cadby.

On, then, to the long and sometimes frustrating trail of the graceful if elusive UFOs : a trail that is packed tight with thrills and excitement unlimited. So mind how you step—be careful ! Here's hoping you enjoy our unusual journeying together into the unknown—

Arthur Shuttlewood.

UFO PROPHECY

CHAPTER ONE

Magnetic Balance and Changing Polarity

Given the proviso that they are divorced from surfacial levels of artificial approach which plague serious inquiry and baulk real progress, pure Science and Religion are not diametrically opposed investigating media and doctrines in compiling Ufological truths.

In fact, they are quite compatible channels and do not conflict, except in interpretation, in basic respects. Here is a concrete example where this applies, if one assumes two things to be factual in connection with increased UFO activity of recent years :—

These spaceships and their crews have been doing an incredible amount of work in reconstructing and reactivating a giant grid aerial system that existed in pre-Biblical days. By this means, they are altering the magnetic field of our Earth, obviously for a carefully calculated purpose.

This implies that there is to be a major polar change effected in near future years, in preparation for a disaster which must not be permitted to overtake our planet and its people prematurely.

This may appear a paradox, a contradiction of terms, indistinct and evasive phraseology, so let us further explore this hypothetical line of reasoning so as to deduce sensibly that some malfunction, as yet indiscernible to us, is causing these interplanetary travellers grave concern. Let us assume that they are worried over their future as well as our own.

Supposing that the hard inner core or central ball of the planet Earth has suffered damage and is defective, its maximum efficiency impaired. This affliction of the gravity centre of a globe, together with its central magnetic fluid content, would make intelligent space visitors from neighbouring planets most anxious.

They cannot stand by, idle and complacent, without jeopardizing their own future preservation as civilized communities. They must act immediately to rectify a worsening situation if at all possible, before it gets completely out of hand, aware that Man on Earth is unaware and blissfully ignorant of a seething cauldron of savage forces beneath his feet, perhaps even threatening his extinction as a species.

Let us assume that this inner core damage was what the callers from the cantel Aenstria in my last book, *The Warminster Mystery*, feared and were alluding to when giving details of fault lines and zones deep underground that their probes and survey missions to Earth for millenia past had proven, computer calculated and undeniable.

If this surmise is correct, then the unchecked effects of a stricken gravity centre could be catastrophic to our civilization and theirs, the magnetic balance of the whole Solar System endangered if disrupted by the destruction of our planet. The seriousness of the position could be heightened by the ravaging roots striking more deeply, although—conversely—in an outward direction.

Even the central pivot of the life and light giving Sun might be adversely affected by changed magnetic conditions thus engineered. So remedial measures and temporary repair operations must ensue by planned precision of aerial activities designed to relieve undue pressure on the defective ball whose 'heartbeat' has been overtaxed.

Simultaneously, there must be healing and sealing missions at strategic underground points by the visitors, aided by knowledgable and trusted people on Earth, to keep the brewing menace of the constant 'time bomb' sufficiently under control until (a) the situation is righted, or (b) a mass air-lift is possible to carry a doomed civilization to places of safety on nearby or fairly distant planets in other solar systems and galaxies.

It may well be that the central core, the very heart of our planet, has outlived its usefulness. The heavy burden, incumbent in dutiful service throughout billions of years in harmonizing with the sun and other solar system planets to thrust Earth around its orbital and rotational path, has taken its toll as scientifically assessed by our space friends.

The ball is tired, exhausted, growing fearfully hot and threatening to explode after unnatural expansion of inner forces whose strength and composition are unknown and therefore ungaugable by us. The planetary heart may be shivering feverishly in its final throes of torment —and the escape of such powerful and fiery shockwaves would absolutely wreck the soft 'outer casing,' bursting through the weaker fabric and decimating all life thereon.

UFO PROPHECY

MAGNETIC BALANCE AND CHANGING POLARITY

In the consequent upheaval, one could expect all sorts of dire results. Violent earthquakes might by the principal warning prelude to the last acts in the drama of a dying planet. Perhaps the Earth will tilt and cease to rotate for a single vital second, or suddenly change its rotational trajectory. Prior to this, as many inhabitants as possible will be mass evacuated by the UFOs and their watchful crews and conveyed to alien worlds.

Unquenchable fires and devastation to come later would cause the planet to burn fiercely and be uninhabitable in the final days of physical breakup. The destruction of all life remaining would be inevitable. Yet physical death is forever transcended by continual incarnatory cycles, so the sting of this demise is extracted on a personal level, as later chapters explain.

It could take a year or more before expert repairing equivalent to renewal of the central core of Earth is accomplished, when fresh vegetation would start the rebirth of the dead world, to be followed in due course by the return of saved remnants of a scattered civilization whose dilated knowledge by then will concentrate on rebuilding the new from the outmoded.

Remedial operations of temporary value, affording a time-saving stopgap in the present emergency, cannot be initiated by Earth dwellers, who have plumbed the mystery of what lies deep under the 'skin' of their planet only to the materialistic and commercial extent of boring down for several miles, extracting oil, gas, water and fuels from the outer arteries of secret fastnesses in the subterranean depths.

Frankly, it might be that Man does not realise the potential of hidden dangers deep within the bowels of his world. More enlightened space people, surveying and studying our planet in depth for millenia, as broadly hinted at by the Aenstrians, would readily appreciate the threats to security and magnetic balance inherent in such a situation. They would know what action to take, swiftly and unerringly, to offset the full impact of destruction and calamity.

Remember, too, the importance of the magnetic balance pertaining between Earth and its tide-affecting satellite, the Moon. This would be roughly jostled out of alignment and equilibrium. The magnetic field of Earth is now very close to a position of 75 degrees 18 minutes latitude and 97 degrees 30 minutes longtitude.

This indicates that the North Magnetic Pole has shifted and that work is proceeding to bring about the corresponding completion of the South Magnetic Pole, which will also be at 75.18 latitude and 82.30 longtitude—and ultimately the Northern Pole will complete its movement. This is conceivable.

Perhaps the planetary records of our visitors show similar malfunctions occurring millenia or even millions of years ago elsewhere in our Solar System, possibly triggered off by nuclear warfare or experimentation—as in the case of the planet Maldek or Lucifer, sixty million years ago blasted to fragmentary ineptitude and now constituting an unfortunate asteroidal belt in our system.

Aware that destruction of one planet will upset the magnetic cohesion essential to continue stabilized and favourable conditions of life for all in a solar system, perhaps affecting preset and natural vibrationary principles of the central orb of the sun itself, they come to the afflicted planet and literally 'play with fire,' imperilling their own lives in order to save those of unsuspecting brethren in their spirit of universal concern.

If this is the case, if we have but an ounce of true religious fervour in us, we must surely murmer, even in grudging terms : ' Thank God they are here ! ' For the manifold problems that beset Man on Earth at this crucial stage in planetary history go further than the physical central core of our physical existence . . .

Additionally, the intergalactic voyagers are anxious to prevent repercussive effects from blasting their own native homes and environs out of the sky. A wayward ball, stripped of its surrounding strata and casing, robbed of its magnetic balancing mechanizm and properties, could create havoc in the atmosphere by sheer freedom and unleashed volition.

Coming into our sky reaches, exploring ocean beds and sounding the unsafe midriff of our planet, our space visitors relieve abnormal pressures by tampering of necessity with the magnetic field, by deftly wrought polar changes, by efforts deep inside the Earth to seal off festering wounds and gaping sores around a damaged heart and weeping arteries.

Impossible ? Unrealistic ? Laughable conjecturing ? I thought so once ; yet it is logical to reason that such a dreaded contingency would explain much, if not everything, with regard to the pronounced UFO activity in our aerial lanes at this fateful hour of time.

A terrific number of interplanetary craft and crews would have to be employed to cope with a threat of these major proportions, united

MAGNETIC BALANCE AND CHANGING POLARITY

in a common goal that must be achieved in the face of hostility from Earth denizens. These people must go about their gigantic and self-imposed tasks quietly, without undue fuss and bother.

They contact comparatively few Earth inhabitants in the rescue operation, these chosen few being acquainted with the position and allotted certain underling tasks. Of an estimated world population of 3,400,000,000 people, I understand just 4,000 have been singled out as completely trustworthy contactees. Religious persons would term them ' disciples ' or ' chelas ' of the modern age, who have earnestly sought Truth and been given it in preparation for a Golden Age to come.

The lack of general physical contact, always a mystery to us, arises from three main factors : (1) The alien helpers are not allowed, by Universal Law that is strictly adhered to by more advanced and truly civilized extraterrestrials, to interfere with the birthright gifts of free will, thought and action in Man, of whatever stage and state of evolution.

(2) By little contact at this worrying phase in Earth history, they desire to obviate the spreading of mass hysteria, alarm and fear among the people of our planet, particularly children and the aged. Distorted and frightening accounts so far published of fairly isolated incidents concerning UFOs, in various parts of the world, illustrate the truth of this and their awareness that they are unavoidable ' trespassers ' in our territory.

(3) Even if language difficulties arise in some cases, so that conversation on common ground is impossible, they constantly bear in mind sharp realisation that Earth dwellers are of suspicious, easily aroused and warlike tendency. This is fact, blunt and inescapable. One cannot refute it, on the evidence of two World Wars among our own native peoples in the past half century alone.

We frequently refer to the ' heart ' or the ' core ' of a problem. Think deep on the unseen activity that is ceaselessly going on at the centre of our planet, on the undetermined nature and character of the 'upholstery' around that inner ball, on the possible dangerous dilemma in which we are unwittingly placed. Now put your thoughts in reverse, so to speak, to this extent :—

Imagine what the turmoil must be, the mounting magnitude of innate pressures seeking egress to thrust outward from the vital heart, if the surrounding matter is pitted and stricken by fault lines, huge cracks, crevices and fissures that are yawning from upper rock strata and pronging downward...

A normal safety valve for this inner energy boiling up through these chaotic chasms in subterranean organs is provided via fiery streams of lava hurled from a volcano. This is Nature's way of expurgation, of curing any internal 'indigestion' irritating the bowels and intestinal tracts of a planet.

But such an 'overspill' is not always applicable, especially when enforced geographical displacement is a factor with which to contend. The present menace deep underground is perhaps far more malignant and ominously far-reaching than can be envisaged by the limited consciousness of Man.

Careful thought brings ready appreciation that giant earthquakes, avalanche hazards and other disasters may be inevitable in future, together with unpredictable and unstable weather conditions; for the generation of excessive heat and explosive pressures from the centre of a planet is bound to affect water masses and currents that give rise —in concert with magnetic pulls of outward influences—to patterns of climate that are usually forecastable.

Soon, therefore, the orderly scientific systems of weather computation will be disarrayed and useless. They will seize up at crisis point as the polarity change is completed. Meteorological reckoning is gradually slipping from our grasp because of the hidden factors that Man is unable to assess.

Using instruments of calculation that are immeasurably superior and accurate compared to our own seismographic apparatus, our Outer Space helpers realise the innate dangers that confront us at present. The water content of our planet exceeds land masses, yet how many of us are cognisant of the formidable ranges of mountains lying deep in our oceans at unexplored levels, or the extent of land density submerged in previous worldwide cataclyzms?

Probably, we shall never see the cities and towns entombed by oceanic overlays, their architectural form and beauty covered and secreted from the gaze of all except those who can plumb enormous depths in amazing machines, flying submarines from outer regions of the Universe manned by intelligent beings who are answering an unspoken 'S.O.S.' that, in our ignorance, we are not even aware of breathing.

As related in a later chapter of this book, one Warminster man

UFO PROPHECY

MAGNETIC BALANCE AND CHANGING POLARITY

claims to have accompanied a UFO pilot, crew and passengers to buried cities and mountain ranges lying between the mid-Atlantic and mid-Pacific oceans. There is one valid reason why I am forced to accept his bizarre story. He was warned of the Earth inner core dangers by his new friends; and this confirmed what I learned from an unusual and surprising source nine months before his journey.

There are numerous stories of UFOs seen hurtling into the seas off our coastlines, or emerging as 'spinning wheels' from the wavecaps. Sir Francis Chichester, intrepid sailor and airman, mentions one instance in an early book he wrote describing his experiences as a pilot.

The crews of these submarinal craft are surely not immersing themselves thousands of fathoms under water, simply for fun? They present us with valuable clues if we can correctly analyse their sometimes erratic behaviour; and the latter is rendered perfectly logical and exceptionally sane when we apply rational thought to motives that steer them on their inspired course of salvation.

In the wilderness of watery depths in the Atlantic and Pacific oceans, so far unexamined by Man in general, thousands of miles of uncharted mountain ranges may exist. Vast cracks could litter oceanic beds. Let the mind dwell on this probability . . . Now consider that, because of radically changing conditions underground, the magnetic frequency of the Earth core is altering, too.

To maintain equilibrium and continuing harmony, faced by this situation, what more obvious than that spacecraft and crews must of necessity be juggling with polarity adjustments of an inordinately skilful and delicate nature at this critical period?

Allow me to draw your attention, here, to that odd natural phenomenon known to geo-physicists as the Fair Weather Variant, which after steadily dropping for the past eleven years still shows no signs of rectifying itself.

Providing there is no deviation from its present rate of fall, the estimated time of reversed polarity in electrical discharges gives all electrical appliances another fifty-two years of effective life. After this, the ground level count of the Fair Weather Variant will render the operation of electrically worked devices impossible. This is surely a staggering prospect.

Furthermore, it is now believed that the detonation of a high yield thermo-nuclear device in Operation Umbrella (1959), by American A.E.C. technicians at an altitude of seventy miles, coupled with the reversal of polarity evinced by the sun and recorded by the Greenwich Observatory in a recent year, has resulted in a steady increase in the incidence of low level static interference along the shortwave bands as well as in the very high frequency band; and may be a major contributory factor in the increased rate of descent of the Fair Weather Variant.

A paper on the observations made by certain classified satellites reveals that, on measurement taken of the gravitation field of our planet, five areas were discovered that show 'bulges' or areas of increased gravity (G plus lx). These comprise five good reasons for seriously considering the content of this chapter as feasible. Here is another intriguing facet:

In the presence of a friend, a nuclear physicist in Britain once demonstrated the impossible. He received television transmissions knowing there to be no stations on the air within receiving distance at that particular time. Even the French stations were off the air.

The frequency range of the transmissions ruled out any known transmitter. It is more encouraging to the researcher to find one sympathetic ear than a hundred clinical scientists with hidebound ideas and sterile reasoning. Fortunately, curious and open-minded scientists do exist and some have occasionally joined our UFO investigating trio at Cradle Hill, Warminster. We make progress in spite of cynics and those who ridicule constructive work, such critics keeping a respectable distance from Warminster for fear of being 'contaminated' by truth.

Scientifically, I submit that all I have so far written is feasible. No realist would deny or defy the significance of startling disclosures of this nature if they are true. They would be utter imbeciles if they ignored warnings the knowledge of the 'sick' inner core and weakening outer layers brings.

Now let us view the identical framework of a horrifying possibility from the standpoint of religious tenets and aspects. There is no clash, I repeat, save in the contexts of interpretation and ideology:—

The second coming of Christ, or Buddha, or Meher Baba, or the Great White Spirit, has often been predicted in recent years, yet failed to materialize. Christmas Day of 1967 was confidently forecast as the vital date by many thousands of good Christian, Asian, Indian and Red Indian people.

Joining them, but with an irresponsible mental raggedness that

MAGNETIC BALANCE AND CHANGING POLARITY

compares badly with the seamless cloak of spiritual progress, were those who epitomize the vociferous outer fringe of religious maniacs obsessed by the shortcomings of Man. They detest him, loudly lament his failings, flay his warring nature, condemning him *en masse*, forgetting he is the living offspring of a Higher Deity in creation and still evolving.

A person I have learned to trust implicitly recently told me that to understand weakness and human frailty in others is difficult. To tolerate it is benign, to forgive it is Divine. Recognition by the individual of his own faults and blemishes is almost impossible. If achieved, to tolerate them cowardice, to transmute them practically a miracle!

Christ promised he would come again to Earth, where He laboured so well and suffered so abominably 2,000 years ago. On May 16th of 1968 we left the Piscean Age and entered the Aquarian. The symbolic fish have died, the water of a new time cycle now washing our consciousness in cosmic cleansing. Religious highlights or peaks of spiritual fulfilment have invariably risen at times of emergency in past ages.

Documentation of these is contained in the Holy Bible. They can be predetermined in cycles of time itself by astronomical and astrological influences patently recognized by gifted students of true Occultism among us; and foreseen farther afield in the sweeping eternity of the living Universe, marshalled by the Great White Brotherhood, Sons of Light, Archangels, Angeloi or Masters of Interplanetary Existence.

Clues pointing to the shape and scope of future events have come in spiritual experiences and visions flooding the consciousness of Man on Earth, after he has passed tests of initiation and learned to use part of his immense mental capacity that is still untapped.

Man advances the more he sharpens his insight on the psychic, paraphysical, paranormal and superconscious planes of dimension that stem from fruitful and self-effacing meditation on things that count in giving Life purpose. These pursuits are closely allied to religion (The Art of Correct Living) in its richer and broader perspective.

Therefore, both schools of thought and approach, religious and scientific, can be proved sound springboards, one-hundred per cent right, in the final analysis. The esoteric and arcane match the coldly factual, clinical and practical, in the prediction of future happenings, so long as there is pure sincerity in the search.

Differing channels of investigation may well evoke the same overall reaction or reality, the same eventual outcome. Each branching search for truth reaches the identical target on the tree of knowledge, so that the two are complementary and not poles apart, along the UFO trail.

Lest alarm and fear are felt by those who credit the 'inner core' problem as probable, their agitation can speedily be put at rest. In conformity with religious belief in pure essence, they can be assured that the Supreme Creator never destroys a single member of His Universe; never blots out the light of Life from any one of His children or creatures. This is dealt with more fully later.

Moreover, it is folly and against natural laws to persuade anyone, forcibly, to accept knowledge. No soul should be pressurized into belief. Man has to find Truth, finally, himself. It glows forth from his own personal experience and contact range. Nor must the virtue of extreme tolerance be forgotten.

No two minds think alike : it would be a peculiar world if that were so. Yet we have seen how two ostensibly opposed factions, religion and science, can live together amicably in our society and reach agreement on urgent issues of human evolution in crises.

This is a reassuring signpost along the paths we are taking towards understanding of major facets of the Great Unknown that blazes a fiery mantle and quicksilver form in our skies, collectively known as the UFO enigma and perhaps comprising the most important subject that will ever face Man on Earth.

To write the last portion of a book at the beginning, as I appear to have done thus far, is deemed fatal to sustained reader interest. There has to be an Alpha and Omega to everything. Perhaps I have transgressed in placing certain contentious hypotheses before you already. I am unrepentant and quite unashamed.

It should stimulate healthy thought and discussion, which is a prime feature of UFO resolving. Reference has been made to the faltering heartbeat of a planet that may be nearing its last shuddering reverberation. Let us briefly consider, now, a further probability :—

A healthy human brain is a phenomenon of almost incalculable power. It is the most sensitively attuned, complicated yet finely adjusted instrument in the whole of the Universe. Intelligently directed, it can project or beam thought patterns over tremendous distances.

It is a remarkable transmitting and receiving machine that can send and pick up mental signals corresponding to radio frequencies and wavelengths of enormous range, when correctly tuned-in to cosmic consciousness.

This is a brazen assertion, yet here we are dealing with the nine-

MAGNETIC BALANCE AND CHANGING POLARITY

tenths of our brain capacity that lies dormant, not utilized during our physical existence on the planet Earth. It is interwoven with cultural, artistic and spiritual development that Man is woefully short of at this junction point of evolvement.

The extraordinary capacity and potential of the human brain and mind, this delicately interlaced network of vibrationary fibres and grey matter, when 'tapped' at a slightly higher octave than the present average, explains how a person in London or Tokyo, Moscow or Peking, can gain instant rapport and communication with one in New York or Sydney without any exterior appendages or artificial aids.

This simple and inexpensive method of thought transference we know as mental telepathy. Our friends from Outer Space are past masters at this practice, economical and swift, effective and proven. Many can move and have their being in realms far removed from the conventional, from the restrictive webs of the fourth dimension and sixth sense that we still soberly contemplate as the ultimate in human development.

We shall shortly be learning that the brain is a chamber of many wonders, a storeroom of almost limitless coherence, a powerhouse of unsurpassable brilliance. It is a vibrant force that can virtually move mountains when the right controlling and guiding agencies are applied —and allowed—in sensible use.

Here we thinly hint at its immeasurable importance when tackling the vast problems of rebuilding a new civilization in devastated areas of our globe, in years to come, after it has been reconditioned to suit the demands of a Golden Age. My last chapter reveals more in this connection and its ancillary offshoots. Were reincarnation not a fact, we should never 'live' to enjoy the 1,000 years of unrivalled happiness our new globe and its people will experience after the 'fall.'

Yet—I stick my neck out here, unreservedly—that 'fall' may not come about in a way our earthly concepts would expect. There are greater forces at work in our atmosphere than we imagine in our limited understanding of mind and matter, of things spiritual and things physical. The full revelation, when it breaks, will shock many . . .

C

UFO PROPHECY

IN THE BLACK HOLINESS

The boy is searching for a little boat.
In the black holiness of the forest pond
He is searching for the boat
That scythes the waters with a swallow's wings.

The night is searching for the boy
With its searchlight moon
And its paper tissue smile.
It has eaten the child's boat—
And now the ship lies becalmed
On a rigid, motionless sea.

In the black holiness of the forest pond
Stretches the moon in an albatross of light;
'Come to me,' say the dark hypnotic eyes,
'I will give you a horse of ebony
And chasms of ancient stone to leap across.'

But the leaning boy finds his little boat
Lodged in the deep mountains of the moon;
In its open mouth of beaked ivory
Sorrowful sails near a deserted shore . . .

He puts out his hands and the moon kisses them.
He curves through the air in a gesture of grace
As the mountains rise and take him.
'Come,' yearn all the caverns of the moon :
'Come, we are hungry, hungry!'

CHAPTER TWO

Fireflies that Elude Scientific Appraisals

Violent vibrations of unearthly quality that battered at house rooftops and thundered against the timberwork of lofts and attics, unnerving strong minds and making stout hearts quail, caused some nervous people to cower and cringe in the Warminster district of Wiltshire, England, in late 1964 and early 1965.

Shuddering in impact, shock soundwaves made window casings rattle, walls tremble and upper doors groan in protest during night hours. Family pets were reported to be demented and demoralized by loud droning noises or high-pitched humming which accompanied the crackling ferocity of an unknown quantity in local sky lanes.

They were aerial blasts, pounding preludes to strange sightings which—while not creating widespread fear bordering on hysteria— at least prompted surprised ' victims ' to wonder at their origin. They were a far cry from ordinary and therefore comprehensible happenings.

It was apparent that here lurked an unworldly force, a savage fiend to be reckoned with if it persisted; and it did just that, as hundreds of local citizens readily testified, although in quieter and less objectionable ways eventually.

The frightening sounds suddenly ceased, to be replaced by visions of dazzling brightness. Now, after well over three years of patient investigation and more than two years of continuous observation of the night skies from a height known to all serious UFO research students in Britain as Cradle Hill, I find a fairly clear-cut pattern at long last breaking through the tangled skein of the UFO enigma.

The buffetings of noise began on Christmas Day of 1964. They formed an unusual introduction to startling glimpses of spectacular spacecraft that showed in our sky reaches after bird-killing and mice-maiming beams of ultrasonic proportion stopped plaguing a peaceful community unused to such unnatural manifestations, as outlined in my book *The Warminster Mystery*.

UFO PROPHECY

It is a unique story, because the chain of events linking together so many instances of the bizarre stretches so far in terms of time; and because we humbly boast that genuine inexplicable flying craft have appeared over our town on nearly every clear night, unmarred by low and dense cloud cover or rain, since February of 1966 to our personal knowledge.

That was when my three-person team began serious study of the phenomena, although weird happenings have gone on, unabated, for well over three years in total. Skyborne 'trespassers' must have valid and pressing reasons for continuing to 'borrow' our air space.

It is equally certain that no force on Earth, or combination of forces, can prevent their doing so while it suits their purpose. Unless one knows of more profound causes, they chose Warminster as a prime focal point of manifestations because of favourable magnetic fields locally.

Sighting reports of a vivid nature keep trickling in to me at regular intervals, coupled with the more ominous aspects of landings made around or on natural watering places and prominent hilltops by alien machines and crews. They are backed by what I have witnessed with my own eyes and senses, experiences shared by scores of other watchers on Cradle Hill in recent months alone.

Spacecraft of differing types, yet coming into a category of three principal structures or forms, have been seen from local slopes by well over 2,800 people to date, inclusive of curious parties from all regions of Britain and overseas. One would conclude that this statistic is sufficient evidence that UFOs do exist.

Yet an unseeing, unthinking and unaware major portion of the world population still doubts the authenticity of sightings. Perhaps they are too easily swayed by 'official' denials that UFOs are actual and are extraterrestrial in origin. They close unimaginative minds, shrug unconcerned shoulders and ignore the warnings expressed by the aerial perambulations of our special visitors.

Cosily complacent that there is a vast Universe all about us that extends into infinity, much of it peopled outside our own small planet, but incurious about interstellar travellers who now haunt our atmosphere in heightening numbers, these deluded souls refuse to accept the possibility of visitors from other galaxies coming to Earth from astronomical distances.

They show not a glimmer of wonder or awe that we are hosts,

UFO PROPHECY

FIREFLIES THAT ELUDE SCIENTIFIC APPRAISALS

willingly or unwillingly, to Outer Space denizens, because their eyes are blinded to reality, ears deaf to a terrific weight and wealth of first-class testimony from reputable witnesses. Personally, I feel desperately sorry for them. The shock of sudden realisation, even after ample warning, may be too much for their shattered senses to stand, when it comes.

To me, this disbelief is as great an enigma as UFOs themselves. How can they spurn as irrelevant and meaningless the strong evidence given by mentally healthy attestors whose characters are beyond reproach? Among these at Warminster have been:

Police, scientists, philosophers, medical specialists, senior teaching staff, astronomers, physicists, magistrates, local government officers, Ministers of the Church, councillors and trade union officials, Army and Royal Air Force personnel, nursing staff and a hospital physiotherapist, college students, an aero-engine designer, the wife of a senior serving pilot.

A number came deliberately to disprove the modest claims made by our trio of observers to Defence Minister Denis Healey that UFOs illuminate Warminster skies on at least half the nights of the year. Others, like a senior English lecturer at a big American school in New Jersey, Richard George from West Orange, come in blind and rewarded faith that they will view their first unaccountable flying object in skies above a town thousands of miles away.

Given the right weather conditions as specified, no earnest seeker of 'other world' evidence has left Warminster without visual proof—certainly not between February of 1966 and September of 1967, when sightings were prolific numerically.

Many examples were given in *The Warminster Mystery*, added to in this second work, testimony that stands concrete firm and unshaken under keenest interrogation. Figures speak volumes. Statistics whet editorial appetites. Facts are what the general public clamour for, successfully, so far as the small Wiltshire town is concerned.

Nor have we ever consciously sought to persuade or browbeat anyone that these spacecraft perform regularly in our atmosphere. I had to see one for myself before I dared credit their existence; and it took nine months from the original outbursts of sound, the uncanny beginning of it all, before I was utterly convinced.

We have made a number of interesting discoveries about these elegant spaceships and their crews. UFOs take the vari-coloured shapes

UFO PROPHECY

of glowing spheres, luminous peardrops, ovular jewels that range from blood red rubies to winking diamonds of flashing light; from lustrous grey daytime pearls of shimmering surface to fiery green emeralds that decorate the nocturnal heavens with fluorescent brilliance, transparent opals to dense white cigar aeroforms.

Seen through a three-inch telescope at night, a hovering spacecraft is a glorious firefly of radiating colour changes, pulsating from centre to outward edges in a continuous stream of flickering and living energy patterns, with white, amber, green, red and blue predominating.

The most common daylight variety is a gunmetal grey that sparkles with silvery majesty when sunrays strike it through lurking fleecy clouds. Basic shapes are round, bell and long or torpedo. Sizes vary, we find, as do conventional aircraft designed for differing tasks and responsibilities on our native planet.

Longer and larger airships, much more rare, are likened by witnesses to aerial submarines, silver white zeppelins or illuminated train carriages in flight, round ended and complete with apparent window slots or portholes along the sides.

The majority of these phenomena are distant and silent in motion, as are smaller types invariably, unless and until they swoop close to the ground—then a distinctive buzzing or droning is audible, reminiscent of millions of swarming bees in a large echo chamber. On Cradle Hill, we see UFOs very low in altitude about once in every thirtieth clear night, on average.

Crimson bellied monsters that shed bright cones of light over the surrounding countryside are also among lesser seen UFOs. They hover over hilltops and have an odd carrying role. Wingless and massive, they swish over the 'targets' with a peculiar whistling noise, to poise there in lambent glory.

Swaying tentacles are dropped from the underside of the craft, down which slide and writhe smaller brethren that resemble agile ants, usually red or orange in colour. These industrious minions probe hilltops and dance over marshy ground before returning as if on coiling ropes to the main superstructure that gives them birth.

It is a fascinating spectacle to watch, the small discs tilting, twisting and foraging while evidently engaged in 'grubbing' duties in topsoil, as though injecting a special substance or energizing beam deep into hillsides and under marshland. Occasionally, a sharp stabbing light

FIREFLIES THAT ELUDE SCIENTIFIC APPRAISALS

appears from the sides of the master craft, revolving slowly once the discs are released.

Operation completed, the lively air ants dart up to the supporting umbrella or canopy overhead, rolling back to base on the slender threads. It is as if they invade the heights to insure them in some mysterious fashion against future cosmic events, as a necessary safeguard to prevent flaws developing at a vital juncture.

Or as though they were purging certain areas of evil and unwanted forces that seek to cripple a predestined plan for Earth. Whatever their primary mission and aim, they are a strange sight to behold, the slender ribbons of red down which the minions swarm and slither of an impermanent quality.

This is proved to the observer, for when the small discoids eventually ' home ' on to the larger aeroform, these threads break up into shapeless wisps of fading light that gradually disperse and vanish from view, sometimes after the carrier craft has left the scene. But they are rare UFO specimens.

Only four such manifestations, of a baffling nature, have been observed in the Warminster district. Cley Hill has been an outstanding example of this sort of happening, just off the main Warminster to Frome road at Corsley. Perhaps understandably so, for this height was notorious in the past for heathenish practises and devil worship of a particularly evil order.

Black magic rites, initiations and lewd ceremonies, I gather from inquiry and research of an historical character, were a commonplace there in past centuries, even surviving in a more subdued light and scale early in this, the 20th.

Apart from the suspicious, predatory and superstitious traits in his makeup, Man is a curious animal, his detective instincts fully aroused when challenged by ' invaders,' friendly or hostile, who fit no established and recognizable Earth concept in behaviour.

When investigating UFOs, however, he must learn to control impulsive action while at the same time smothering natural fear, if he is to arrive at correct answers to the constant puzzle they present. Commendable caution is advised every watcher on the ground—yet unreasoning fear of the imponderable unknown is unwarranted.

Familiarity must never breed contempt, either. Take my sincere word for this. Especially active in speckling the sky over Cradle Hill, the most common UFO is what I can only term ' a thinking light ' or 'brain beacon.' These normally fly at high altitude, according to the eye, but this is an optical illusion that stems from their miniature status.

They are tiny, flitting mosquitoes in movement; simply bright lights of circular physique that change direction rapidly, sometimes at bewildering speeds. They are usually amber or white and surrounded by a glowing aura or halo, on edge looking like a shallow plate no more than a foot in diameter. Scientific appraisal is difficult, although certain clues give a pointer to their specific role in the UFO plan.

In June of 1966, using the yardstick of thirty feet in diameter which we associate through experience with the ordinary dome-topped saucer type, and based on a triangulation measurement method aided by astro-compasses or theodolites, a British Unidentified Flying Object Research Association (BUFORA) team headed by Edgar Hatvany checked the speed of one UFO scorching sky reaches over Cradle Hill as between 56,000 and 72,000 miles an hour.

One member of my regular team, Bob Strong, calculating from his past service as a Royal Air Force bomber crewman, has shrewdly estimated flight rates of some UFOs as topping the 100,000 mph mark. He knows conventional aircraft 'inside out,' so his help and advice are invaluable to me. The majority of UFOs, however, obviously desirous of being seen by disbelievers attracted to the hill, obligingly saunter across at little more than satellite speed—and perform all manner of strange aerobatics to prove they are not Earth artifacts.

If we can rely on these assessments, as expertly organised as possible in determining the factual, here surely is evidence that only the fantastic and incredible—to us—are feasible at the cosmic level of technological evolution that our visitors have attained.

Let us study more minutely the 'thinking light' kind, for they are quite interesting. When seen near the ground, hovering over copse or hedgerow, the myth as to far distance, when seen earlier, is exploded. They are no larger than the dimensions of a football and comprise a shallow shining disc like a plate or soup tureen.

We are confident that these are robots of a remote-controlled mechanical and electrical nature, sent out from bigger craft on close survey operations. They gather data needed by the 'senders,' storing knowledge and details in electrical memory cells and on film plates.

They are electronic 'brains' with metallic casings but having all-seeing, all-hearing and all-recording potentials. These unmanned

FIREFLIES THAT ELUDE SCIENTIFIC APPRAISALS

surveyors must be of tremendous value to interplanetary travellers farther aloft, anxious to learn all they can about our reactions, our peaceful and warlike tendencies, as exemplified in past history perhaps to their own forebears.

Tiny devices such as these can plunge low with impunity into dangerous territory, into battle exercise areas for Army troops and heavy armoured fighting vehicles to the North of town on Salisbury Plain and at Imber, where even the most fleeting touchdown of manned craft might be a suicidal risk.

On beneficial missions to Earth the small subsidiaries can study sub-strata, crops, vegetation, water content, human reaction and emotion at their noticed advent, at a leisurely pace. They can reach places, underground shelves and oceanic caves, etc., which are inaccessible to the larger craft. We have had several 'brushes' with them in the copse at the top of Cradle Hill, as explained later.

Watching their purposeful actions carefully, my co-observers and I are sure they are intermediaries, able to chronicle and record whatever is 'seen' and 'heard' for prompt relay to humanoids aboard the launching airships, waiting expectantly hundreds of miles farther up for all available information they can amass.

Superbly constructed and motivated, the robot thinking lights are self-sufficient for their 'linking' duties. Unless one is steeped in UFO lore, well acquainted with mystical habits and manoeuvres they exhibit, one can be forgiven for imagining that such minor revelations are only as substantial as figments of fevered thought trends from a space fiction writer, in futuristic word creation.

Conclusively, eye-witness accounts verify that these 'servant' spheroids of pygmy stature have giant capacities despite their physical frailty. No fanciful embroidery in description or strained mental logic is necessary to guess the exact relationship between small and larger UFO craft. Robot mechanizms are patently working in perfect unison and co-operation with major spaceships, supplying ready replies to questions flowing from their occupants.

Experiences where the pygmies are seen to plunge straight into the bellies of the bigger ships after completing their missions are too strong to be rejected, too corroborative to laugh off as 'nonsensical' or 'illusionary.' And a common denominator that applies to all these celestial chariots, giant and fairylike, is that they are phantoms of an elusive quality.

UFO PROPHECY

Their speed in flight and weaving alterations of course and direction, on occasions, openly mock laws of gravity and frictional atmospheric barriers. To be absolutely fair to the unversed, one has to see these unhalting veerings at speed to credit that the eyes are not being deceived.

Whoever or whatever is in charge of these hallucinated machines has overcome problems of gravity pull and anti-gravity leverage, working in harmony with natural magnetic fields, force lines and energy elements in and beyond the atmosphere of Earth. In short, they persistently rebel against present scientific limitations that curb our own flight progress at phenomenal rates.

In addition to complete mastery of electro-magnetizm in its broadest concepts, do they harness certain strengths and lengths of solar rays for storage in a central column to provide positive and negative force facilities they can manipulate as and when needed?

Can they, by skilful extraction of some of the superfluous energies of Nature and knowledge of polarity reversal factors, produce extra power, drive and impetus under all conditions of flight and manoeuvrability? The full explanation of technical and scientific perplexities they create for us, yet have conquered themselves, would give Man the Open Sesame to undreamed of conquest in outer regions of the immence Universe.

As this would undoubtedly be warlike in approach, rather than peaceful probing, they lock such secrets from us and throw away the key: not to be found and used by us until we are spiritually equipped to join interplanetary brethren and sisters on voyages of discovery in interstellar realms.

I am not easily fooled. I dare not be. I have built my reputation as a journalist on the bedrock of integrity. Nevertheless, soberly judging by facts collected from solid citizens whose eyesight is not defective, whose temperament is equable and senses rational, I have to conclude that these machines are not of this Earth.

This assuredly applies to the majority, although—as explained later—a few have been manufactured on Earth, by amateurs who have been permitted to learn enough of hidden secrets of the cosmic brotherhood because they can be trusted more than professionals. Even so, these craft are inferior to the interplanetary versions.

Weighing all testimony to date, evaluating it carefully on the local UFO front alone, our team concedes that these wonderful machines fail to comply or conform with the behaviour, performance and char-

FIREFLIES THAT ELUDE SCIENTIFIC APPRAISALS

acteristics of conventional aircraft. Therefore they correspond to unidentifiable and unrecognisable factors and must be classified as extraterrestrial artifacts.

A stubborn pointer giving the lie to any assumption that they are prototypes of vertical takeoff craft, or ground to air missiles on the secret list of the British military, is that they have been sighted in no fewer than seventy countries.

Furthermore, no aircraft on this planet is soundless in flight, unless one considers gliders having severely limited altitude and capabilities. A guided missile, even if capable of hovering, does not possess the circular or teardrop shape of the majority of UFOs. It is pencil slim and can travel relatively short distances.

It definitely does not have the propensity for hovering in one spot for over an hour, a feature of UFOs that bathe Cradle Hill with radiance. A helicopter or whirlybird is no suitable candidate for the UFO race handicap, either. It is far too raucous, noisy and unmistakable even at maximum altitudes it can achieve.

A relevant query is : Why on Earth, or out of it, should so many alien air vessels haunt Cradle Hill in particular ? Service aircraft that are capable of doing so (and the number of these is restricted) are not allowed, under strict regulations and stiff penalties, to hover over populated communities. This single transgression of our visitors led me to approach highest service authority.

Back in the spring of 1966, having seen decided UFOs every clear night from local hilltops during a six-week period of constant observation, I wrote a personal letter of invitation to our Minister for Defence, the Right Honorable Denis Healey, telling him of our astounding findings and cordially asking him to journey to Warminster to view these spacecraft for himself, in company with other Cabinet Ministers.

I was politely rebuffed by a Mr. M. H. Toft, who wrote to me from the Ministry offices in Whitehall. Thanking me for my invitation, he pointed out that the Minister was a busy man and could not spare time to avail himself of my offer. Then followed a list of the usual frustrating kind of stereotyped, official ' brush-off ' versions in explanation of most UFO sighting claims.

The preferable alternatives included Venus, atmospheric disturbances, sun-dogs, balloons and meteorological apparatus, sun reflected from wings of high-flying birds, satellites, optical illusion, hallucination, imagination, spots before the eyes ... You name it—they gave it !

UFO PROPHECY

WARNINGS FROM FLYING FRIENDS

We were quietly stunned. It was as though we were trying to sell Her Majesty's Government the Eiffel Tower in Paris or the Empire State Building in New York illegally, as opposed to being co-operative and presenting them with first-hand evidence that genuine UFOs are not rare ornithological specimens around Warminster.

The probable explanations glibly trotting from the pen of Mr. Toft, on behalf of Mr. Healey and his colleagues, made us smile after initial annoyance, although it was tactfully admitted that about ten per cent of reported sightings are inexplicable. Actually, the letter was worded to the effect that more than ninety per cent are explainable.

Since then, I have not tried to convince H.M. Government that UFOs exist or—as my friend Bob suggested—that the whole ten per cent must be dancing a lively jig over Warminster every week! Whether official departments like it or not, the Air Ministry must know what the position is from pilots' reports.

If the Ministry ever insisted, I could show them several letters I have received from Royal Air Force men, serving officers and leading aircraftsmen, also NCOs, asking me for ' all possible information ' I can kindly give them about Unidentified Flying Objects, as these now form a part of their course in extra study training.

We were prepared to be co-operative right up to the hilt. In fact I submitted witness accounts and photographs for exhaustive testing and examination by Air Ministry experts, up to August of 1967. The ' no comment ' notes attached as evaluation on the return of prints and negatives have been zealously hoarded and filed.

' No comment ' is reasonable enough for us, for it is clear why no government dares commit itself to acknowledging, publicly, that UFOs are real and not derived from this globe. Had it not been for their abject refusal to take advantage of our offer, I could well sympathize with Ministry officials and departments who are obviously more baffled by UFO perplexities than our team are, in their dilemma.

Materializm and the commercial profit motive are anathema to progress along a trail to shining truth, especially in this field of research. That much we have learned. However, government support nil, we sensibly ignored the depressing and discouraging official attitude which brands high-grade witnesses as liars and continued to plough furrows of lonely investigation regardless.

Statistics to date may crystallize the local situation and sublimate to some extent what people may think to be exaggerated and extrav-

UFO PROPHECY

FIREFLIES THAT ELUDE SCIENTIFIC APPRAISALS

agent claims meekly made by our team of stalwarts. They are of more than scant interest, even to the scientist who prefers the concrete to the abstract, the tangible to the untouchable.

Up to Christmas of 1967 Bob Strong had seen 563 genuine UFOs, all but sixteen at night. Sybil Champion, our housewife observer, lynx-eyed in spotting the real and the 'phoney,' had chalked up a total of 559. My humbler tally was 536, my profession making wide inroads into evening hours spent reporting council meetings, trades council gatherings, dinners and assemblies of local organizations, etc.

Since February of 1966, Bob has taken no fewer than 3,523 camera shots of elusive spacecraft, of which only 101 have developed convincingly. However, we modestly claim that these comprise the finest collection of authentic pictures in the world, of their specialist kind, taken over a span of two years and a month to date, March of 1968.

On the majority of occasions, witnesses have been in our company when these photos were taken. Bill Nixon, of Pathe News, has taken movie black and white and colour shots of UFOs from Cradle Hill. Nothing developed on his film. Why? Simultaneously, Bob was taking still pictures on a comparatively inferior camera. He captured the images of UFOs. Why?

Nowadays, Bob employs two high grade cameras, a 300 mm magnification lens, a 500 mm magnification telephoto lens, a three-inch telescope, a 15 x 60 x 60 instrument for easy handling and swift assessment of craft coursing above us, inclusive of satellites, conventional Earth aircraft and all strange luminous bodies that spell or shriek 'UFO.' A reflector telescope and powerful binoculars are other necessary purchases.

To those who are misguided enough to imagine we capitalize on research and photos, I stress that we have spent well over £500 from our own pockets in essential equipment to record pictorial UFOs, faithfully. If we wished to get rich quickly, I am certain we could 'unload' some of our pictures to American and European magazines for colossal sums which, in aggregate, could net us a small fortune.

We abstain because each of us instinctively realises that 'there will be a time and a place for everything.' It is better to bow to such dictates, which may be generated by those who 'allow' us to reap their images on film...This is not as fantastic as it seems, judging from experiences we have shared.

Naturally, best results come when UFOs are hovering obligingly, or when they sweep in from the opposite direction of a full moon setting, at night. If spaceships are distant, the three-inch telescope gives crisper detail than binoculars if the angle is not physically impossible to align on or follow.

This telescope is the most vital, yet oldest, part of our research gear. A legacy from Bob's grandfather, it reminds us of early attempts at photography through its lens by pressing a thirty shilling camera against it in hopes of non-wobble at crucial moments! Successes were few but worthwhile.

Acute disappointment resulted from early efforts, however, in the main. Instead of UFOs on film, all we ended up with were bizarre shapes—of animals, birds, fish, serpents, pyramids in series of triangles, stone columns and arches, ridges illustrative of stairways or ladders... How the 'experts' and cynics would have reviled us, had we shown them these peculiarities, seriously purporting them to be UFOs!

Not oblivious to this, yet extremely puzzled by the odd impressions, we destroyed most of these negatives and prints. We wish, now, we had retained them, if only as historical and personal museum pieces of testimony; for much later we learned what they represented in symbolic terminology, as outlined in another chapter. There was method lurking behind madness, here. They were not as effete and unproductive as we first thought.

Yes, Warminster sky spaces have been hosts to thousands of alien craft in the past three years and three months, from December 25th of 1964. The gentle aerial strolling of 'maiden aunt' satellites we discount. They are so obvious, so neck-stiffening to watch in their laggardly though graceful movements.

Clement Freud visited our hill one night and described these satellites as elderly dowagers at a sedate tea party on rolling lawns. We also discount high-flying jet fighters, identifiable by their trailing sound wake after darting across the heavens at maximum altitude. UFOs have been seen 'dancing rings around jets' travelling at full speed, or 'playing leapfrog over them,' as referred to in *The Warminster Mystery*.

The hard fact remains, and this sometimes disheartens us: These amazing airships, these chimeric chariots that bejewel the skies in a multiplicity of shapes and colours, elude precise scientific appraisals. Logically, there must be valid reasons why their occupants dare not permit too close contact.

UFO PROPHECY

FIREFLIES THAT ELUDE SCIENTIFIC APPRAISALS

If one could entice a spaceship to land and be available for putting under a slide for microscopic analyses to be made, with content, composition, motivation power ascertained by examination in depth, scientists would be absolutely satisfied that here indeed is something not of this Earth.

Yet I am thankful there are sufficient scientists with open minds who are inquisitive and concede there are other dimensions to be explored beyond the hypothetical fourth, senses existing beyond the extrasensory sixth; and are ready to accept the challenge that UFOs present to brains and minds of the curious.

Sorting out hundreds of inquiring letters in my post intake, I am content that doctors, surgeons, physicists, geologists, archaeologists and some of the finest teachers in the world, practical and spiritual, are at last taking seriously the greatest mystery in the history of Man on Earth so far, in this present civilization.

At this point I take an opportunity of complimenting sincere Ufologists everywhere. Intelligent and dedicated devotees are among students the world over who are questing for ultimate proof in this important pioneering field. The resolving of UFO conundrums cannot be achieved by sceptics with closed minds who jeer conscientious efforts to probe deep into unexplored fastnesses and grapple with unknown factors in search of utter truths.

Much of value can be accomplished by the many quiet, industrious and methodical investigators on a voluntary basis who spend leisure hours to get to the very roots of the acute problems and mysteries with which UFOs beset us. The final outcome could well be that those who blind themselves to reality, as mutely attested to by millions of disbelievers already ' toeing ' the ' official ' lines of misreasoning, will be those who abjectly 'fall by the wayside' when the profound meanings behind UFO appearances are eventually revealed for the clear understanding of us all. This book, I hope, will give shrewd insight to some of these meanings . . .

For we are earnest seekers of truth in the absolute. Nothing short of that will appease the insatiable appetite of our trio of investigators. This is no lighthearted escapade or cheap gimmick on our part. No governmental or private backing of a financial sort has assisted us, although BUFORA and the International Sky Scouts (now Contact UK) have been helpful with loans of equipment now and again, making our tasks easier.

UFO PROPHECY

Although I am a journalist, the UFO activity in and around Warminster constituting a 'scoop' of unparalleled magnitude to me, no one can accuse us of not giving full, up-to-date information to those seeking further knowledge. Many in all sectors of our globe, we know, can substantiate this. It is often more blessed to give than to receive.

During the past two years I have lectured on UFOs to numerous Rotary Clubs and other interested organizations over a wide area of the United Kingdom, by request from them. In September of 1966 I spoke at the annual Northern Conference of BUFORA at Bradford, Yorkshire. I then modestly prophesied that by May of the following year the world would know a great deal more about our 'visitors' and their purpose in coming into our atmosphere in increasing numbers.

When the reader reaches Chapter 16 of this work, it will be noted that—had I then been able to find an agency for the startling information given to me by an unworldly 'person' named Karne—this prediction would have been enhanced and completely justified.

COROLLAS OF GOLD

It was a silver bell that came, quiet as oblivion,
Brighter than mirrored jewels in still water.
It was a bell dropping the shadow of a black butterfly
Where the land shakes its shoulders in a gesture of mountains,
Stretching their wavering mists between the hills' hollow hands.

Often I think of the strange faces
Pressed like flowers behind glass;
Marble white at dawn, with ivy glances
Luminous as fresh oak leaves full of sun
In the green wonder of their eyes.

They did not seek the daylight—
And yet it found them trespassing the morning,
Trembling the meadows and the wine-dark earth.

Somehow, only the simmering corn
Saw the grace of their profiles,
Cut like a cameo in the pale sun's corollas of gold.

CHAPTER THREE

Trifling Pointers are Embryonic Clues

Do UFO crews resemble us in stature, looks and mannerisms, bodies having similar chemical contents, organic properties and cell structure? Do masks that cover their mouths—a peculiarity noted by several witnesses when our visitors have landed in the Warminster area—denote that they are singularly anxious to avoid contact with micro-organisms or viruses which might infect or reinfect men, women and children on their native globes, upon return to home bases by space explorers?

Conversely, are the extraterrestrial voyagers concerned that they might unwittingly pass on to us germs of unknown disease potential, harmful to respiratory systems and causing blood stream impurity, or radioactive substances gathered and absorbed during long interstellar journeying into our atmosphere, mindful that they 'trespass' in our sky lanes on missions not requested by Earth people initially?

If they appreciate that our present medical science cannot guarantee certain antidotes, or that we have no natural barriers of immunity and resistance to counteract new and possibly deadly bacteria from interplanetary reaches beyond our ken, they hesitate to land and openly contact us more than is necessary.

This is one humane principle that could be associated with higher intelligences dedicated to preservation and conservation rather than wanton destruction of life and moral values. Or—the most probable explanation, I feel, on rational assumption—do these humanoids breathe a different sort of air from us in their own natural environs?

If they do, then oxygen might well prove fatal to their particular brand of lungs, heart and blood. Their bodies need not be carbon-based, their cell structure entirely at variance with ours, so that air composition and gravity density might vary considerably between galaxies. Even atmospheric pressures could differ.

This challenge to a technologically advanced civilization could be

UFO PROPHECY

overcome in alien conditions by the use of adaptable and adjustable mechanical aids and the carrying of their own air supply cylinders equipped for conversion, assisted by special masks or respirators, during trips to Earth.

Only fools would deny the existence of life on other planets in an immeasurable Universe. It need not automatically follow that Earth type atmospheres and magnetic field strengths, coupled with identical gravity density, are essential for its emergence and sustenance on various sized planets.

Just as we have pygmies and relative giants in our society, plus a number of colour ranges according to pigmentation, our visitors doubtless differ in proportion with life-giving elements applicable to their respective planets or solar systems.

Reliable stories of 'little green men' and 'seven-foot giants' with crimson faces and large nasal organs, containers manipulated at their chests by gauntleted hands, rubber tubing running to masks, simply endorse this prospect of infinite variety and conditions dissimilar from our own. Evolutionary changes must occur physically as well as mentally.

Tiny clues, trifling in themselves, are of paramount significance when added together to present a coherent picture and collective logic in assessment of UFO crews and their spaceships. For example:

From extensive sleuthing work at and around Stonehenge, we can make deductions of a fairly sensible nature. Here we find a wide radius of burial barrows, tumuli and ancient earthworks that bring us to the fringe of certain probabilities.

We are acquainted with round barrows, bell barrows and long barrows. Young Douglas Chaundy, of Burnham-on-Sea, and housewife Mollie Carey, amateur archaeologist living in the village of Stockton, near Warminster, to whom we are grateful for intense interest and enthusiasm in their task, have helped us actively in this aspect of research.

Thus we discover that the old burial barrows, in shape and sometimes in actual dimensions, conform to the three most common varieties of UFOs seen in the area. This is a quietly exciting find, for under our very noses on the ground are symbolic layouts of what may have been haunting Wiltshire skies for millenia. Trifling pointers like these are clues in an embryonic stage, surely.

The barrows are: Bell, which contain an amount of flint in their

UFO PROPHECY

TRIFLING POINTERS ARE EMBRYONIC CLUES

composition and correspond to the typical flying saucer. Round, representative of the 'translucent bubble,' a spheroid usually green at night and glowing with alternating dull and bright luminosity, likened by researchers to an implosion device that neutralizes excess radioactivity. And long, matched by cigar aeroforms sometimes classed as 'mother' ships when releasing smaller discoids into flight at distances far from Earth.

What is more relevant, perhaps: Take away the smaller barrows when making an aerial survey of the long barrows in isolation, drawing a ground floor map of the clearly defined positioning of these on Salisbury Plain, and you notice that they give an accurate presentation of constellations of stars, including Ursa Major or The Plough, in the Northern sky.

One can make reasonable conclusions from these factors. Either primitive Stone Age inhabitants or ancient Celtic communities were on more than mere nodding terms with greatly advanced civilizations from these Northern sky regions in the past, thus building their burial barrows as mute evidence that this link once existed; or they constructed interment grounds in this way to 'guide in' friends from Outer Space to these areas in the long ago when indigenous Man was in his mental and spiritual infancy, welcoming expert assistance.

Archaeologists have often argued over the purpose and history of enigmatic Stonehenge, but we must try and override sacrosanct territory of the 'experts' here, in searching for UFO truths. Much on the ground can be correlated to permanent and impermanent phenomena in the heavens. Are these Northern constellations, copied so faithfully by long burial barrows on the plain, where the designers and perhaps even builders of Stonehenge came from originally?

A local farmer found, one morning in the summer of 1965, that several acres of land left fallow near our town were 'a mass of weeds' —they were silvery thistles of a rare type that virtually ceased to flourish in England in the year 1918, proclaimed the experts who rushed excitedly to the scene.

The amazing story made headlines in regional newspapers, but we did not dream of connecting the sudden eruption of unusual growth with space visitors or their machines. Naturalists and botanists from all sectors of the United Kingdom flocked to the farm to see the astounding crop, the overnight wonder, which was unique.

They included highly qualified staff from horticultural and agricultural schools and colleges, botanical gardens, universities and natural study groups. They came in awe to view the acres of an extremely scarce plant that never grows in more than the odd one or two clumps in any county in England.

Although we did not link such freakish growth with UFO manifestations overhead, it could be that the force field power of spacecraft had unlooked-for effects on plants of specific kinds.

Checking carefully on reports, I discovered later that inexplicable flying objects were regularly seen over this particular piece of farmland on successive nights before the wild thistles mushroomed in prolific and abnormal quantity.

Harold and Dora Horlock, over whose garden in East Street 'a large red poker' hung suspended for some while, as explained in *The Warminster Mystery*, then flew off with a noise 'like the crackling of frying bacon,' made news copy and a BBC 'Points West' programme after ordinary thistles in their front garden soared to a prodigious height of almost twelve feet as opposed to the expected 3ft. 6ins., that same summer.

The Warminster area farmer begged reporters to keep the precise whereabouts of the astonishing thistle crop secret, fearing that if it was publicized hordes of the curious would trample down agricultural crops growing in adjacent fields.

At first, he confided, he was strongly tempted to hoe down the thistles. He took them to be offending weeds, but a naturalist friend prevented such desecration just in time, aware of their identity and rarity. Other minor revelations broke locally that year, not mentioned in my last book for the simple reason that their possible connection with UFO activity did not prong my mind at that period.

For instance, Warminster gardener Joel Sibley grew a plant that broke world records for the number of cucumbers on its stems. A leading horticultural journal seized on this news, with illustrations. It made quite a splash in the gardening world.

Odd stories of a spring that surged overnight into a Church Street cottage garden from an apparently untraceable source, of gravestones vanishing from their kitchen paving status and reappearing in courtyard form outside a farm labourer's dwelling in Kingston Deverill, made us ponder on the macabre. There was no relationship between the bizarre news items and UFOs, we thought.

Printing compositor Roger Hooten, whose garden became a miniature

TRIFLING POINTERS ARE EMBRYONIC CLUES

lake, dug frenziedly with a spade before starting and after finishing his daily labour, to let gushing water escape when it began flooding rooms he rented from George Knock.

To accommodate the terrific inflow that spurted from a spot at the bottom of the garden, he eventually dug seven feet in depth over a period of three days. Even so, the pool measured ten feet in width and twelve feet in length when the unwelcome water stopped gushing.

Much to his relief and that of his landlord, the local police and water board officials, it abruptly dried up and evaporated—as poor Roger was contemplating converting the lake into a duckpond to amuse scores of child visitors! It was a baffling eruption, although it was rumoured that an unmapped underground water pipe connecting with the supply to the Lord Weymouth School nearby had broken. Incidentally, water flows under a large proportion of Warminster dwellings.

Three women have told me, each making a separate approach, of the strange 'floating' sensation they experience when crossing a footpath through a cornfield near the heights of Battlesbury, in Warminster, not far East from our favourite night sky observation point at Cradle Hill.

Blindly, we did not immediately connect this with our space visitors, either. More enlightened nowadays, we realise that these small truths, meaningless and effete when taken out of the context of the overall UFO pattern, are significant.

Occasionally, Cradle Hill watchers have felt uneasy, dizzy, as though standing or walking on jellified legs. It is as if some unaccountable force is being generated from underground, matched by vibrations of an unearthly sort beating invisibly downward from the air.

The three women near Battlesbury had to part the corn stalks with shaking hands to make sure their numbed feet were still treading the narrow path. Their uncertainty is expressed by one housewife, Anne Parham of Boreham Road.

She told me in late July of 1967 that the loss of feeling in nether limbs 'made me very unsteady and unsure of my balance for over a minute as I walked along the path. I felt I was simply floating along without using my legs at all. Imagine yourself in a very fast car, speeding over a humpbacked bridge.

'You seem to leave your stomach in midair as you mount the highest point, your heart leaping. That was the effect this had on me.' she continued. 'Not that I was walking fast—I only had that impression.

UFO PROPHECY

As though I was lifted bodily and suspended over the wheat, feet pushing down hard without meeting any resistance.'

This phenomenon happened on two occasions, both at night when the women were taking a short cut to the military camp from the Boreham district. They have laughed over the peculiar feeling of 'weightlessness' since, although it quite scared them at the material time.

There is an obvious clue here. Do UFOs 'home' on high frequency signals generated from apparatus buried deep underground in that area, possibly millenia ago, by forbears of our present race of UFO aeronauts; perhaps a transmitting device placed there deliberately, in shrewd foresight or pre-calculation of a future cosmic event, scientifically computed in the long ago?

Our team have a pretty good idea where such an instrument might be located, but realise the deadly danger resulting from foolish excavation in reaching it. By tampering with such apparatus, by attempts to remove it from its embedded power centre, the whole of the nearby barracks and an extensive section of the town itself might be blown asunder by the terrific detonation.

Another brain-teasing imponderable is: The closer the spaceship to the observer, the less chance there is of capturing a 'scoop' picture. This is amply proven by what took place—or did not, rather—at Starr Hill, between Battlesbury and Scratchbury, on the night of Thursday, April 13th.

Bob Strong took no fewer than thirty-two 'shots' of an orange-glowing and hemispherical topped spaceship that silently hovered over a shoulder of the hill in haloed glory for several minutes at about 11.56 p.m. It was as bold and prominent to the eye as a lighted house window on edge, no farther than 250 yards from our vantage point near Middle Barn overlooking deserted East Hill Farm.

It showed detail in design we had never seen previously. Yet nothing developed on the plates except wavy horizontal and vertical lines indicative of scorching. Why? There could be several sound reasons, from the viewpoint of those aboard the fiery monster.

The force field from the 'sitting target' may have been too overpowering at that close proximity, not sufficiently strong to harm the onlooker yet adversely affecting a camera mechanism. Again, the people on board the slightly tilting craft may not have wished such revealing film (if we had been successful) to get into wrong hands,

UFO PROPHECY

TRIFLING POINTERS ARE EMBRYONIC CLUES

subsequently, with power-crazy cliques on Earth thereby learning too much from print-filling closeups of the exterior. Or again, they were simply demonstrating a warning of dangers from venturing too near harmful radiation.

We now have a scientist friend, employed in chemical engineering, who is working on a colour inversion principle and formula to help us decide what type of film to employ for best results when within hailing distance of these tantalizing UFOs.

Colours and sounds are important criteria in dealing with a technology and way of life that out-strips our own in many respects, as incidents in this book will amplify. Various entities, in a dimension beyond the infrared and ultra-violet, exist and are invisible to the gaze of Man at present.

The blunt and inescapable truth is: Numerous facets of UFO behaviour fail to fit snugly into conventional pockets of Earth thinking and scientific attitude. In the past year alone, our team trio have shared a total of 1,365 voluntary skywatching hours from local heights that embrace Cley Hill, Battlesbury, Scratchbury, Westbury White Horse, Starr Hill, Lords Hill, Willoughby and our beloved Cradle Hill.

This averages out at more than twenty-six hours a week additional to our employment. We enjoy company if it is sincere and dedicated, although a sense of humour at ' flat ' periods of non-sighting is cheering when the blood is cold.

On winter nights we have been frozen to the marrow by bitter North winds and gales in shelterless and exposed locales; drenched by lashing rain or pelting snow and hail, shoulders bowed yet spirits unbroken in face of the perpetual challenge UFOs evoke.

With bouts of bronchial trouble, influenza and heavy colds to combat at personal level, it has been a difficult and exhausting labour of love, only the sightings of spectacular aeroforms pumping the blood warmly through chilled veins and limbs.

Humility in approach is a prime requisite in a thrilling if exacting quest. We appreciate the subject to be of supreme importance in the destiny of Man. It is far bigger than consideration of a single person, group, organization or race. Minds should not be clouded to this truism.

If not seeing, hearing and recording things of worthwhile import, which help maintain our solidarity of purpose, we should stand accused of being the most stupid fools in Christendom, certifiable for entry into any mental institution. Of course we should.

UFO PROPHECY

Never are we more conscious of dangerous ground we tread than when facing verbal battering from cynics with closed minds. We were formerly over-sensitive to barbed criticism, which now bounces off an impregnable defence of thick hides and impervious minds. One cannot afford to be deterred by senseless tirades of abuse from sceptics whose inertia of body, compared with freedom of tongue, ties them idly to armchairs instead of engagement in active field work.

More than once, especially when forced to gape in frustration at results of early filming, we were tempted to 'throw up the sponge' and refuse to take any further health hazards on those hills. My book *The Warminster Mystery* gave at least two examples of the fantastic unpredictability of UFOs, when transmogrification impeded our photographic progress and diminished our enthusiasm.

Remember the 'flying bat' and 'pyramid' pictures in my last work? We were in fact seeing typical UFO shapes through the telescope and camera eyepiece when taking those shots; and winced at unaccountable travesties of original forms which marred prints after development by Edwin Till, commercial processor in George Street, Warminster.

Fruits of three months of filming elusive and fleeting airships, we ended up with prints emblazoned with weird animal heads, bodies and legs; birds running an inscrutable gamut between domestic duck and giant eagle; wriggling snakes and serpents; scale-coated fish; triangle arrangements; series of stairs and towering stone columns, fancy ridged and as if pounded by seawater . . .

Frankly, we despaired of getting anything sensible and realistic on our negatives, something we could show to collaborators and critics alike as pictorial evidence of UFOs. The spacecraft in our camera sights were extremely uberous—but not, unfortunately, of their own true ilk.

Thankfully, when we were verging on pulling out from an uneven contest, from investigation of an enigma that gave no encouragement of final success to the serious student, as though sensing our acute dismay and shivering disconsolation on lonely hilltops, the crews of the alien airships changed their tactics and allowed us more convincing glimpses of spacecraft physique on film.

What was their object in presenting us with 'false' images in the first place? It took us a long while to analyze, correctly, their motives. They had valid reasons, as later chapters define and clarify. Demonstrably, their erratic behaviour made us think deeply. A culinary

UFO PROPHECY

TRIFLING POINTERS ARE EMBRYONIC CLUES

metaphor is that proper stirring of thought often produces an appetising dish of discovery!

Bob, Sybil and I will not easily forget a September experience in the middle of the copse atop Cradle Hill in 1967, where we were discussing the singular events of Tuesday, August 29th of 1967. Let me deal with the latter first, to avoid any out of sequence complication:

After a positive landing of a cone shaped UFO that dropped like a fiery stone to the copse, before veering immediately to a final resting place about 1,000 yards away and near a second wooded belt to our right, as can be supported by over two dozen people with us that early morning, I advised onlookers to stay at a safe distance while I explored the area.

The landed airship was shooting out beams of bright light from a conical and revolving rim. It will tax the credulity of the reader too harshly if I recount, at this stage, exactly what transpired some 300 yards from the glowing UFO, and 'whom' I spoke to near a rustic gate separating two large fields. Perhaps I can steel myself to narrate this story in another book. I became terrified, shortly afterwards, in spite of the reassuring 'meeting.'

The spaceship blacked out after six minutes and I went along by a hedgerow skirting the edges of both copses. Walking back, I was struck by the utter silence, night birds ceasing to trill around me. I passed the second copse and for a few seconds stopped to glance up at the beautiful stars speckling the heavens with enchanting globules of light, the overwhelming majesty of the vast Universe spreading a velvet canopy overhead filling me with wonder.

I placed a hand on the top of the bordering hedge to steady myself as I stood on a low bank. My reverie was wildly disturbed, shattered by what happened then in a frightening knockout count of ten seconds. Right above my head came the awesome sound of a gigantic bird flapping leaden wings.

It was a heavy, thumping noise, so ponderous that the whole hedge trembled under my palms and my hands were lifted by the sheer vibrationary power pulsing beneath them. Imagine the downbeating thrust of the wings of a swan in flight; this aerial intruder was a thousand times as large and disquieting. I felt my hair blown into confusion by this blasting pressure and swayed on my heels by the rocking hedgetop.

The phenomenon passed. My dazed eyes saw nothing to mark the winged monster's flight. This has always been a great mystery to me since, unsolvable. When I suffered a second similar experience, a fortnight later, I was in company with another male. As badly scared as I, all he could say was ' It was most interesting, but definitely negative.'

My companion on that occasion was an advanced student of the Occult, much more wise and knowledgable than me. When we arrived back at Cradle Hill copse, observer Margaret Cooper from Bournemouth was complaining to her husband Alan (once a soldier serving at the School of Infantry) that some practical joker had thrown an empty five-gallon petrol can over the copse, narrowly missing her head as she stood on the periphery.

I checked when this occurred: it must have been seconds prior to the ear-crushing bird wing sounds that assailed us. Had Margaret not known me as a serious person not given to tomfoolery and the playing of outlandish pranks, she would have accused me of hurling the can at her unprotected head from the rubbish tip just inside the copse.

What connection was there between the monstrous bird and the tin-throwing culprit? Oddly, no one back at Cradle Hill copse heard the reverberating beating of the giant wings that raised such a cacophany and audibly smote a friend and myself only 300 yards away . . .

These macabre incidents formed the central talking point for my team as we stood in the middle of the copse at the end of September. Bob, too, had suffered strange personal contacts and effects from ' invisible' walkers. When ascending the track to the copse, even in daylight, he was uncomfortably aware of someone or something invisibly following him.

Once, when he heard footsteps yet saw no pursuer, he could detect grass being ruffled on a windless afternoon in rear. Whoever the instigator was, he or she was not a physical entity. Nor, in the absence of a sighting, was the outsized bird whirring over the hedgerow to plague my inner calm. Puzzling, these pointers produced clues later.

Other watchers were with us that night in late September, but only our trio saw the ' ghost ' light that sped through a clearing at the copse. It halted near us, in the centre of the trees, about five feet from ground level. Thinking it was some practical japer riding a bicycle along the track, Bob yelled: ' Come on—let's nab him!'

He and I ran towards the light, which resembled a circular lantern when we closed in. When we were four yards short of the point at which

UFO PROPHECY

TRIFLING POINTERS ARE EMBRYONIC CLUES

it was steadily hovering, it suddenly sped towards the second copse at blistering speed. As it left the tree-darkened undergrowth, we saw it was certainly no cyclist, nor was it conceivably of Earth construction.

Sometimes ball-like in appearance, at others almost cylindrical, it weaved a little from side to side as we hotly chased it along the track by the hedgerow. It went straight through a high gate—around which was barbed wire fencing—without stopping or soaring upward to negotiate the top of the barrier. Straight through! That made us gasp . . .

Sybil came up in rear of us while we stood there, by the gate, puffing and panting from concentrated efforts to catch the glowing circle, now receding into the far distance towards Imber. Bewildered, we shook disbelieving heads and muttered in annoyance at the escape of the small spheroid.

Sybil leaned against the hedge and laughed at our nonplussed attitude. She pointed out: ' Whatever it was, it obviously knew us pretty well. I am not a bit frightened. Are you ? ' I looked at Bob. He gazed askance at me. Then we both burst into peals of laughter.

No, surprisingly, we were not scared at all and knew at that vital moment, undoubtedly, that we had encountered one of the thinking lights or small brain beacons sent out from a larger spacecraft. ' It tested our reactions and emotions,' I opined. My team mates agreed. We laughed all the way back to Cradle Hill.

Other observers gathered there glanced at us as though fearful that we were ' blowing our tops.' Maybe we were—but this lighthearted release of tension did wonders to restore our faith that these UFO occupants are not hostile. They were testing us—and we felt it to be more reasonable to laugh and joke about an inexplicable experience than sob with emotion or cower with fear, which was unjustified.

No one else saw the gleaming light in the midst of the trees. The others would have derided and mocked our story, we sensed. So we kept quiet about it apart from telling Dr. John Cleary-Baker, Fred and Pat Harding, now more hopeful than ever before that real contact would soon be established between us and ' them.'

Trifling things, almost of no consequence in isolated separation, begin to make sense when collectively assessed. Numerous witnesses of UFOs at Cradle Hill and Starr Hill can confirm that articles have vanished from cars and vans, even when vehicle doors have been locked

—then miraculously turn up again when drivers and passengers arrive home.

George Wood, a Merseyside area Ufologist who has braved inclement weather at Warminster several times, following long journeys South by train or coach, found on reaching home after his first Warminster visit that his tape-recorder next morning had been tampered with, skilfully, by 'someone unknown.'

It had been expertly taken apart, components laid in reverse order on top of the mechanizm. A silly prank? Barely possible, as no one in the house could have had access to the instrument. It made him ponder afresh on the weird capabilities of space people who work in mysterious and devious ways to make 'victims' use their grey matter.

I autographed a copy of my last book, published by Neville Spearman, for a Birmingham member of the International Sky Scouts, now termed Contact UK. He placed it in his bookcase at home, locked the glass-paned door, took the key to his bedroom when he retired for the night. Next morning, he discovered that the book was missing from the shelves of his library. It reappeared several days later, in the exact position between two other books where it was originally placed.

One UFO research group bought a new 'pop' record while staying in our town for a few days. The disc was recently cut and issued. The record was in the locked car of one of the lads at Starr Hill. As the driver, having secured the car, joined us at a gateway fronting a disused farm, he saw a shadowy figure silhouetted against a car window, inside.

He counted the people at the gate, realised the figure belonged to no one in our observation party, so ran back to the vehicle and unlocked it. No one was therein, but in the thirty seconds or so of indecision in which Neil Beverly enumerated the watchers, 'someone' had been in the car. What is more, the new disc was grossly misshapen, wax-soft and depressed at the edges by obvious thumb impressions.

It was warm and sticky, grooves spoilt and useless, ruined. A camera in the glove compartment by the dashboard had been dismantled, film turned around. Developed film had been taken from a container, replaced the wrong way round. All manner of odd things had happened to the boys' property in that amazing thirty seconds!

Our investigating trio have encountered many mind-taunting puzzles like these, mystifying and challenging in the extreme, confronting us at regular intervals. We have helped others search, in vain, for 'lost' property and items such as spectacles, knitting needles and

UFO PROPHECY

TRIFLING POINTERS ARE EMBRYONIC CLUES

wool, packets of cigarettes, small food hampers, coffee flasks, cameras, etc., which have invariably been ' found ' eventually, either during or after homeward runs of the losers.

What can we deduce from these perplexing disappearing and conjuring acts extraordinary? Simply, that entities capable of manifesting in a duality of physical and spiritual forms, of solid and astral shapes, have been industriously at work to make disbelievers goggle at impossible feats.

These ' visitors ' with the magpie tendencies and illusionary capacity are not malicious or actually thieving in intent: they are not exhibitionists or extroverts without good reason. They are merely calling upon us to employ our faculties to the maximum. Here is another pointer to their remarkable talents and abilities that rise considerably higher than the mundane:

On the Chitterne to Tilshead road, in daylight, our team have seen gunmetal grey UFOs materialize and dematerialize as if at will. They appear and disappear on the same aerial spot! Only one sane conclusion is possible when we have ascertained that our eyes are not deceived by flight speeds.

These craft (and their crews?) can raise and lower at whim the frequency of atomic particles of which all flesh and matter is composed. They achieve an ultra-rapid vibrationary rate that alters the molecular and cellular composition of matter, animate and inanimate, so that they are visible one moment, invisible the next. The craft revolve their photons, or units of light measurement, at such fabulous speeds that this is cold fact and not fancy to the patient observer.

Fantastic though this is, there can be no alternative explanation. As will later be explained, they are capable, also, of changing their size, shape, form and dimension under pressing circumstances. The only absolute proof of this comes with personal visual experience: and here we are perhaps highly privileged to gain such information in a UFO ' infested ' area . . .

Here is a recent news report which concurs in almost every detail with the story of a Warminster housewife on page twenty-five of *The Warminster Mystery*. Observant readers will remember it clearly. The following cutting is from the British Sunday press organ, *News of the World*, dated March 31st, 1968:—

Police are sending a report to the Ministry of Defence this weekend, giving details of an unidentified flying object seen by two officers in a squad car. It was spotted as the police crew were driving in Union Street, Torquay, Devon, about 3.15 a.m. on Thursday.

Supt. Harry Brooks, head of Torquay police, said yesterday: 'This is something that cannot be dismissed out of hand. The officers, patrolmen Michael Kirby and Basil Warren, are very reliable and we questioned them closely. They describe the object as being very like a railway carriage travelling across the sky and estimate that it was flying at about 150 feet.

'A line of illuminated portholes down one side was clearly visible. The officers also say it was only in view for a few seconds, but was considerably larger than a Vulcan bomber.'

Ufologists must have wondered at the number of 'close range' victims who instinctively fall to their knees when confronted by a landed UFO. This was my own reaction when I first saw a celestial chariot not far from where I was standing at the back of the copse on Cradle Hill. What invokes this temporary collapse of the nether limbs, dominated by a bewildered brain?

Is it fear? Is it awestruck wonder? Or is it a movement of unconscious reverence, perhaps, which one book tells us befell those who long ago came face to face with angels? A Warminster case of matching significance happened on the evening of Sunday, December 10th last year, 1967, when engineering foreman Bill Horler was taking his usual stroll across fields at the rear of his home in Bath Road, Warminster.

He lives at No. 34 and at 7.35 p.m. set out along Gashouse Lane with bright, starry conditions overhead in this wintry month. He turned left, along the lane, and entered the first field. Starting to cross the meadow, he was aware of a bright light overtaking him from behind. It passed overhead and made no noise. It was long and cylindrical in shape and dazzling white.

Bill Horler, not at all an imaginative person, gasped in amazement as it came down in front of him in the field, landing and glowing with a fierce, hard brilliance about two hundred yards away. 'Until I saw the shape above me, I thought it was the beam of a searchlight,' he told me later. 'It sounds silly, and I really don't know why I did it, but I immediately fell to my hands and knees, starting to crawl away from the object.

'I was very frightened, because I had never seen anything like this before. I crawled through a hedge into another field, proceeding in this fashion for about 100 yards. All strength seemed to have left my

UFO PROPHECY

TRIFLING POINTERS ARE EMBRYONIC CLUES

legs and I virtually pulled myself along with my hands. When I looked back the object was still there, fearfully bright and pulsing with white light. It did not change colour.

' By this time, I had managed to haul myself to my feet. Then I sank down on my haunches and again began to crawl until I reached the end of the field. My strength returned, so I got up and ran all the way home.' His wife was puzzled because he was so shocked and overwrought. One thing he said, straight away, increased her unease.

' Turn the light out—please ! ' he begged her. She did as he asked and noted how red and blurred his eyes were. He suffered eye pains and discomfort for several days and described the sensation as ' Something like arc-eye, which you occasionally get when welding under intense heat and light.' It was not until 11.30 that night that Mr. Horler told his wife what had happened—and she had to badger him for hours to get the information . . .

Both then went outside and walked over the relevant field, searching the ground closely. They found nothing—there was no trace or sign of earth disturbance where the UFO had landed. However, both looked upward at that point and were conscious of a pear-shaped aeroform in the sky, moving at a steady pace yet bigger than any star and brighter than any satellite. It was headed in a direct line for Cradle Hill.

What I, as a serious investigator, find of great interest in Bill Horler's narrative is the all-revealing admission on his part that : ' I was very frightened, because I had never seen anything like this before.' The great and spectacular unknown must surely have caused a great deal of natural fear in past ages : but it must be met squarely today for understanding to dawn, gradually, and enlighten minds still dulled by superstition and suspicion.

Bill and his wife have told few persons about the experience, for fear of public ridicule. This, too, is an obstruction to progress in determining beyond reasonable doubt the very nature and purpose of our Outer Space visitors and their chariots. A cruel and thoughtless public attitude is as bad as the close-minded response from some scientists to these phenomena, killing vital evidence at birth !

CHAPTER FOUR

Visual Communication Possible with UFOs

A late October experience in 1966 is still ineradicable, vividly etched on the minds of a building plasterer contractor and his wife who live in St. Johns Road, Warminster. Checking carefully on their testimony, I firmly believe they witnessed a UFO landing and takeoff on Saturday, October 22nd at Chitterne, a village lying a few miles from Warminster in the general Eastward direction of Stonehenge.

Dennis Tilt and his wife were then newcomers to our town and honestly did not know what to make of their unusual sighting, except that it was 'certainly nothing to do with the military.' They were driving homeward from Basingstoke and neared the quiet village at around 11.28 p.m.

Just on the far side of Chitterne both noticed ' three flame-coloured lights in triangular formation on the ground, on land belonging to a farm on our right.' Dennis stopped the car, his curiosity aroused, stepping out on to the road to enjoy a closer view of the brightly shining trio of spheres.

A trifle nervous, sensing that all was not as it should be along the otherwise darkened highway, a deathly silence blanketing the air with the cutting of the car engine, Mrs. Tilt advised her husband to get back into the vehicle and continue their journey.

Although her eyes probed the darkness as avidly as his own to focus on the pyramid of lights in the field, he obeyed the apprehension in her tones as she called out. They drove along a bit farther, therefore. But when they turned heads to glance back, they noted that the strange lights had fused together.

The object had lifted off the earth and was now huge in the sky. Both testified that it resembled, at this joined stage, ' a frying pan without a handle.' It was hovering some fifty feet up, looming large and ominous, deadly silent.

Dennis, prompted by his wife passenger, put his foot hard down on the accelerator pedal, sharing the unease at that moment of his wife. As the car surged into full power and tore along the night-shrouded road, the couple kept looking in rear and further saw that the spaceship did not appear to change its distance from them one iota, although Dennis was proceeding at top speed.

The wife maintained constant watch on the UFO, which gave off a fitful yellow glow, and Dennis peeped backward as he negotiated bends and corners. Both found it disconcerting and a little frightening that they were unable to shake off their aerial pursuer for several miles of that memorable homeward run.

When they eventually reached St. Johns Road the shining apparition overhead had faded from their gaze—and the upset couple breathed sighs of relief. There was one more shock to come . . .

When Mrs. Tilt later went up to the bedroom of their children, glancing out of the window as she straightened the curtains, she was staggered to see the flying object again for a few seconds. It was a ball of shining glory in the heavens before suddenly changing to an elongated egg shape and blacking out.

Because it is so preposterous in the light of Earth concepts, one hesitates to decide what must have actually happened when the UFO ceased to shed blazing light down upon the car in the final stretch to their home. The glowing spaceship must still have been present yet out of vision, according to its last dramatic reappearance at the curtain close.

So it is permissible to accept that these spacecraft are able to ' black out ' whenever it suits their purpose of mystifying people and provoking thought, giving a false impression that they are no longer present in the atmosphere. This confirms observations made in the last chapter concerning the advanced art of materialization and dematerialization.

Even while the Tilts were excitedly and agitatedly discussing the vanishing act of the skyborne giant, it was probably right overhead and invisibly dogging their car tracks on the run in from Heytesbury to Warminster, unknown to Dennis Tilt and his wife.

So sure were the couple that they had indeed witnessed something untoward and absolutely inexplicable by Earth standards, that Mr. Tilt arose early next morning, Sunday October 23rd, and was at the farm making inquiries about the resting place of mysterious objects that merged together before flying unerringly in rear of his car the previous night.

UFO PROPHECY

VISUAL COMMUNICATION POSSIBLE WITH UFOS

He drew a blank, however. The farmer was incapable of enlightening him with regard to what the ' one ball from a triangle of lights ' was doing on his pastures long after dusk on a strange nocturnal spree. In spite of a diligent examination of the field, and search of the surrounding area, the plastering contractor could not discern the precise spot where the spacecraft had taken off.

Dennis was only able to guess the approximate region, and there were no telltale marks or indentations on the farmland. His investigation, that of a sensible person bent on dealing intelligently with unknown factors, proved to his own satisfaction that what he had seen was not even remotely connected with military activity.

He contacted the Army and asked relevant questions, answers convincing him that troops were not the culprits. When first seen by the young couple in the car, the three lights forming a triangle were flame-coloured or orange-red. The composite object chasing the car was silverish and gave off a pulsating glow or radiation.

Dawn Flanigan is a keen Warminster equestrian, living in Bath Road, who loves nothing better than a stiff breeze rippling her fair hair as she gallops or canters over the downs on horseback.

She and a friend had several peculiar visual experiences in May of 1966, shortly after my last book was submitted to my publisher. Here is her description, given to me at her home in the following month, of patent UFO aeronautics:—

' While riding over Salisbury Plain, in the general direction of Imber village, we saw to our left—about five miles away, I would estimate, to the North—a long object, silvery and metallic, that remained stationary over a wood.

' Frankly, we paid little attention to it at first, as we are accustomed to seeing strange sights over the plain. The Army and Air Force are often on manoeuvres in that area, although we keep out of their way when riding. The afternoon was warm and sunny and the object glittered ever so brightly.

' The glint caught our eyes and we stopped to have a good look, then. It was a brightly flashing pencil of silver in the sun. The next day, about mid-afternoon, we saw a similar thing. But this time it was moving slowly over the tops of some trees. Again we stopped and watched.

' We expected it to twist and turn, or perform some aerobatics, as we now presumed it to be a glider. But it simply vanished from view completely, only to reappear a few seconds later at the far end of the wood. Then it sank slowly down behind it and out of sight.

'The belt of trees seemed to swallow it up. We now realised it was not a glider or anything like that, because it had an elongated shape, was without wings, and shone much too brightly in the sun. My girl friend and I changed direction and prodded our mounts towards the wood as fast as the rough terrain would allow.

'On arrival there, we could find nothing to link with the strange air machine. Nonetheless, the horses were most reluctant to enter the wood—and quite impatient to leave, we noticed. They grew ever so restive and began snorting, tossing their heads.

'All in the same month of May, we saw this sort of thing happen on several occasions. In fact, we investigated another three times. In each case we found nothing on the ground. There is one particular occasion, the last, I shall never forget.

'That was when our horses became so frightened that they reared up and bolted across the plain for home. Needless to say, we did the same rather than be stranded out there in the wilds,' she admitted soberly, reflecting that there were certain copses in the area that horses will not enter. It is as though they possess a sixth sense, warning that danger lurks in the undergrowth there.

During the third week in November of 1967, the retired surveyor and chief public health inspector of Warminster and Westbury Rural Council, Frank Merrett, was out shooting pheasants on the Rye Hill Farm estate of Claudius R. Algar, who is chairman of Warminster Magistrates' Court and farms at Longbridge Deverill, a few miles South of Warminster.

Shooting friends and beaters were with Mr. Merrett on that Thursday afternoon. A shadow uncurled on the ground—and the surveyor sportsman immediately raised his gun into the firing position, expecting to see a covey of game birds winging overhead.

But there was no whirring sound that one associates with such mass flight. Above the farmhouse itself, casting its shadow in accordance with the position of the wintry sun, was a long torpedo shaped object that shone grey-white and sparkled along the top where sun rays struck and bounced off its casing.

It was more rounded at one end than the other. What appeared to be dark slots or windows darkened the side facing the shooting companions. Frank told me bluntly, in front of a dozen people: 'I have always

UFO PROPHECY

VISUAL COMMUNICATION POSSIBLE WITH UFOS

thought you and other so-called witnesses of these phenomena mad, you know.'

His eyes gleamed as he shook a wiser head. ' All I can now say is—if you are insane, I am proud to join you. It was in sight for over three minutes altogether and made no sound. I ran along by the hedge to warn a gamekeeper friend in the shooting party, but when I reached him the object had gone.'

When he left his co-shooters, it was moving over the house and slowly heading towards the downs to the North, he told me. Having actually seen something unworldly and incomprehensible, the former disbeliever was adamant that it is futile and resolves nothing if such information is kept secret. He was quietly thrilled to have had his sighting, I could tell.

Other witnesses affirmed that the aerial torpedo continued its gentle course towards the downs, then vanished. One moment it was still there, the next non-existent. Changing of form is not restricted to night-time alien craft.

The following Warminster sighting report, which I gave the Air Ministry in the summer of 1966, really interested them a great deal. I could sense the mounting excitement of my Ministry contact at the revelation over this alteration of one particular UFO shape at speed. He was insistent on full details.

These I willingly presented : we have nothing to hide or be ashamed of in our town. There were over a dozen young people present on this occasion. Let us listen to the words of one of them, Marion Bull, a 14-year-old schoolgirl :

'The date was July 28th. The time was between 3.30 and 4 p.m. and I was in the local swimming baths in Weymouth Street. I was looking South towards the Ferris Mead housing estate when I saw a silver object come across, just above the trees.

' It was quite big and shiny. It seemed to be flat to start with, then—as it came over the pleasure park next to the public baths—it appeared to turn on its side. It then looked like a bowler hat, with a slightly upturned brim.

' It kept on going backwards and forwards for a while, then its shape changed entirely. It was now for all the world like a bone, slim in the middle, large and bulbous at either end. To me, it was just the same as a large bone any dog is fond of gnawing.

'One girl thought it was rather like a man's bow tie, only it was a silvery white in colour. Once more it shot from side to side across the park— then it fled from sight, leaving no trace,' said Marion.

This ability to alter shape in motion is one of the tantalizing features that UFOs exhibit. Later chapters give clues as to what this strongly suggests. Spacecraft, and those aboard, are capable of transformation in physique, size and dimension. This sounds ridiculous taken out of context, for we at first concluded—when trying to analyze such reports and their consistency—that force fields around these airships are responsible for making them ostensibly produce differing shape patterns.

The craft outlines are blurred by swift movement that upsets the power field surrounding them in flight. This is what we initially felt, yet we were not entirely correct in our diagnosis. Here is another puzzling little cameo from the overall UFO jewel box:

It was on Boxing Day of 1967, when farm worker Michael Coleman set off to feed a herd of cows on the hill overlooking Heytesbury, three miles from Warminster, that another example of the bizarre and unworldly sounds erupted without warning, scaring the beasts of the field as well as causing the phlegmatic employee concern.

He had distributed the food to the cattle and, turning his tractor round to face the wind and rain so that his seat would not get too wet, he dismounted from the machine and started to count the animals. Immediately his feet touched the earth, however, he heard a tremendous clatter of noise that shook the sides of the hill and almost made him topple off balance.

It was so unexpected and savage that he clung to the side of his tractor until it subsided. The weird buffeting of soundwaves he termed ' much like giant hands shaking huge loads of galvanized sheeting all around. The cattle fled from their piles of food with feet flying and tails in the air. They were terrified.'

Michael pointed out that it is a rarity for cows to run from food, especially in bad weather. After the thunderclaps of noise abated, they were still reluctant to return, taking ten minutes or more to settle back to former equanimity and content.

' It was funny, though,' he told me sombrely. ' Some cattle in the next field, no more than a couple of hundred yards from us, never even flinched.' This surprised him considerably. They chewed the cud quite happily, unconcerned at blasting sounds nearby. Why?

Perhaps this was an earth tremor, I suggested, but Mr. Coleman was

UFO PROPHECY

VISUAL COMMUNICATION POSSIBLE WITH UFOS

insistent that—although its effects made the ground tremble at its height—the loud sounds originated in the atmosphere. 'It made my head and ears sing, it was so fierce,' he told me. The geography of the hill fields supplied the answer.

The sounds were localized in one section; the adjoining field was around a curving slope of the hill. Mr. Coleman then recalled another unaccountable incident back in December of 1961, when he worked for farmer Harry Wales. The employees erected a new fence, digging in sleepers some three feet into the ground to act as strainers.

Going to the field next morning, they found that all the cattle had strayed from their pasture during night hours. The fence had been violently uprooted, the sleepers torn out and littering the area in jumbled confusion. Yet not one of the beasts was hurt and there were no tracks of any vehicle visible around the soil disturbance mounds.

In February of 1962, working for his present boss, Stanley B. Pottow, by the same field only over the boundary, Michael found that a similar phenomenon had again struck one night. The employer thought the fence had been smashed by the impact of a vehicle driving through it.

No tracks of any transport were discovered, however; and no cattle were anywhere near the scene of devastation, so their footprints could not have obscured wheel marks. The tractor driver from Knook thought no more of these incidents, apart from their constituting unsolved minor mysteries, until he read a newspaper report that Geoffrey Gale, of Parsonage Farm (near Cradle Hill at Warminster) had suffered fencing damage in January and February of 1966.

An account of the latter appeared in *The Warminster Mystery*, preludes to sightings of UFOs with clockwork regularity over Cradle Hill itself, a few hundred yards from the farmhouse lying in the dip before the steep approach.

These happenings all took place in the same area, Michael revealed, practically on a direct line between Chitterne and Warminster. He saw nothing overhead at the material time. Nevertheless, he did experience a nasty electric shock on one occasion, while travelling on a tractor early one morning.

He attributed it to a shorting fault on the machine. Strange climax to this true story is: When the tractor and its engine was thoroughly examined by a specialist, its electrical wiring system was faultless. Now here is a story about cows that some readers might have deemed 'a lot of bull' at that period . . .

UFO PROPHECY

WARNINGS FROM FLYING FRIENDS

This minor mystery hit national headlines in late summer of 1967. A herd of several dozen cows disappeared from farmland at Chitterne one morning. In fact, they were absent from pastures and milking sheds for more than a day. An extensive search was carried out for the missing beasts by the farmer, his dairymen and other labourers, to no avail.

The Army was indirectly blamed, one gathered, for broken fencing. They denied responsibility. No troops were in that vicinity at that time. Because of a baffling lack of tracks which should have been left by the fleeing creatures, the several hours of searching over a wide area found the cattle still missing parade.

The hunt was called off by a worried farmer and his staff. Then, next morning, the cows were all back in the field, closely herded together and lowing contentedly, as though nothing extraordinary had transpired, no page ripped out of their calendar. They were unharmed, a cursory inspection proved.

Forty sheep vanished from a farm near Norridge Wood (like Chitterne, also mentioned in *The Warminster Mystery*), shortly after this. Despite an exhaustive search of the area for many miles, not a hide or hair was found of the flock. It was assumed they had wandered afar or were lost in thick woodland.

They came back—or were brought back?—to their grazing grounds a whole week later, wagging their tails behind them! Either we have abnormally adventurous cattle around Warminster, capable of flying into the night sky without wings; or they were deliberately abducted by aliens for necessary experimentation and organic examination, safely returned undamaged and perfectly happy afterwards.

A foreman fitter for a firm of agricultural engineers told me of his encounter with a cigar aeroformed UFO on the night of Sunday, December 10th of 1967. George Radbourne and his wife Ruth live at Southleigh View, Warminster.

At around 11.35 p.m. they had passed through the crossroads at Chapmanslade and were approaching the straight stretch of road leading from Thoulston Bends to Warminster, returning home after an evening out in the Bath area. They blinked when the large airship hove into sight.

It swept from left to right across the bonnet of their car, from Warminster downs towards the Cley Hill direction. It was white in colour but had a curious green sheen at its centre, the craft to the eye

VISUAL COMMUNICATION POSSIBLE WITH UFOS

the size of a human adult hand at arm's length.

'It jerked up and down slightly, in a rather erratic motion,' attested Mr. Radbourne. ' Then it curved gracefully to low height, away to the right of us. The sharper ended " nose " of the craft dipped—and the whole structure blacked out just short of Cley Hill. It was silent in flight and seemed to bob about like a duck on pondwater in its forward movement.'

Ruth, in the front passenger seat, corroborated his story. They were comparative newcomers to our district and knew nothing of the town's amazing UFO history. Neither wanted publicity, to begin with, relenting when I stressed that names and addresses are so important when enumerating and evaluating testimony on a subject which is, unfortunately, still largely futuristic and embryonic to the majority of people.

'It was a little bit like a weather balloon when we first spotted it,' said Mrs. Radbourne, who was not frightened by the experience. ' It maintained constant speed in crossing and was doubtless under control. The movement was not the same as that of a balloon and the object appeared solid at its nearest point. We assumed it had landed when the light went out.'

Ronald Dew and his sister Dorothea, together with their parents, had an unexpected visual feast on the night of April 23rd, 1967. This was a few months after the family took over management of a cafeteria in High Street, Warminster, and Mr. Dew was driving to their Westbury home at the end of a working day.

Dorothea and Ronald, likeable young people, supplied me with this news story interlocked with UFO outbursts around Warminster. Dorothea said: ' It was about 9.25 p.m. and we had just passed Colloway Clump into the climbing stretch of straight road leading to the junction with Upton Scudamore village.

' Cley Hill was to our left when we saw a large bright light hovering in the dark sky. It was a mixture of orange and red, we thought, then we could see that this effect was produced because smaller red lights flickered from the base of the large object. They lit up the countryside for a great distance around.

' We all watched intently, Dad having stopped the car. Our eyes were glued to the bright spectacle, not knowing what it could be at that location. It then went out, like a candle being extinguished, after growing smaller and fading.'

UFO PROPHECY

Ronald confirmed this account, saying the small lights seemed to shoot back into the main light before all vanished. He thought the smaller red globes were darting down to the hilltop and returning to the main structure from time to time. ' It was an intense light coming from the larger ball. The little ones glistened and were full of movement.

'When the tiny globes of light disappeared into the huge ball, this became egg-shaped, yellow in colour, changed to a dullish white and was reduced in size. Then it went out.' His father had seen something equally as dramatic shortly before this, but did not desire any publicity. I respect such wishes.

American poet and senior English teacher Richard George, of the Dean Carteret School in West Orange, New Jersey, flew from the States to London, then travelled by road to our Cradle Hill on the night of June 30th, 1966. He came with the express intention of seeing a UFO. He is Dean of Boys at the school in the USA, also, formerly served in the Royal Air Force and is not easily fooled. An ideal visitor.

Richard was accompanied by Joseph Hall, his brother-in-law, and another welcome volunteer in our skywatching party the same night was Owen Roberts, chemist and opthalmist from Merthyr Tydfil in Wales. (Nothing wrong with his eyesight, surely?)

The ironic part is that Geoffrey Gale and his wife Robin, living in the farmhouse nearby, came along for the first time—and saw an unidentified flying object—although the 'Thing' had been virtually haunting their very doorstep for four months by then.

They drove up in a Land Rover to see a UFO in silver-ringed and pulsating splendour blazing a semi-circular aerial trail over their farmland. Richard George journeyed several thousand miles to see one of the incredible craft. He was not disappointed and all present were impressed. ' If this is not absolutely inexplicable, I do not know what is,' exclaimed Joseph Hall.

Our visitor from America was emotionally moved enough to quote verse in the silent solitude of 12.55 a.m. Owen Roberts said : ' I am over sixty and my wife thinks I am crazy to believe I shall ever see a UFO. I have been convinced life exists on other planets as far back as I can remember.

'After what I have seen tonight, I can go home and tell my wife I have at last seen a space vehicle from another world that can travel in the region of 30,000 miles an hour at least,' he enthused. He snatched

UFO PROPHECY

VISUAL COMMUNICATION POSSIBLE WITH UFOS

a brief period of sleep on our living room settee, later, sending my wife a large bottle of perfume in appreciation of her hospitality, from Merthyr Tydfil.

Whereas satellites glide gently for over a dozen minutes to cross from horizon to horizon, aching to the neck to watch even though travelling at 17,500 miles an hour, we had seen a pulsating UFO with orange body and silvery aura tear across the sky in 46 seconds. Bob Strong handed round hot coffee and Sybil ladled out biscuits as we quietly thrilled to the noiseless magic of the ring of fire.

Richard wrote to me from America on July 5th: 'Thank you for the opportunity to observe with you the unusual astral phenomenon over Cradle Hill. I found the entire experience stimulating and fascinating. It is easy to doubt and scoff, much more difficult to accept.

'To tell you the truth, I keep trying to understand what I actually saw. It was " out of this world " and yet " into this world." Once again, thank you for your invitation to come along at any time in future, and for the extraordinary sighting on June 30th. All good wishes. *Ad Astra* —Richard.'

Cynics laughed when hearing of a modest claim I was able to make by July of 1966 that I had reached a stage on Cradle Hill where I could persuade UFOs to descend to low altitude with the aid of certain light patterns shone from beams of a torch into the night sky. This small measure of personal contact has been achieved by a mixture of patient and persevering methods, helped by uncanny foreknowledge of UFO appearances stemming from experience.

Spacecraft hover after occupants have seen my signals. The craft drop to our estimate of about 600 yards up and barely a mile outward from the site where the signaller stands. Whereupon, they promptly 'reply' to the flashes from ground to air. Whatever signal is sent, Morse code or a haphazard series of dots and dashes at random, is responded to faithfully, without mistake.

This is no stupid boast: I shall always wear the same size in hats. It is sheer fact, attested to by many witnesses on the hill. It would be arrogant and foolhardy to guarantee I can do this every time I climb to this vantage point. It would make nonsense of a truthful claim, meekly made.

When a 'message' is torch transmitted to a spacecraft enticed to low height, the same signals bounce back boldly from the whole lighted portion of the UFO that is visible. Usually it is repeated within two seconds. One must surely gather, from this factor, that people aboard the airship are not hostile when permitting this tentative exchange of greetings. The pointer of doubt swings in a positive direction to indicate genuine desires for friendly relations.

Dr. John Cleary-Baker, once chief evaluating officer for BUFORA and still its journal editor, was a leading speaker at a public meeting in Warminster to inquire into UFO phenomena over and around our town, in August of 1965. Fourteen months later, he had not only seen many of these flying mysteries at Cradle Hill but affirmed that:

'On the evening of October 14th 1966 I went to Warminster with Mr. Arnold West and his daughter Edith. We arrived in the dormobile at Cradle Hill about 10.30 p.m. Almost immediately it began to rain very heavily. This downpour continued for several hours and all of our plans for a skywatch that night seemed futile. Accordingly, we went to sleep in the vehicle.

'I awoke at about 3.40 the following morning and on going outside found that the rain had ceased; the sky was completely clear except for a bank of light clouds, low in the South East, and conditions were ideal for skywatching.

'I told Mr. West that I was going to begin observing and he came out of the dormobile to join me within ten minutes, leaving his daughter still sleeping inside. At 4.10 a.m. I drew his attention to a bright object like a star of the first magnitude.

'It was moving in the sky a little above and to Westward of Betelgeuze (a. Orionis). We watched this object for three and a half minutes, during which interval it described an arc which carried it near to and a little Eastward of the planet Jupiter, which was very conspicuous in the constellation of Cancer; then down towards the South-Eastern horizon, where it was finally lost to view in the bank of light clouds previously mentioned.

'The object's speed varied while under observation, sometimes quite rapid and sometimes very slow. Its brightness also varied and at times it appeared no more luminous than a star of the third magnitude. It seemed to me that changes in speed were related to changes in brightness. "The faster the brighter" would appear to sum this up.

'On three occasions during the observation, Mr. West flashed a powerful electric signal lamp towards the object. On each of these three occasions, after a short but appreciable interval, the object

VISUAL COMMUNICATION POSSIBLE WITH UFOS

appeared to flicker as if in reply. No flickering was noted at any other time while it was in view.

'The brightness changes were not rapid or regular like those which would result from irregularities in the surface of a lighted sphere in rotation (as, for example, a partially deflated balloon satellite). The changes were not due to haze, for stars in the vicinity remained uniform in brightness and could be used for comparison purposes in assessing alterations in the brightness of the object.

'It is no more than just to point out that this observation is strongly corroborative of the claims of Mr. Arthur Shuttlewood to have witnessed many similar phenomena from Cradle Hill,' he added. The UFO investigating veteran wrote this report from his home at Weeke, Winchester, in Hampshire. His confirming letter to me, which was unsolicited, could be used as I thought fit, he assured me.

Now for another little 'missing' animals story, which appeared in the British Sunday newspaper, *The People*, with the February of 1968 headline of 'Riddle of the Lost Pigs:'

Detectives at a small village are investigating their most baffling case ... the mystery of fifty stolen four-week-old piglets—without tails. The pigs, worth £250, disappeared two weeks ago from a farm managed by Mr. Leonard Griffiths at Everleigh, Wiltshire.

The mystery deepened last week when Mr. Philip Hues was astonished to find thirteen strange tail-less piglets on his farm at Conock, near Devizes, seventeen miles from Mr. Griffiths's farm. Mr. Griffiths said: 'It is amazing how they travelled seventeen miles.'

Why no tails? Mr. Griffiths explained: 'We dock them to stop the piglets biting each other's tails. We are the only local people to do this.' (Author: Here is one extraordinary case of animals which came back, in part, without wagging their tails behind them! In my last book, *The Warminster Mystery*, I wrote on page 200:

'It should not surprise if the fact comes to light that—in kindly and harmless fashion—Earth people have been subjected to rigorous examination by Aenstrians to discover radiation levels and blood differences since nuclear tests were started. Humanely hypnotized or given a memory-sleeping drug to make them unaware of these experiences.'

Distorted stories in the USA about this sort of 'kidnapping' and 'treatment' of Earth people by aerial 'invaders,' bearing out the

UFO PROPHECY

hypnotic reference in my book, may have led to animal specimens now being employed for this life-saving purpose by our space friends...)

THE ROARING SKY

The burnt sun hurts my eyes
And if I walk I fall :
They say I cornered their surprise
For wishing down their ecstasies—
The Dazzling All, the Dazzling All.

They come like molten herds—
And, if I look, I die.
Their smiles scythe down the muted words,
Assail with love my throat of birds :
The Dazzling All—the roaring sky !

CHAPTER FIVE

Technical Secrets of Crashed UFO 'Hushed'

Easily providing sufficient material to cram at least one book full of incident, hundreds of definite UFO sighting reports have reached me from all regions of the United Kingdom in the past two years. Able to segregate the false from the genuine, our team know they are authentic, because they tally with our observations and follow flight paths and habits we can verify from experience.

Some coincide with our own sightings, time varying within minutes or seconds either way, depending upon distance from Warminster and aerial route spanned. Joseph McKie, headmaster of Elsdon School in Northumberland, for example, gave me a great deal of information concerning UFO aerobatics near Newcastle-upon-Tyne, which have persisted for upwards of five years.

Royal Observer Corps personnel and a member of the British Astronomical Association were among those present when unearthly wonders flew over Blaxter. C.O. R. S. Telfer and Messrs. F. Coulson, A. Coulson, J. N. McKie, F. Corbett, V. Grieve and G. Storey testified to the following recent sighting:

Four fiery gems in formation, breaking off and heading in different directions later, featured in a series of exciting UFO displays one night. Speeds varied from almost stationary to fast moving, for the quartet of shining spheroids also hovering unblinkingly while in formation. Joe estimated that at maximum velocity they would have journeyed from horizon to horizon in anything between six and ten seconds.

They turned at fast speed and what could only be described as 'impossible angles.' Two observers detected a greenish tinge about one of the objects. Joseph said that, as far as he knew, no such phenomena are listed in any standard works of astronomy.

Personally, I quietly exulted to hear that alien spaceships appear in the far North of England. During an early period of my schooling, I attended a place of learning in Ashington, Northumberland.

UFO PROPHECY

Marie L. Martin cherishes perpetual memories of a certain day in January of 1953. She then lived in the Norfolk hamlet of Marham, a half mile from the aerodrome where her husband was an air crew engineer. She saw three silvery discs, which were then hardly ever publicized. Here is a relevant part of her story:

'My husband and I had a very great interest in astronomy and in any flying aircraft. I became quite well versed in the several types. It was a brilliant day and, as there was a visiting VIP making the rounds of the Norfolk air bases, all flying was grounded that day.

'I had seated myself on the settee by the caravan window, intending to read a book, with a puppy dog on my lap. It was about three o'clock in the afternoon. The beauty of the sky was so arresting that I did not bother to open the book.

'Instead, I sat gazing upwards. Suddenly, extremely high up, a jet aircraft came into view. The rate it was travelling, even for a jet fighter, was extraordinarily rapid, especially for that altitude; so I knelt up for a better look.

'Then, to my horror, I saw the two "wings" leave the fuselage, expecting them to come hurtling down and the jet crash. My clenched hands flew to my cheeks in anguish. Here was tragedy, stark and horrifying, in front of my eyes . . . But it did not happen.

'Instead, without any loss of speed, they went round, one behind the other, so that in a straight line they continued to race across the sky. Just as abruptly, they came to a dead halt in midair. I could then determine that they were round, shiny and metallic, glinting brightly in the rays of the sun.

'After pausing for a matter of seconds, certainly no more than half a minute at most, they suddenly rose together as one and sped into the blue above and out of sight. This was viewed by another friend in an adjoining caravan.

'When I told my husband about this at teatime, he was not at all surprised or excited, as I fully expected him to be. He just said that they had seen such things, particularly the jet pilots who had faster and higher speed instruments than the bombers he was in.

'But all personnel were firmly warned not to breathe a word about them to the public—not even to members of their own families. My husband was true to his code and had not told or hinted anything to me before I told him what I has seen that afternoon.

'Not until the "later" discs had left formation and joined into a

UFO PROPHECY

TECHNICAL SECRETS OF CRASHED UFO 'HUSHED'

line did I realise the significance of what I was seeing. I felt very elated and mentally sent " them " a heartfelt welcome. Since then, I have had a lot of inexplicable things happen, as though my life has been mapped out for me, contrary to what I thought I wanted to do.

' Unfortunately, my husband died in a crash soon after my sighting, and I have had two children to bring up, but I have had much help and comfort. I have also had " experiences " which indicate that we are not " seeing " all that there is to see in this dimension; and I do not mean this in the psychic sense, either.'

Mrs. Martin has the right attitude of mind, the instinctive attunement to cosmic consciousness, which leads the UFO student to final truth, as explained in later chapters. She now resides in Hove, Sussex. Frank, fearless and revealing, her true narrative makes mockery of ' official ' denials that UFOs abound . . .

Contrast that personal story with the following, from a woman whose testimony would have reduced me to cynical laughter a couple of years ago. But her letter was dated March 17th of this year, 1968, and—ridiculous though it may seem on the face of it—I believe what she writes. She is only one of a growing band of ' contactees ' who are occasionally ' missing out ' on minor revelations :

' I am writing this letter, with apologies for troubling you, as I realise that you must already be rather over-burdened with work when you really need peace and quiet for what you want to do—just as I do, myself.

' Quite a number of years ago now, whilst " listening in " for general guidance and not considering individual link-ups at all, I was told that I was in contact with people speaking from a flying saucer who wanted me to meet them on a mountain near Abergavenny in Wales.

' To cut a long story short, I went to great lengths in an effort to get there, as the voice was so imperious. But there were a great many obstacles, and although I reached the district and the flying saucer came (and was written up in the local press as the first appearance there), I did not succeed in getting to the top of the mountain.

' There have been several other efforts at contact, but I have been suffering from the after effects of a series of very serious accidents, which condition has affected the bit of natural clairvoyance and clair-audience I had on certain occasions.'

Two factors combined to convince me that this lady speaks truth : I met acquaintances who corroborated her Abergavenny rendezvous as factual and known beforehand to them, and have learned the hard way that mental telepathy is not the improbable foreign science I once imagined it to be, when an uncompromising realist. No, Veronica Gee did have an actual experience.

A journalist has to be on guard against hoaxers and those wishing to gain notoriety by relating sensational stories with no shred of truth in them. If, for instance, a person comes to me with a vivid UFO sighting report, then specifies that although his name sounds like ' Smith ' it must be properly spelt as ' Smythe,' I shy instinctively.

This especially applies when taking a deposition on Ufological matters. If, on the other hand, a witness of good repute comes along with an unusual account connected with strange flying craft, requesting specifically that I must not mention his name or address, I am impressed.

There is no personal motive present. In a normal type of news story, I might respect the wishes of a person to remain anonymous, in fairness warning him that his name, in any event, must be delivered to an editor. With the oft reviled UFO subject it is imperative that names, addresses and full description of what is seen should be presented to strengthen authenticity of ' unlikely ' stories.

A prominent businessman as well as justice of the peace, my next witness debarred use of his name. He told me sincerely : ' I do not wish to cash in on this. People will simply say I am advertising for the sake of my business. Take the story or leave it—it is up to you.'

Therefore, I omit personal particulars in this single case. I am sure there is substantial truth in his narrative, for I too faced an almost identical situation once, verging on and leaning over the precipice of the incredible, at a point not far from Cley Hill. In essence, here is his experience :

' It was a clear and bright night in August of 1966. As my Jaguar sped along the Westbury road from Warminster, where I had stopped for a late dinner, I rounded a sharp bend past the first turning off to Upton Scudamore. To the right was Colloway Clump, reached by a narrow hedge-lined track on foot. The time was just short of eleven o'clock when I rounded the corner and began to enter the straight.

' I saw a huge red ball, fiery and glowing, which rolled slowly over a clump of trees and above a hill on the right. It hung suspended for a time, the rolling motion ceased, and I drew to a halt to watch more closely. My wife and the eldest of our three children were with me.

UFO PROPHECY

TECHNICAL SECRETS OF CRASHED UFO 'HUSHED'

'We were astounded. Up till then, we had laughed and joked over these "things," as Warminster people call them. Gradually the large ball commenced to turn on its axis, revolving and changing colour, as though cooling down from immense heat. It was now a fluorescent egg, flattened out somewhat, a brilliant orange in the sky.

'A deep crimson band spread along or through the centre of the egg, jutting out slightly from either end. We looked on, amazed, as four small red balls of light shot out of the main scarlet beam and protruded into the air for what we estimated to be about twenty feet or so. At no time were these smaller balls disconnected from the main object.

'They seemed to be linked to it by a thin thread of paler red light that swayed like the tentacle of an octopus. They remained in that position, dancing vaguely from side to side, for about two to three minutes. Then they quickly shot back into the larger shape once more and disappeared from sight.

'It was a fast and straight back action, no hesitating or messing about. Although I have been passing this spot pretty regularly for the past fifteen years, I have seen nothing to match this wonder, before or since. My wife kept talking about it for months afterwards. And our son told a number of friends, who did not believe him.'

There are so many sighting reports I could list in this book, yet am sanguine the thinking public are a trifle weary of these. The meanings that lurk in rear of glittering facades must be captured by diligent research and broadcast to those interested in the more profound aspects of alien visitations.

Let us look for a brief spell at a few of the events of UFO character that caused sensations in some of the defence departments overseas. It was in February of 1960 that the first discovery of a mysterious 'spy' in the sky was made. It resulted in a furore of excitement, carefully concealed from the unsuspecting public by the United States defence department.

The North American air defence system radar tracking gear had picked up what appeared to be a giant satellite weighing at least fifteen tons—which is far in excess of anything capable of being put into orbit by Earth agencies and propulsion methods; certainly in 1960, at least.

The satellite had not been launched by either Russia or the USA. That much was speedily determined. For one thing, it was in the wrong kind of orbit, apart from its vast size at that period. The mystery satellite's path was taking it over the North and South Poles, where the orbits of satellites blasted into space from the Soviet Union were invariably inclined at sixty-five degrees to the Equator, which took them on an aerial course over South America and North Africa.

The stunning satellite of February 1960 was only the first of a whole puzzling series of unusual space phenomena, serving to baffle scientists for the past eight years. It was revealed on September 3rd of 1960, seven months after the first sighting, that an inexplicable object giving off a reddish glow had been seen several times in the past fortnight.

It was photographed in the sky over New York by a tracking camera at the Grumman Aircraft Corporation factory on Long Island. This object was following an apparent East—West orbital path, whereas most satellites are launched in a West to East direction. The speed evaluation was three times that of Echo 1, metal balloon satellite of America.

There ensued a three-year lull in aerial activity from satellites alien to Earth concepts, but they emerged into the news again after a Mercury capsule, carrying Major Gordon Cooper, was hurled into space on May 15th of 1963 from Cape Canaveral on a journey of twenty-two orbits of the Earth.

The astronaut told the tracking station at Muchea, near Perth in Australia, that he was seeing a glowing greenish object ahead of him that he could not identify on his final orbit. It was travelling very fast and approaching the Earth spacecraft.

It was picked up by the tracking radar at Muchea, so must have been solid, and was circuiting from East to West. There was no aerial collision, thankfully, the astronaut's sighting reported by the National Broadcasting Company. They were covering the flight step by step, stage by stage. However, when Cooper eventually landed, the public was no wiser.

Reporters were barred from questioning him over his strange visual experience in the aerial No Man's Land. No official statement concerning the incident was ever released. Ostensibly, the matter was discreetly hushed-up and, as the Americans would say, ' expediently put under wraps.'

Russian astronaut Vladimir Komarov was a gallant man who had the steely resolve of a space pioneer and relentless curiosity of the true scientist. He was acknowledged to be one of the most able and experienced spacemen in the Soviet Union.

UFO PROPHECY

TECHNICAL SECRETS OF CRASHED UFO 'HUSHED'

Therefore it was all the more pertinent to question the reasons he had for bluntly directing his two-man crew to shift the giant spacecraft Voskhod One on to an emergency course back to Earth, under conditions that amounted to panic, four years ago.

What could he have seen from the observation windows that shook his composure to such a degree that it compelled him to make this decision, a drastic one in view of the lead Russia was bent on achieving and maintaining in the great Space Race? Maybe the world at large will forever be ignorant of this.

Voskhod One was scheduled to orbit for at least five days when it was fired into space on October 12th 1964. Yet it returned to Earth after twenty-four hours. Why? The Russians have never revealed, publicly and precisely, what their astronauts saw on that memorable day. It is doubtful they will.

There are strong indications, judging from recordings of radio transmissions between Voskhod One and ground control, that the crew of the Russian spacecraft came face to face with something frightening and unaccountable while in orbit: something that terrified them so acutely that they were forced to make a swift and unscheduled descent from space regions.

Sadly, Vladimir Komarov is unable to help untangle twisting strings of the mystery news parcel. He was killed outright when his Soyuz One capsule plunged to Earth with unopened parachutes in April of 1967. Rising above the veiled horror of the Voskhod incident, he and other cosmonauts insisted on returning into aerial seas of the unknown.

Perhaps this reassuring factor proves that the initial experience of being confronted by the Great Unknown in lonely space fastnesses is not necessarily of horrifying impact, but more of a salutary visual warning that Man in his present evolutionary stage can go so far, but no farther, by the dictates of more enlightened beings...

Russians are not the only cosmic pioneers to sight, and even photograph, inexplicable flying objects beyond the immediate outer space coverings of our globe, UFOs utterly unlike anything ever put into orbit by the Soviet or the West. It has been reliably testified that certain of them were so enormous that there was no rocket gear in existence which could have thrust them successfully into space.

No nation will officially discuss the mystery satellites orbiting our Earth. The United States set up a special committee to gather facts about them. Its findings were not disclosed to the public but put under strict secrecy wraps. This still applies. I am indebted to fellow journalist Bruce Sandham, who wrote a stimulating series called 'Invasion from Space?' for the *Western Daily Press*, Bristol, for the following:

In June of 1965 astronauts Edward White (later to die tragically in the Apollo capsule blaze) and James McDivitt were passing over Hawaii in their two-man Gemini spacecraft when they saw a weird-looking metallic object some distance away. The thing appeared to have long arms sticking from it.

McDivitt took pictures of the thing with a cine camera—pictures that were never released. The official U.S. Air Force explanation was that the astronauts had seen America's Pegasus satellite 2, which is equipped with broad, protruding 'arms' to register hits from micro-meteorites.

But the Air Force had forgotten one thing: when White and McDivitt passed over Hawaii, Pegasus had been more than a thousand miles away. So what did the two astronauts see? From America's National Aeronautics and Space Administration there is still 'no comment.'

But one NASA specialist, in an unguarded moment, did let slip to reporters that the object photographed by McDivitt 'looked like no satellite launched from Earth.'

In December of 1965, Gemini astronauts James Lovell and Frank Borman also saw something strange in space during the second orbit of their record breaking 14-day flight around the world. Borman reported that he had located an unidentified spacecraft some distance away from the Gemini capsule.

Gemini Control, at Cape Kennedy, suggested that perhaps he was seeing the final stage of the huge Titan booster rocket which had hurled him and Lovell into orbit earlier that day. Borman confirmed that he could see the spent booster rocket all right, as it was shining brilliantly in the sun.

But what he was looking at then was something entirely different: He had never seen anything remotely like it. What have all these men seen? Many highly reputable scientists are now convinced that the mystery satellites in orbit around the Earth can only have been placed there by an alien intelligence.

In other words, someone is watching us—just as our space probes observe the planets in the solar system. 'Who they are, what they want... only time will tell,' adds Bruce, who later in his short series

UFO PROPHECY

TECHNICAL SECRETS OF CRASHED UFO 'HUSHED'

of articles tells of the hushed-up case of the crashed UFO. It is worth recounting here:

The pilot of the Norwegian Air Force Catalina flying boat was bored. For over four hours, as the aircraft droned deeper into the long Arctic shadows, he and his crew had seen nothing but a vast expanse of grey sea and white ice-floes.

Only occasionally was the sombre scene lit by a shaft of dim, watery sunlight that coloured the vast ice-pack off Norway's North Cape a delicate pink. It was May of 1952 and the Catalina was on a routine ice survey mission from its base in northern Norway.

Ahead of the aircraft, the jagged snow-capped peaks of Spitzbergen rose from the icy sea. The pilot turned slightly, bringing the Catalina over the western shores of the islands. Dwarfed by the mountains that towered above it, the aircraft cruised on.

Another half hour or so and it would be time to set course for home. Suddenly a flash of reflected light caught the pilot's eye. There was something down there, something that glittered among the icy crags. Skimming past a sheer mountain wall, the pilot brought the Catalina down for a closer look.

Whatever was down there appeared to be metallic . . . The long polar shadows made it difficult to pick out the exact shape of the object —but it looked like the crumpled wreckage of a crashed aircraft. If it was, there might be survivors, and in that freezing climate help, to be effective, had to be quick.

As the Catalina climbed away from Spitzbergen, its radio operator flashed a priority signal to the Norwegian air rescue service. Within half an hour, rescue teams were on their way by air to the island. While the Catalina flew homewards, its crew were unaware that their discovery on the barren island of Spitzbergen was destined to become one of the biggest mysteries of modern times.

It was a mystery which has remained a closely guarded secret for the past sixteen years. Whatever the rescue teams actually found on Spitzbergen, it was certainly not an orthodox aircraft. And a few days later, the Norwegian government released an amazing statement to the newspapers.

It claimed that the object found on the island was, incredibly, the wreck of a flying saucer—a disc shaped craft that was ' definitely not of this Earth.' The statement added that a thorough investigation and analysis of the alien object was being carried out by Norwegian, British and American experts.

Journalists flocked to Europe, into Norway, seeking more information, but the Norwegian government refused to make any further comment. After the initial earth-shaking announcement, the security wraps came down. From then on, there was only silence and complete secrecy.

The silence was broken very briefly a few months later, when an unnamed United States Air Force spokesman told newsmen that the mysterious craft had been of Soviet origin and carried Soviet markings. The newspapers were by no means satisfied but they filed away the story as unusable through lack of reliable information—and forgot it.

Then, in September of 1955 the Norwegian government revealed that a Norwegian general staff board of inquiry had practically completed an investigation into the nature of the mystery object, and was about to make its findings public.

The chairman of the board, Norwegian Air Force Colonel Gernod Darnbyl, stated emphatically that the wrecked craft could not have originated on Earth; for the materials used in its construction were completely unknown and had defied every attempt at analysis.

The statement that it was of Soviet origin was false. Furthermore, a detailed examination of the disc had revealed certain technical features which were beyond the grasp of terrestrial science. Colonel Darnbyl went on to say that a team of air force specialists—who had been keeping a close watch on the Arctic regions since the crashed disc was discovered—now believed that the area within the Arctic Circle was being used as a base for alien craft.

The specialists, moreover, had logged a great deal of Unidentified Flying Object activity during their three years of surveillance. The statement concluded that the true facts behind the affair were of sensational importance and should be made known to the public without delay.

The full report, it was said, would be published after discussions with the British and U.S. governments. But the report was never released. One rumour was that a NATO partner—either America or Britain, or maybe both—had clamped down on any release of further information.

Certainly, since the early Fifties, both the United States and Britain have been classifying information about UFOs under the heading of

UFO PROPHECY

TECHNICAL SECRETS OF CRASHED UFO 'HUSHED'

'secret.' To issue the standard type of explanation in connection with the Spitzbergen saucer would have been futile, particularly in view of the announcements already made by the Norwegian government.

Is this why the whole affair was cloaked under a veil of 'no further comment'? And what finally happened to the Spitzbergen saucer? Did the Norwegians find its crew dead inside it? Were its technical secrets ever unlocked? These are questions which, for the time being, must remain unanswered.

One day, perhaps, public opinion may force the authorities to lift the curtain of secrecy that hangs over that May afternoon when invaders from space landed amid the Arctic ice.

I was especially pleased when one visitor to Warminster saw something unusual. It could not have happened to a nicer young man... Ian Girvan, whose father the late Waveney Girvan was a pioneer in flying saucer investigation, an author and one-time editor of *Flying Saucer Review*, came up to Cradle Hill one summer night in 1967, accompanied by his farmer brother-in-law.

Ian badly wanted to vindicate his father's opinions and works concerning UFOs, so was particularly anxious to enjoy his very first UFO sighting that night. Through a pair of powerful binoculars, which they quickly aligned on to the first pulsating type spaceship that came over Warminster, both saw no fewer than six other UFOs flitting in rear of the main one.

'The large one we could see clearly without the aid of binoculars,' said a highly delighted Ian, like myself a journalist and hard-headed realist. 'But it was only when we used the binoculars that we could see the others far beyond, very distant but discernible through the lens.'

With the naked eye, these half dozen would have been invisible and therefore uncounted. Bob, Sybil and I may have inadvertently been missing scores of more distant UFO brethren, by not always employing binoculars in skywatches.

CHAPTER SIX

Flying Crosses and Excaliburs Nothing New!

Flaring flying crosses are nothing new in aerial phenomena over the notorious Warminster area, although there was a spate of such descriptions in late October of 1967, widely and fairly reported in the British national press at the time.

Reliable witnesses include police, senior Royal Air Force officers and Army personnel. To recount them all would be both boring and tedious within the context of a work seeking to raise thoughts of the enthusiast to higher horizons than a narrow skyline of mere sightings that are now so numerous.

Suffice to point out that similar testimony was given by witnesses in my last book, *The Warminster Mystery*, as observant readers will recall. Then the terminology was 'four-pointed stars' moving at varying speeds and trajectories. They were particularly active in September of 1965, as page 169 of the book stressed.

Sometimes testifiers likened them to 'flying swords' and one even referred to this type of UFO as an Excalibur, the legendary sword of King Arthur of Round Table renown.

When low in altitude, one can see around the vivid outline of the 'cross' itself a more subdued amber casing in circular form. Thus, they conform to the usual UFO rounded contours and shape in overall character and dimension. For the four-armed 'spiral' to stand out clearly and outshine the outer casing, the spaceship must be viewed at extremely low height.

According to scientific concepts in engineering design of conventional aircraft, these interstellar chariots are aero-dynamically unsound and utterly wrong in flying principles. If only because of this reason, they have no right to use our air space, say the obstinate and those who stick to dogmatic dictums, spurning the serious testimony of reputable witnesses.

Yet all the experts decried the unsuitability of the delta-winged

UFO PROPHECY

bomber at the designing board phase some twenty years ago. It flew —and very well, as it happened, ramming the conservative opinions of the ' experts ' down their throats.

Recorded in historical documents apart from the Bible, becoming more prolific in numbers since the last war especially, UFOs have been seen by so many people in all major countries of the world that a discerning and growing proportion of a no longer gullible public is amassing sufficient wisdom to refuse, nowadays, to be fobbed off with weak explanations far short of truth.

Surely the most maligned planet in our Solar System, the poor old Venus ' cow ' must have been milked dry ages ago by the alibi furnishers and the manufacturers of alternatives to UFOs. As a shining scapegoat, she does not stand up to hard scrutiny from the rational and open-minded. As for the puerile ' plane refuelling ' myth freely propagated by the ' damp-downers,' this has been detonated by the very Americans held to blame for flying cross manifestations.

During the October ' flap ' of spaceships that treat gravity pulls with contempt we dare not emulate, in different parts of Britain and especially the West Country, UFO activity heightened at Warminster, too, although it has left its indelible impression on the town for well over three years to date.

During the weekend period from October 28th to 30th, my voluntary team observed no fewer than fifteen alien spacecraft in a total of eleven skywatching hours at night. Aside from us three, who now plough a less lonely furrow than formerly in earnest field research as opposed to armchair criticizm, at least eighteen others witnessed some of these luminous moving objects.

A few at random are: Post Office employee Hilary Chadderton, George and Sheila Scott, John and Neil Champion, Gil and Pauline Roberts, Alan and Margaret Cooper, Ken Rogers and Johan Quanjer, printing compositor Ian Davies, garage worker Alan Ford, my son Graham, Dorothy and Clive Fear, Mollie Carey and Brad Taylor.

Alan Ford, in fact, saw a most unusual combination of spacecraft at 6.42 p.m. on the Sunday, before our main party set off for Cradle Hill. His account was: ' They came over Cop Heap like a string of coloured lights, oval in shape, and four of them seemed to be joined together at the edges.

' All were a pale yellow in colour and pulsating from dull to bright

FLYING CROSSES AND EXCALIBURS NOTHING NEW!

as they sped fast towards the downs to the left, to the North-West. It was a wonderful sight and so unexpected. There was not a whisper of sound when they raced across.

'They were fairly low down, but I can give no real estimate of actual height. At one point they almost brushed against treetops. Each was about the size of a sixpenny bit at arm's length away from the eye. As they shot up and away, out of sight, they changed into circles of light at the last moment, as if turning on their sides.'

Housewife Dorothy Fear, of Boreham Field, went further and attested to a positive landing of an orange glowing craft with a hemispherical top or dome on the shoulder of Battlesbury Hill a few minutes short of midnight on Wednesday, October 25th.

Her son Clive confirmed this. Had it not been so late, she told me, she would have sent Clive to rouse our investigating team. A claim of a second landing came from Peter Lawless, who then worked with the Lions of Longleat enterprise at Horningsham, a few miles from Warminster.

My informant said that a small and round-edged spinning aeroform glided gently down to land near beauty spot Heaven's Gate on Tuesday, October 24th, late at night. Marks of grass being slightly depressed measured around thirty feet across, in a circular pattern, the following morning.

Ian Davies told me he saw 'a large fiery object the size of a pea to the eye, but not green of course. It was rather low over the downs to the North. It passed over the golf course at Elm Hill and changed from dim to glittering every second or so, fluctuating from pale orange to red.

'For some time it simply hung in the sky without noise. That is when I first noticed it. Then it moved off at a tremendous speed.' This was on the night of Wednesday, October 25th, after the alleged landing at Heaven's Gate.

Other accounts reached me soon after. About the time that two Devon policemen saw something peculiar in the sky on Tuesday, October 24th, Lieutenant Michael Casey, on military exercises near Imber, the deserted 'ghost' village on Salisbury Plain, saw something similar in the Bulford direction.

He is based at the School of Infantry, Warminster, serving with the 1st Queen's Regiment then stationed in Lingfield. His home is at Purley, Surrey. 'I have got an open mind regarding what it was,' he told the *Wiltshire Times* later. Then sensibly continued:

UFO PROPHECY

'At the time I thought it was a satellite or a bright star. But when I saw the television news on Tuesday evening, I realised that what I had seen was very much on a par with the Devon police sightings. So I reported it to Warminster police.

'I was on exercises about one-and-a-half miles South of Imber at 4.30 a.m. We were on a two-man patrol, but I did not mention it to my partner because he was busy map reading. It was about thirty degrees above the horizon. It was a white blob with four prongs, roughly twenty times brighter than the North Star and ten times bigger.

'It appeared to be stationary and I watched it for about fifteen seconds, although it may have been there longer. There was no sound and what I saw was apparently much farther away than what the policemen saw. I have done some basic astronomy and it certainly was not Venus, as somebody suggested after the police sighting.'

We are extra careful in our meticulous assessment to define true UFOs, yet I always welcome descriptions given in this frank and excellent way. Concise, to the point and breathing very truth. One cannot ask for, nor expect, anything more in a sometimes bewildering quest for the factual.

Let us now consider what Michael Wakely, chairman of the Wiltshire UFO research group, had to say on January 12th of 1968: 'Reports of unidentified flying objects are still being received by research groups up and down the country. Warminster is still an active area. The object of these groups is to investigate fully these phenomena. This is something the authorities will not or cannot do!

'The public showed quite recently that they were not satisfied with investigations into the Flying Crosses seen over Devon and elsewhere. Two main explanations were given by the Ministry:

'(1) That the lights were the planet Venus. This was emphatically denied in a great many cases. No police officer is likely to go around chasing planets at eighty miles an hour. Is any trained observer, such as a police driver, likely to be so simple as to give chase to any planet? In many instances, Venus had not even risen by the time the crosses were seen.

'(2) That the crosses were aircraft refuelling. This was absolute rubbish! Major Westgrove, the director of the USAF base at Ruislip, denied that any of his planes could have been mistaken for crosses because (a) red lights were very prominent (only white crosses were

FLYING CROSSES AND EXCALIBURS NOTHING NEW!

noted) and (b) all exercises had finished by 9 p.m. (most of the crosses were seen in the early morning).

'Until the *Sunday Express* of October 29th mentioned this, the Ministry of Defence had stuck to these weak explanations. Afterwards it said: "It looks as if there is still no rational explanation for the objects the policemen report having seen."

'All I can say is—they did not try very hard to find one. They just buried their heads in the sand in the hope that the crosses would soon go away. If we had another "saucer" flap tomorrow, we would be given the same putrid and inconclusive "explanations" that even children of nine and ten would fail to accept. They are insults to the intelligence of the thinking public.

'Research into UFOs is being carried out by major powers all over the world. The USA have given £107,000 to the University of Colorado under Professor E. Condon to investigate aerial phenomena. The USSR, under General Anatoli Stolyerov, have formed a panel of eighteen top Soviet scientists to investigate the problem.

'U Thant stated publicly a few months ago that "Next to Vietnam, UFOs are the world's next big problem." UFOs have been seen in their thousands since 1947. Over 250,000 claim to have been seen. Now, I am not saying that every single light seen in the sky is extra-terrestrial.

'Most of them can be explained away as hallucinations, sundogs, refractions through ice crystals, etc. But not all! I feel very strongly about this subject and ask that we eradicate this neurotic apathy or ridicule that surrounds Ufology.

'Something has to be done to investigate the subject fully. We feel that people have a right to know what is going on in the skies above us—and we are trying to find out as much as we possibly can. We want thinking members, people with open minds,' he urged in a recruiting drive.

'We do not want cranks. We are a scientific study group, using science wherever possible to investigate these phenomena; trying to remove the pathetic apathy and antipathy towards the subjects and looking for a logical, sound solution. Our evaluating committee are willing to investigate all sightings sent in to us.'

This straight from the shoulder viewpoint is shared by all earnest research students. As library assistant Margaret Clayton, of Westbury, puts it: 'I do not think the public realise just how much difficulty Mike Wakely has had in forming a successful group.

'Most people think that when teenagers meet, all they do is drink, smoke and pursue the frivolous things in life. However, this is not so. The local group of Contact United Kingdom consists of just over thirty people, nearly all of whom are teenagers. We are trying to do serious research into telepathy, psycho-synthesis, and of course UFOs. But how can we carry on with this if we do not get public support?

'If we appeal for any information, people just will not come forward. They are much too worried about what their neighbours or friends would think if they did. They regard us as set apart from " people ;" some even think we are queer!

'Don't people realise that this is a sincere attempt by serious-minded people to "crack open" these unexplained phenomena? It is about time that people looked around them, to see what makes them tick and what makes the Universe tick. They are no better than cabbages. One will not make a move without the other.'

A letter to the *Daily Telegraph* from Camilla, Countess of Erne, stated: 'With reference to the Defence Ministry's astonishing claim that British and American aircraft on refuelling exercices accounted for most of last week's UFO sightings, may I point out the following?

'1. Wing-Commander Eric Cox states categorically in his report that the objects he noted in formation were whitish to yellow-coloured, were noiseless and were like nothing he had ever seen before. Is it conceivable that a man of his experience would not be able to recognize a formation of conventional jet aircraft when he saw them? Yet this is what the Defence Ministry managed to imply.

'2. With regard to the same report—would four aeroplanes be expected to hover in the shape of a cross, static for three solid minutes, while taking part in a refuelling procedure? I maintain this is not valid, and no doubt there are many who will agree with me here.

'3. Police reports state that an intense white light was seen, both moving slowly and accelerating up to amazing speeds. They maintain also that no sound emanated from the source. Indeed it must have been a miraculous aeroplane, or aeroplanes, to have been capable of manoeuvres of this kind.

'4. The same must apply to the planet Venus, not normally given to performing such antics in the heavens.

'To sum up, we are left with the indisputable fact that fiery cigar-

UFO PROPHECY

FLYING CROSSES AND EXCALIBURS NOTHING NEW!

and cross-shaped phenomena, saucers and brilliant white objects have been seen over wide areas (including Ireland) by many reliable witnesses; and that these sightings mostly vary in sizes, shapes and speeds, apart from the tallying evidence of the Devon and Sussex police, which also coincides with certain civilian reports.

'Is the British public seriously going to accept either a "normal aircraft refuelling exercise" or a "particularly bright aspect of Venus" as an overall explanation of the former observations in our skies?

'Or will we swallow anything so long as it is not the bald statement that we are being scrutinized by extraterrestrial visitors at the present time?' wrote the Countess from her home at Newtownbutler, County Fermanagh.

Recapping on the flying cross stories that hit headlines in all British newspapers at that period, two policemen had an 80-90 mph chase after what they described as an unidentified flying object over a Devon road. A spokesman for Devon and Cornwall police told reporters that the policemen said it was very large, bright and in the shape of a cross.

According to one news medium, the constables later reported seeing the object again, when it was this time joined by a second, similar object. Two Earthbound Venuses in one go? How remarkable!

PCs Roger Willey and Clifford Waycott were in a patrol car at 4 a.m. when they first saw the glowing object, on the Holsworthy to Hatherleigh road. PC Willey is based at Okehampton, PC Waycott at nearby Winkleigh. Both are married men in their thirties.

The nearest they got to the object, they attested, was about forty yards, when it was 'at about treetop height.' The spokesman said: 'It followed a course virtually over the road on which they were travelling and they were doing 80 mph at one time. Then it left them. It appeared to stop in a field and they stopped also and got out—but it disappeared.'

The constables were joined by a motorist, Christopher Garner, of Hatherleigh. 'He told the constables that he thought he was having a nightmare,' the police spokesman added. The men finally reported the disappearance of the objects at 4.58 a.m., almost an hour after the initial sighting from their patrol car. In the course of keeping them 'under surveillance,' the constables had journeyed a distance of about thirty miles.

Exeter police HQ checked with Chivenor RAF station and Exeter airport. At Okehampton, a senior officer was waiting to interview the

UFO PROPHECY

FLYING CROSSES AND EXCALIBURS NOTHING NEW!

added 'how on Earth did you know?' Frederick Harding and his wife Patricia supported this. Bob and Sybil knew of my forecast, too. I have never told anyone of my source of information. Everyone can learn it in chapter 16 of this book.

For more than an hour, seven coastguards watched a giant cone-shaped UFO through high powered field glasses as it hovered above them at Brixham, Devon, from noon of April 28th 1967. This story made news headlines, also, although our Warminster team trio had actually logged landings on our sightings list by then.

In fact, at Starr Hill on the night of Thursday, April 13th, we not only saw the glowing bodied craft at a range of 250 yards weaving over the shoulder of the hill, large as a house window at thirty paces to our eyes, but observed a wonderful display of conical lights flashing from its revolving rim as it practically 'sat' on the ground near a deserted farmhouse about a mile away.

Later we heard 'human' coughing sounds coming from the lower slopes of Starr Hill and noises of jackboots or wellingtons squelching in soggy ground and soft mud around a barn near our parked car. We told a few people about this, and how we kept close watch for several hours until—quite frankly—the gurgling footsteps of apparently invisible walkers preyed on our nerves, stretched them to tension point.

They could stand no more of this tremendous pressure, so we hurriedly left the eerie scene at about 2 a.m. Who would credit we were not simply 'shooting a line' and fabricating such an astounding sequence of events? Reporter Ned Grant of the *Daily Mirror* seized on the story, promised to come along with us to follow up the next act in the drama, yet failed to appear.

One so-called paraphysical expert from the Salisbury area openly derided us and contended that what we had seen was a farm tractor with its lights on. This was an incredibly naive indictment. Between 11.45 p.m. and 2 a.m., would a 'flying' tractor have been operating with three balls of light that sped from left to right and returned at lightning speed to a blacked-out craft, dizzying to the gaze?

When true narratives of personal experience were laughed at and unwisely scorned by the obtuse 'experts,' we withdrew and kept certain information strictly to ourselves in future. Remember, we have nothing to gain from falsifying evidence and everything, including our good names, to lose . . .

I may relate these landing details (we saw several spacecraft touch down on Earth in April, May, August and September of 1967) in a future book, when space visitors have impressed their presence more strongly on people's minds. That time will soon arrive.

The world is not yet fully prepared for such revelations and our team are inclined to forget the vital point that we have been active in close studies of UFOs at Warminster, and so favoured by contacts impossible for an unseeing majority to place absolute trust in, not having experienced them.

Back to the cone-shaped UFO at Brixham... As the object hovered, it slowly revolved, revealing some sort of door in its side. An aircraft approached and circled around it, then flew away. Eventually the conical giant vanished behind cloud after climbing to 20,000 feet.

Scores of onlookers, according to a front page story in the *Sunday Express*, telephoned police stations along the Devon coast to ask about this aerial pyramid. The report from the coastguards regarding the object was forwarded within minutes to the Ministry of Defence by the RAF at Plymouth.

The Ministry reaction to the report, sought shortly after the incident, puzzled the coastguards. For the Ministry at first denied ever receiving such a document. Later a spokesman said:

' Further inquiries reveal that we did receive a report, but somehow it was not logged. We can only suggest that the object may have been a reflection of car headlights or some sort of meteorological phenomena. I cannot comment further.'

This led to one of the biggest Ufological titters of the year. As the chief officer of the coastguard station in Berry Head, Brixham, Harry Johnson, said: ' It is just laughable for anyone to suggest to a body of highly trained observers that this was the reflection of car headlights.

' It was midday! The object was obviously made of something very highly polished and reflected the sunlight almost like a star.' Coastguard Brian Jenkins said: ' I was able to make a detailed drawing of it, which I showed to an air vice-marshal who called at the station a few days later. His only comment was: " Most interesting."

' They must have known it was an unexplainable object,' Brian added. And a senior RAF controller at Plymouth went so far as to say: ' We reported all the details. I cannot tell you where the aircraft came from, and you will have a job to get anyone to admit that one was in fact sent up. I understand the UFO was also tracked by radar.'

Shortly after my book *The Warminster Mystery* reached my publisher

UFO PROPHECY

FLYING CROSSES AND EXCALIBURS NOTHING NEW!

in May of 1966, it was reported by the *Birmingham Post* that two mysterious objects were seen in our neighbouring county of Gloucestershire, near each other, within a few hours.

The first, metallic in appearance, was suspended in daylight over Leckhampton Hill at Cheltenham. The second, ' brighter than any star,' was seen at 12.30 a.m. next day. Keith Beard, Cheltenham photographer, described the first as ' round, with a kind of disc fixed to it, like a cup and saucer.'

He was travelling in a car and immediately asked the driver to stop so that he could capture the UFO image with his camera. But it had disappeared when he looked again. ' It was hovering between 500 and 600 feet above the hill and looked very metallic to me,' he added.

About twelve miles away Roger Eggleton, a law student, of Tuffley Avenue, Gloucester, had just said goodnight to Miss Averil Scott when he saw a strange light in the sky over the city. ' It was oval and bigger and brighter than any star. Behind it there was a long tail of light.'

Miss Scott said: ' When I saw it the tail had shortened, but it definitely was not a high flying aircraft because it had no navigation light. I have seen satellites. They were not like this. I was not frightened at all. In fact, it quite fascinated me. I just could not take my eyes off it—and wanted to follow it.'

The *Western Daily Press* of Bristol featured a story of a UFO seen by two policemen stationed at Hindley, near Wigan, Lancashire. They were PCs Lionel Haw and Steve Parsonage, whose police chief accepted their unusual evidence for official filing.

First, they had a thorough interrogation from Chief Superintendent Tom Andrews, of Wigan division. The entry in the notebook of PC Haw, aged thirty, for August 10th of 1967 reads: ' 12.43 a.m. Liverpool Road, Hindley. Saw an object in sky, high altitude, travelling East, fast speed, round shape. Not plane or comet. Also seen by PC Parsonage.'

Aged twenty, PC Parsonage said: ' I have never believed stories of people seeing flying saucers, but now I have seen one for myself. I was on the beat when I glanced up and saw this object in the sky. It was glowing white. I could not believe my eyes. Then I saw PC Haw driving a patrol car towards me.

' I waved him to stop and we stood looking at it, when it suddenly started to move.' In the police force eight years, PC Haw testified: ' We watched it move across the sky for two minutes. It certainly was

UFO PROPHECY

not a comet, weather balloon, plane or trick of light. In this job you are trained to observe.

'We had time to have a good look at it. I would estimate its size as round about 100 feet in diameter. I drove back to the station and rang Jodrell Bank to see if it was a satellite, but they assured me this was not possible. I checked with Manchester Airport just to make sure—and was told there were no planes in the vicinity,' he ended.

It is significant that two other officers of the law reported seeing a UFO on the night of Thursday, August 10th of 1967, confirming observations by PCs Haw and Parsonage. They were Cheshire officers PCs Peter Morris and Robert Young, stationed at Bredbury, near Stockport, thirty miles from the site where the Lancashire lawmen witnessed a similar flying object at Hindley.

The Cheshire UFO was a few hundred feet up and glowing white. PCs Morris and Young estimated the size as 100 feet in diameter—same measurement furnished by PCs Haw and Parsonage. The Bredbury sighting was mentioned in the official report submitted by the Hindley officers, sent to Lancashire county police HQ by Chief Superintendent Tom Andrew, head of Wigan division.

Constable Morris refused to comment to pressmen at his home in Romiley, near Bredbury. 'I am unable to confirm or deny the report,' were his only words to newsmen. But Mrs. Norma Morris, his wife, said: 'They say they saw it on the same night as the two Hindley officers. My husband told me not to do anything.'

At Hindley, Constable Haw said: 'After we had seen the flying object I checked with Jodrell Bank radio telescope and they told me they had received a similar report from police at Bredbury. I rang Bredbury and spoke to Constable Morris, who told me what they had seen—and that it was only a few hundred feet from the ground and measured about 100 feet across.'

PC Parsonage said: 'We saw the object at 1.43 a.m. on August 10th and the Bredbury policemen had their sighting some three hours later. This has been included in our report.' The *Daily Mirror* featured a double UFO story in 1967, headlined 'Mystery of Flying Saucer 100 Saw.' It read:

'Two mysterious objects from the skies were yesterday frightening hundreds of people and giving experts a headache. Mystery No. 1 was at Clifton, Nottingham, where 100 people claimed to have seen a flying saucer landing.

UFO PROPHECY

FLYING CROSSES AND EXCALIBURS NOTHING NEW!

'The crowd of adults and children had gathered on high ground near Fairham Comprehensive School after a report swept the area about a flying saucer. They all claimed to have seen a disc-shaped, silvery saucer about 30 feet long landing. Many people gave an identical account of its size, colour and movements.

'Mystery No. 2 was down in the New Forest, Hampshire. Camper Ron Woods, from Farnborough, saw a huge ball of white light flash over his tent, crash close by, and explode. Ron and dozens of other people phoned the police about the object, which came down between Brockenhurst and Highcliffe. Coastguards at Southbourne who saw it said that they believed it was a meteorite.

'But by last night not a trace of it—or any damage—had been found.'

Ufology is a serious business, although delightful touches of humour leaven the sobriety of nocturnal observations at times. Everyone knows the various brands of English chocolate, for example. This leads me to the type of wicked puns we crack when sightings of UFOs are temporarily at low ebb on Cradle Hill.

We had a party of about forty-five BUFORA members with us on this particular occasion and several UFOs had obligingly 'dropped in' to keep us entertained. It was nearly two o'clock in the morning. A girl was eating a bar of chocolate near the awning of a canvas tent where she was camping out.

To keep spirits high after a fifty-minute period minus sightings, I asked her: 'What is that—a Mars bar?' Her friend caught the pale magic of a poor joke and brightly asked: 'Or is it a Milky Way?' Biggest laugh of all came when the girl, poker faced, looked at the wrapping and coolly announced: 'Sorry, you are both mistaken. It is a Galaxy!'

Now for one of the most astounding stories my shorthand notes have recorded in the exciting yet exacting unravelling of tangled UFO clues. It is truly fantastic and will probably form the central theme for my next book. For the male who took a trip for eight hours aboard a celestial chariot, in company with people from an alien planet, is going to release much more data to me 'when the time is ripe.'

Readers will scarcely dare to credit that it can be true. For excellent reasons, as explained at the end of the chapter, I cannot believe that it is false... Not in its entirety, anyway. It must be substantially true.

UFO PROPHECY

WALKS THE WILD ANGEL

Walks the wild wind angel of malice
    In a field of snowdrops,
Where happy morning children star the grass,
Some to gather seeds and larksong,
Some to run like golden honey in the sun.

Their voices dream like summer rivers with fine mists;
They only hear their own sweet, minnow sound.
All they desired was the treasure of buttercups,
Or the great leaves to drop storms of dew,
The sun in haloes spinning round their heads.

The children did not know the afternoon . . .

Through the snowdrops waiting like white assassins,
Walks the wild wind angel, listening with its eyes;
Dragging the sad moan of cut flowers
On the metal edges of its wings . . .

CHAPTER SEVEN

Bizarre Changes of Form and Dimension

Study the following dramatic story carefully, before condemning the two people concerned as outrageous liars. Both are absolute realists with nothing to gain from verbal weaving of untruth. They do not hanker for notoriety or dubious fame. Their character and standing in Warminster are high.

Here, in brief, is the astounding series of personal involvements in the aggregate that presents us with evidence that UFOs and their crews make a special appeal, when it suits their purpose, to the most practical and down-to-earth persons in bizarre ways.

It was on the night of Monday, January 15th of 1968 that they drove up Portway (where the author lives) and headed towards Elm Hill, about a mile short of Cradle Hill. Both of placid temperament, they were completely at ease until the short burst of aerial activity broke their phlegmatic calm.

They had reached the traffic roundabout at the junction of the foot of the hill and Westbury Road when a fiery UFO swept across their vision, from right to left, from Cop Heap towards the silent downs. The car engine began to seize, choke and splutter.

It did not affect the woman, who was in the passenger seat next to the driver. She shielded her eyes from the bright glare of the spaceship in close proximity as it swooped down to the front of the car and swiftly upward. She was then intent on looking left to see where it went after blistering their sight.

The man, however, felt two terrific stabbing pains, high up on either side of his chest. He collapsed at the wheel, slumping over while managing to brake the vehicle to a halt. He remembers little else, yet at work next morning a friend confided: ' I do not want to worry or depress you, but I dreamt last night that you died.'

The vividness of the dream awoke the friend, who looked at his bedside clock and noted the time. To the minute, this corresponded with the time of the car driver's ' death ' and ' double chest wound ' when the UFO flooded the cab with blinding light in a split second ' attack.'

Shortly after this, the ' dead ' man received a strange phone call, urging him to be at Heaven's Gate, on the Longleat Estate of Lord Bath, at 9 p.m. three days later. He and the woman went on the Thursday, not knowing what to expect, staying in the car park opposite.

At three minutes past the appointed hour, the female espied a UFO. It tilted from side to side, overhead, then flew straight to Heaven's Gate and dropped with the suddenness of a stricken bird. The two companions keeping a weird assignment with the unknown clambered over chainlink fencing and tore across the grass.

They sped along the avenue, between trees and bushes, and on the downward slope just beyond the ' gate ' proper (one has a glorious view of stately Longleat House from here) was the saucer. Shocks were in store for the middle-aged couple.

It ceased to spin, the glow lessened in intensity, as it virtually lay on the sloping ground. They found it difficult, almost impossible, to grasp an amazing fact which staggered them in that tense moment . . . The craft was literally no larger than a soup plate ! The two rendezvous keepers gasped.

Then a golden ladder, fine in texture as gossamer, appeared from the base of the miniature spaceship, down which climbed tiny elfin figures no more than four inches in height. There were more than two dozen of them altogether. Stepping away from the landed craft, now blacked out, each in turn zoomed up to the height of the man and woman standing there, dumbstruck, aghast and refusing to credit the testimony of their eyes.

They shook hands with the two Warminster people politely. They were perfectly normal and friendly, as though knowing them well. After a few minutes of small talk, inconsequential yet enlivened by broad smiles from the ' visitors,' they invited the male to take a journey with them in their machine to see some of the hidden wonders of his own world.

Staggered still, yet no longer fearful in face of their warming presence, he agreed. The woman was left behind, holding his car keys and personal effects. To her further amazement, all were again dwarfed in size—including her companion, this time. They ascended the golden ladder, cobweb fine.

UFO PROPHECY

BIZARRE CHANGES OF FORM AND DIMENSION

A whistling noise accompanied the lift-off, the craft rising with a spinning and slightly agitated motion until in free flight. It became larger as it soared up, stopping momentarily well above the treetops before continuing its flight. It soon faded from sight.

The woman, alone in the darkness, waited there for eight hours until past 5 a.m., when her friend returned, dismounted in pygmy stature from the reminiaturized craft and assumed normal height of almost six feet on nearing her.

I will quote what she told me, descriptive of her mixed emotions as he went into the shining spacecraft with the occupants at about 9.10 p.m. ' Arthur, you may think me mad—that is up to you and makes no difference to me. But I swear it is true.

' I could have stooped down, plucked the saucer from the ground and held it in one hand, everyone aboard, it was so small. When I saw B— reduced in size, the same as the others, before he went up the ladder into the machine, my heart almost broke in two. I could have cried over him ! '

Frankly, in spite of the quiet and sombre way in which she gave me the bizarre story, I laughed out loud at this remarkable revelation, until the man—who had not spoken at all, leaving it to his friend—released one specific piece of information which I had already gained from a contact.

To the best of my knowledge, very few others knew of it at that time. It concerned the state of the inner core or central ball of Earth. The man knew of this, now; that was all he was ' permitted ' to tell me to substantiate the fact of his journey. It was enough to convince me that the couple had indeed undergone a chimerical and unnerving experience that was more than a vague imprint on their minds or a traumatic nightmare.

Further details he gave me, later, in an indirect way as though it germinated from his own reasoning and not that of others, with regard to buried cities, communities and mountain chains lying deep under large oceans, caused me to guess intuitively where his trip had carried him on the glowing spaceship.

Yet one has to be furnished with personal proofs before one accepts the almost incredible as truth. These ' people ' have the ability to change form, size and dimension. This, with applied thought, explains much that has puzzled us in the past during our investigations. Maybe

UFO PROPHECY

I am still obtuse and blind, but I have inward doubts that all our 'visitors' are benign. More of this anon.

Remember the 'floating' light in the middle of the copse atop Cradle Hill, which flew right past us and through a barbed wire fence and gate? The 'funny' photos taken at the very start of our joint researches? Queer animal and bird images, pyramidic triangles, ancient stone columns, apparent stairways—all these unpredictables instead of flying craft our eyes were patently seeing?

These were clear pointers from the positive types of UFOs and crews, peculiar clues to make us blink and—more important—think. The signs were emphasized for a purpose we had failed to appreciate, uncomprehended because of minds rendered un-co-operative through pursuit of ruthless realism...

Content of this chapter so far will stretch your credulity. It is bound to, by its very unorthodox and unconventional concepts. I realise that plainly and sympathetically. It could be, nevertheless, that we are becoming more and more sane each day, now, as opposed to the rabid 'mad hatters' some will consider us.

There is no brooking the reality that we are confronted by extraordinary phenomena and beings capable of moving and thinking in dimensions that—if at all assessable according to Earth lights of logic—would possibly frighten conventional conservatives to death!

Whom to trust, welcome and instantly recognize for good or ill? Whom to avoid like a plague, or attempt to convert? What protective clothing or symbols to wear when in proximity of aerial 'intruders'? These are cardinal questions we are beginning to find answers to, in our nocturnal adventuring, not yet foolproof, finalized or conclusive at Cradle Hill. It is an exciting quest and occasionally nerve-sapping, particularly by the dark and lonely copse.

Two women have gone into a disturbing trancelike state, as though mesmerized, at Cradle Hill. On the night of July 8th 1967, which was a Saturday, I was in my native Essex on holiday, taking a short and welcome break from sleepless nights tangling with the Unknown.

On this memorable date, Bob and Sybil stumbled on a rather horrifying example of ostensible hidden menaces in Ufology, on the road at the base of the hill proper. Motoring to the hill from Starr, where they had watched since dusk, they reached our favourite observation point near the midnight hour. A distraught, nail-biting husband was pacing up and down near the white gates, beside a parked car.

UFO PROPHECY

BIZARRE CHANGES OF FORM AND DIMENSION

Worried and wringing his hands in anguish, he made a swift appeal to the welcome newcomers. The stranger told my team mates that his wife had wandered off to neighbouring bushes to 'spend a penny,' but that was twenty-five minutes ago; and now the poor man was demented, staring with dread up the rough track to the dark silhouette of the silent copse.

Grabbing torches from their car, Bob and Sybil rushed along the rutted trackway, sensing something amiss. The husband, braver now he was with company, groped in rear of them. Short of the trees, and to the left side of the copse, their flashing beams brought into bold relief a tall figure standing at the edge of the wood.

He was clad in what my team termed ' some sort of dark and close-fitting garment, shining as if made of leatherette. It seemed to be a one-piece outfit and he wore a hood or black helmet on his head, which was turned towards us and showed a pale face in the glow of our torches.'

When the two torches focused and fused their blazing light full upon him, the man suddenly vanished from sight. Panting from the exertion of a headlong dash on foot up the incline, Bob and Sybil then saw the white raincoat of a woman they gathered was named Lydia beyond the vacant point where the black-garbed figure had been.

The woman, almost in a state of total collapse, clung tight to her rescuers and sobbed : ' It was horrible—he was evil ! Don't leave me—please get me away from here.' She was in a severely shocked condition, distressed in the extreme, shaking from head to toe, weeping and wailing alternately.

Between them my friends helped her down the track, half carrying her back to her husband, who stood by the gates anxiously, head in hands and murmuring ' Thank God she is safe.' From his car he brought hot coffee, which calmed his wife's upset nerves and quietened her outbursts of emotion.

She told the three how she had been drawn, magnetically, to the copse on the skyline by a deep and compelling buzzing sound. It was like ' millions of angry bees swarming ' and originated from behind the small cluster of trees and bushes. She confided that she felt no actual fear at this juncture.

Walking alongside the copse, she heard a rustling noise coming from the undergrowth to her right. Then the tall form of a man, wearing a tight fitting suit of dark and glistening material similar to shot silk, rounded helmet on his head, plodded slowly towards her.

Lydia stood rooted to the spot, feeling the ground thump under her as the heavy tread brought the stranger nearer. Her limbs were numbed and useless as he came within a few feet of her. She almost fainted then. She remembered most of all the 'staring eyes' and the still audible humming of bees, now at a distance.

The figure lifted his hands as though to assure her he meant no harm, but this terrified her more than ever, she taking it as a distinct threatening gesture. When she tried, on tottering legs, to push past him, he obstructed her—and for a fearful second she brushed against the glistening raiment he wore.

It crackled. She lurched backward. There she cowered from him, her own gaze transfixed by his steady and unwavering eyes, large and bright, for what seemed a fear-fraught eternity, until my co-observers ran to the copse and released her from her plight. By then, she was holding on to a tree trunk for support in the darkness, bemusedly gaping into the twin streams of light from their torches.

Was the figure hostile or friendly? A clue may be found in the most unaccountable part of the true story... After Sybil and Bob had safely escorted Lydia from copse to road, and she narrated the astounding tale of what appeared to be a near kidnapping to husband and rescuers, she sat in the car for a while, regaining her composure, recovering from shock.

Then—without warning, except for noticeable dilation of eyes and sudden restive hand movements—she leapt out of her husband's car and hared back up the track! It was a move that caught the trio unawares. When they realised the magnetic impulse was still present, the creature in the wood attuned to the same mental wavelength as Lydia, calling to her silently yet surely, Bob and Sybil once more rescued her.

This time, they were forced to drag her down physically, ignoring her whimpers of protest, in spite of her wildly flailing arms. By this stage they were anxious, for her own safety and peace of mind, that she should be driven from the area as quickly as possible.

When her ashen-faced husband locked the car doors, having bundled her brusquely into the vehicle, they breathed sighs of relief. Sybil was naturally upset at the ordeal, also, and my friends decided to 'call it a night' and drive homeward after the couple left. They were exhausted and a trifle unsettled emotionally, themselves.

UFO PROPHECY

BIZARRE CHANGES OF FORM AND DIMENSION

One more surprise, an explanatory one in a way, was in store before they forsook the scene. A sound as of a large dynamo powerfully pulsing into life, or the droning of thousands of hornets, filled the air. Torpedo shaped and glowing red as a ruby, the UFO telescoped over the treeline, casting its crimson aura over the countryside.

It hovered for seconds, tilted its sharper end upward—and sped in eye-dazzling fashion from view. Here, then, was the aerial culprit responsible for discharging the tall figure in black near the copse, so that he could fasten on to the woman's mental frequency and lure her up to where he awaited contact with an Earth female. Or was it the droning of the craft that attracted her?

In daylight on the Sunday, Bob and our female co-observer examined the locality thoroughly. They found a peardrop or crescent impression in clumps of long grass some 650 yards in rear of the Cradle Hill copse, away from the spot where the dark figure had been standing. Large footprints were discernible in damp earth in the copse centre, leading to the side. None was found around the craft tracks.

The footprints were of unusual pattern, criss-crossed bars on the soles, deep and made without doubt by a heavy person or someone wearing weighted boots, perhaps lead lined. Unlike George Adamski and his doctor friend, my companions had not conveniently brought along any plaster to take casts of the foot impressions.

(I am not being unkind or uncharitable, here, for Adamski, much maligned and criticized before his death, had much truth in him). Nor were my friends able to take photographs, although Bob tried. Disadvantages were the darkness of the undergrowth and a then grey sky. Pouring rain followed to wash the criss-cross design away, in any case.

Confirmation of this astonishing story came a few weeks later, in the same month, when a similar nightmarish thing happened. This time, several valiant young lads of the Birmingham branch of International Sky Scouts—currently styled Contact UK—carried out the rescue of a frightened lady attracted to the copse by what was apparently the same dark uniformed male.

A girl of sixteen was a second 'victim' that night. She went into a mesmerized trance, by the gate, for ten minutes, and had to be restrained from following the older woman up the track. Her mother, brother, uncle, a friend and the ten Birmingham Ufologists (who have assisted our team most conscientiously from time to time) attested that the girl was emotionally overwrought for some weeks after a harrowing experience.

Can we sensibly doubt that an extraterrestrial landed from a nearby spacecraft and 'tuned in' to the mental wavelengths, the electrical frequency, of both woman and girl? Yet was he hostile in intent? Probing their minds, evoking response, was he merely desirous of imparting information without any wish to cause harm?

Is that why he attracted them to him, showing himself boldly, not touching them physically, trying to etch unspoken words in thought or picture form on their mental 'receivers'? We may learn more about this possibility later, meanwhile being given much of serious import to think over and digest.

We strongly discourage children or old folk from venturing near the copse at night, especially when unprotected by adults, for there are possible dangers we are constantly alive to and on guard against. Steel nerves and iron willpower are necessary human qualities when dealing with powers of the ineffable Unknown.

Many varied factors make Ufology a difficult and frustrating labour of love and scant reward. All fellow research students, whether active in the field or in evaluating offices such as the excellent *Flying Saucer Review* (editor, Charles Bowen), *Bufora Journal* (editor, John Cleary-Baker) and *Orbit* (editor, Leslie Otley), will know what we mean, for scarcely anything surprises and shocks any longer.

Have you ever heard of the Golden Ram of Satan? This highly coveted talisman of the Devil, according to practisers of black magic rites, lies hidden somewhere in Europe. The fortunate finder (although I would disagree violently with this assumption) will have his every wish come true, could he but hold it in his hand after digging it from its burial ground.

So the legend goes—and this brings in the aspect of dark and evil forces continually warring against those of Truth and Light. Witches and sorcerers, male and female dabblers in both white and black magic, are not the rare human commodity we imagine them to be, in a civilization which has wisely learned to reject the supernatural yet clings to narrow doctrines of hate and war.

Nothing in this world or any other is supernatural. Everything and every entity, visible or invisible, is explainable in natural terms throughout the whole Universe, although there are so many dimensions and planes of existence undreamt of as yet by Man on Earth.

UFO PROPHECY

BIZARRE CHANGES OF FORM AND DIMENSION

Cley Hill, at nearby Corsley, has been notorious in the past, up to and beyond the turn of the present century my investigations tell me, for ceremonies that encourage devil worship. There is a female witch, well into her eighth decade of life, still living in the village; but she practises white magic, which is of a different order entirely.

Journalists know what a problem it is to unearth sufficient 'hard' news stories around the Christmas period, notable for extensive advertizing prior to the festive day and lack of news material afterwards, in a 'flat' week for provincial news organs.

At Christmas of 1966, therefore, I avidly pounced on a likely story, receiving the 'tip off' from Andrew Bowen, publicity officer for the Marquis of Bath. He is also P.R.O. for the Longleat Estate. My stopping place was the Royal Oak at Corsley, where the landlord and his wife, Mr. and Mrs. Jack Hampton, also a cockney barman named George, told me eerie tales about the ghost of a hooded monk.

He materialized in a brown habit from oak panelling in the lounge and sometimes from steps at the top of an underground cellar, then went through bedroom and bathroom walls as though such obstacles did not exist. The pleasant inn used to be a refectory or breakfasting house for the monks of a monastery burnt to the ground well over 400 years ago.

It occupied the site of the present Longleat House, where the son of Lord Bath, Viscount Weymouth, lives in a wing of the huge building. It was not so much the seasonal ghost story and spooky manifestations of the cowled friar that fascinated me so much as a minor revelation forming the prime content of my 'off beat' Christmas story.

It came to light while I chatted to the friendly landlord. On the ceiling of an upstair room, used by the Hamptons as a drawing room, was a brown face that could not be erased or obliterated. Jack and his wife had distempered over it, whitewashed it, painted and even wallpapered it, to no avail. Still the face persisted on that particular spot, reminiscent of a hooded monk with long red hair.

The tale went over pretty well and found its way, eventually, in a leading evening newspaper. It was several weeks later that the landlord dropped a bombshell at my feet; although it was to me a fizzling 'dud' at that time, meaning nothing explosive in effect.

He solemnly told me he had a visitor at the inn one night—a tall, thin man with fanatical dark eyes who claimed that the triangle of passages and tunnels under the inn, leading to a farmhouse at Whitbourne and from thence to Cley Hill and back to the former refectory, held the most precious secret or earthly relic of the devil.

First of all the odd caller with the cadaverous features, wearing a long black cloak over evening dress, asked the licensee whether he could venture down to the wine and beer cellars and explore behind the built-up screening wall that separates the inn from the ancient tunnel. (This passage, also the triangular pattern of underground lanes leading to Cley Hill and the farm, was mentioned in my newspaper article.)

When the landlord refused permission, pointing out that Viscount Weymouth as the owner and the brewery as lessees would certainly not approve of this pulling down of a bricked structure, the stranger confided his firm belief that the talisman of the devil, the golden ram of Satan, lay buried in earthen walls of the tunnel, probably interred under Cley Hill itself.

I did not use this story as a follow up sequel to my Christmas ghost yarn. I felt it a little too macabre for readers to digest. It was not until much later that news reporter Peter Hiscocks, a friend of mine, delved more deeply into this aspect and concluded that it might link with UFO concern and manifestations in our area. A triangle, again . . . The three-sided symbol keeps popping up in our research findings.

When one of my contacts 'sanctified' and freshly 'charged' certain hills and circles around Warminster, in late 1967 and early 1968, dealt with more fully later in this book, he discovered that Cley Hill was or had been 'a particularly bad centre of evil forces and their works.' He had quite a struggle in 'laying them to rest and converting them.'

It was one of three pronounced witchcraft centres he had to cope with in his necessary operations. It might have been a case, although I did not appreciate the significance of it then, of 'laying a ghost to catch a ghost.' Peculiarly again, the three hideous venues of former devil worship form an accurate triangle geographically!

Going up and away over Cradle Hill . . . Just caught before leaving the camera behind ! Bob Strong photo.

UFO PROPHECY

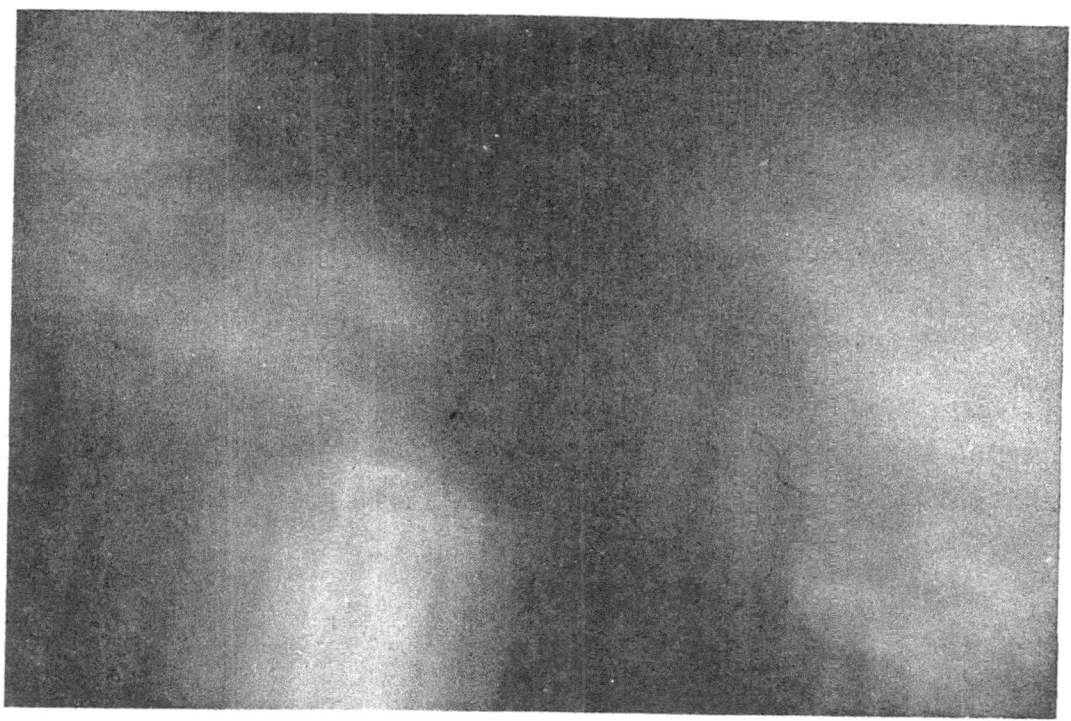

Should have been a UFO, but
Ridged columns of stone, as though sea-washed.

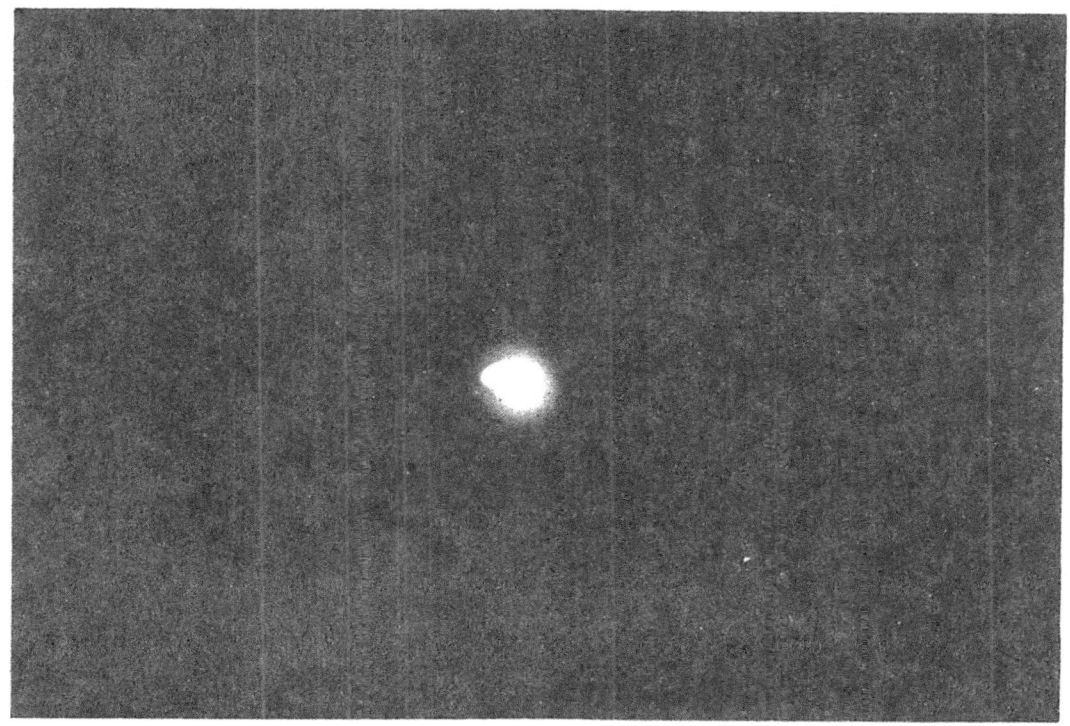

Giant UFO, green, like one that ensnared Capt. Mantell's Mustang over Godman Field. Cradle Hill, Autumn, 1966. Photo by Bob Strong.

CHAPTER EIGHT

Possible Methods of Spacecraft Propulsion

Much has been theorized about the motivating power of alien spacecraft, the methods of propulsion they might possibly use, also the relevance of the often observed 'fuzziness' at the edges of discoids when in flight. Resolving these answers must be an important part of research to quench the thirst for knowledge on the UFO front.

These questions should engage serious attention of experts in aerodynamics and technical engineering who have suitably open minds to explore them. They doubtless arouse curiosity of governmental departments involved in defence, throughout our planet, even if this is adroitly sheathed from the public by repeated denials that UFOs exist.

Unfortunately, we are prone to suffer from xenophobia, the dislike of strangers and fear of aliens that may yet prove the biggest drawback to complete and uninhibited understanding of our visitors from Outer Space. In our Solar System, the Sun is the principal life and light giving agency. We have not learned all its dazzling secrets so far.

We are now aware of how to harness its radiant energies for several purposes—let us hope, predominantly, for peaceful utilization—but possess only the barest conception of terrific potentials in this field of inquiry, achieving a mere mouse-nibbling minimum instead of a Man-saving maximum of knowledge.

Assuming that our aerial visitors are so technologically advanced that they have mastered many wonders of Nature beyond the elementary realm of splitting the atom, capturing and 'tapping' enormous reserves of power through working in harmony with natural forces, we can catch fragmentary glimpses of our future destiny in space travel providing we ever become civilized enough to earn parity with interplanetary brethren.

Suppose the saucer type of UFO should contain in its interior two pillars, rods or columns which represent positive and negative poles of power. These power fields are best described in lay language as 'electricity'—that is, power which is 'pumped' through the solar system by our sun. This electricity is, in fact, the same sort of force we are already conversant with to a limited degree.

However, in the saucers its use is different, its composition not quite the same. Crews are able to relate their extensive knowledge of electricity and its true nature to the varying kinds of ray which emanate from the sun in any reachable solar system.

This would probably apply only to the bell or saucer shaped aeroforms, although the general principle is not all that dissimilar when it comes to propulsion methods employed by larger spacecraft such as the ark or mother ship that releases smaller discs into the atmosphere.

Ufologists are familiar with the three 'balls' sometimes seen at the base of the saucers. They are usually defined by writers as landing gear constituents. This could, in part, be erroneous. Two of these balls represent the base portion of the two rods or pillars inside the saucer and are exterior appendages.

The positive electrical rod is related to the main positive ray of the sun. On the other hand, the negative rod is related to the longest ray of the sun, which may be employed as a required negative counterforce to control differing movement and trajectory.

These two columns serve to propel the saucer forward, upward, backward or downward. They are operated by a special control panel in the spaceship. To make the latter drop, the negative rod is brought into action. To propel the airship upward, the positive is used.

When greater speed is needed, the positive rod is manipulated accordingly. The negative is allowed certain degrees of 'play' in order to slow the craft down; and the two forces are balanced to permit the spaceship to hover. The positive pole is half 'shut down' and the negative probably permitted maximum boost to achieve this delicate counterpoise.

For the spaceship to effect a landing, both forces are switched off. This is consistent with accounts of saucers shooting away at immense speed or, conversely, dropping towards the Earth with an oscillating motion 'like a leaf falling in a breeze.'

The main positive electrical ray of the sun would not be comprehended by the majority of people on Earth; but genuine scientists, who find that conventional training and traditions do not obstruct inquiring minds that are willing to accept challenges, may readily grasp what is implied.

UFO PROPHECY

POSSIBLE METHODS OF SPACECRAFT PROPULSION

It corresponds most nearly to the Yogi term of Sushumna Ray—our Outer Space visitors would not use this terminology themselves, perhaps, but it fits—with which Yogis in India are familiar. Students of the true Occult should not be mystified by the expression, either.

The fuzziness or blurred effect often seen, even with the naked eye, is caused by the particles of air (that is, of nitrogen, oxygen and other gases in the atmosphere of Earth) being forcibly expelled by the electrical power generated from the saucer.

When all gases in the air are so expelled, a vacuum is created—so as to see light clearly, it must be reflected from atomic particles to hold it steadily in view, as it were. Consequently, light coming from the aerial vehicle would be 'fuzzy' as it enters the field of this vacuum.

In short, the faster the airship is travelling, for example, the greater and more noticeable the extent of blurring. This is a factor one must weigh carefully when attempting to photograph a craft in motion. Both the positive and negative charges are far more powerful than our known positive and negative force fields.

This enormous energy thrust and content is responsible for the frequently reported 'cutting out' of engines in ordinary Earth vehicles, whether aircraft or road transport, when in the immediate vicinity of a flying saucer. Unless and until we learn to harness special sun rays, we shall never possess the equivalent of such terrific power potential.

There have been hosts of instances where car and lorry engines have seized up or cut out when in the proximity of a low-flying UFO, neutralized until it has flown far enough away from stalled engines to allow their revitalization after usual reliability and performance has been adversely affected.

Observers will find that fuzziness, for want of a better term, does occur most with UFOs of the saucer variety when the positive rod is obviously in predominant operation, according to movement and velocity of the craft. The slower the saucer is journeying, the less fuzzy is its appearance.

It is difficult to measure degrees of haze or fuzziness, but these explanatory details may present sincere Ufologists with something to work on and by in watching hours, for determination purposes connecting with speeds, rates of ascent and descent, etc.

As the primary motive power is electrical in nature, this accounts for a fact that has puzzled many observers and 'victims.' Petrol driven engines normally are afflicted by the surging power of UFOs to a great extent. Diesel powered engines do not seem to suffer too badly in comparison, statistically. This discrepancy is worth examining by specialists.

If a saucer craft—I do detest that inane term!—is dropping down to the ground, there is little or no appreciable amount of fuzz at the outer rim or edge of the spacecraft. This, if you like, is simply theorizing on a workable motivation unit, or units, as applied to the flying saucer.

But how can one do otherwise in endeavouring to decide exactly what does make a UFO 'tick'? Short of taking a trip on board these wingless wonders and inspecting at close range and first hand the inner mysteries of the incredible craft, one must posit certain probabilities.

Let us survey and consider other hypotheses which might fit in as alternative or complementary sources of power. We may be hazarding shrewd guesses at ultimate truths somewhere in this chapter, having eliminated propulsion media which are palpably suspect.

Imagine that the entire Universe is an orderly system of magnetic vortices, each vortex having power going into it and energy coming from its point or centre—this energy released by the condensation of solid material out of magnetic energy.

Interplanetary vehicles could possibly manipulate this same energy to achieve high speed motion in any direction required. However, before any motion can exist, there must be energy initially converted into motion. This power pocket could be tapped by a series of collector rings from magnetic forces ever present and available in the Universe.

The Universe is composed of magnetic fields within magnetic fields; and when these are combined they display a fantastic amount of power sufficient to create suns, planets, satellites of planets and satellites of satellites, even, not to mention vast clouds of nebulous material, small meteorites and comets.

Power from these fields could be employed by spacecraft if it is tapped and extracted at all ranges of magnetic frequency. Because of this, gigantic displays of energy would be possible, even from the smallest craft. The energy could be gathered by a series of collector rings and transmitted to a storage cell, which would then feed it to a distributing computer.

From there it would proceed into a computer-controlled frequency variator or stabilizer, and from thence to the propulsion sphere itself: usually located just below the top and inside the umbrella shaped

POSSIBLE METHODS OF SPACECRAFT PROPULSION

collector rings. The propulsion sphere is segmented and each portion activated in relation to the other portions to effect the desired motion or combination of motions.

One could sensibly surmise that the small circular robot monitors, which are unmanned, have three collector rings and one propulsion sphere; whereas much larger circular craft are equipped with the same number of rings for propulsion power, plus a smaller one for power supply to satisfy the other necessary functions of the ship of the air.

Let us assume that larger airships have a series of collector rings and propulsion sphere combinations, in addition to collector rings that supply power to the computers, lighting units, air conditioning plant, magnetic beams and the manual control systems.

One could envisage that the propulsion power is generated separately in all ships except the unmanned robots or ' brain beacons.' This is a precaution in case one system or network fails, another then substituting to supply energy so that the craft will not be totally disabled in emergency.

We can conceive, therefore, that any spaceship can operate to a limited extent on any one collector ring; but for the intermediate spacecraft and the huge arks, a disaster of this kind (loss of other collector rings) would be most unlikely.

Yet in such an unexpected event the craft would function, but very slowly and falteringly, on any one collector ring under pressure. Such an operation would involve and require shutting off computers, the air conditioning, majority of the lighting, and reliance on space units.

Such emergencies, one can well imagine, would seldom arise, for these graceful yet power-packed space machines are almost perfect. No doubt all who fly aboard them are instructed what action to take in case of power failure, meticulous training finding a well schooled response in dire situations.

Malfunctions would be rare and a spacecraft would virtually never wear out. Crews must be prepared for all sorts of eventuality, experiencing different types of atmospheric, magnetic or thought conditions prevailing, having to combat much that is actively aligned against successful and trouble free flight.

It is possible that spacecraft could run into unfavourable magnetic conditions; have been fired upon by hostile denizens of other planets that are less advanced morally and spiritually; beset by one of many undependabilities of an internal nature; any of which could cause malfunctioning. The minor element of uncertainty keeps the crews ever alert.

It may be that the majority of interplanetary or intergalactic trips are equivalent to joy rides for veteran travellers, yet they can never tell when the next one will be that single journey out of a million which turns into a nightmare.

As well as being monitoring devices, unmanned robots or 'thinking lights' may also be defensive weapons. In each miniature discoid are cameras and highly accurate receivers of speech, thought transfer, electromagnetic radiation (radio and television) and magnetic 'sensors' to explore the character of the surrounding magnetic field.

All these could receive impressions to send back to the master station or spacecraft, there to be recorded. Occasionally, unmanned robots may be on 'detached' duty, free from the mother ship, in which case all information gathered could be stored in cylinders placed on board the robot craft for this express recording purpose.

There might be only a crew of two or three humanoids aboard a thirty-feet machine, whereas the sixty-feet craft crew consists of a pilot, co-pilot and six monitors who operate the nine unmanned robots. At other times, all functions could be handled by just the pilot and co-pilot.

We are broadly assuming certain prospects and possibilities, here, but based on evidence that individually and collectively matches them. If necessary, one person could handle the entire ship and unmanned robots. But this would be in emergency and not general practice.

Even with the assistance of a computer system, one person would find it a strain to perform all duties for any length of time. One or two people could handle the ship comfortably, and cope reasonably well with most assignments, providing they called for very limited robot employment.

Assume that a sixty-feet spaceship can carry twenty-five passengers in addition to crew members. In emergencies, more could be conveyed by lining the walls of every corridor, occupying kitchen and storage spaces, access routes to computers, loading central hallways and jamming as many as possible into the pilots' compartment.

This practice would be discouraged and frowned upon except in cases of absolute necessity. Have you ever heard of Diophantes of Sirius 2? According to the Rev. Margaret J. Barnett, First Minister

POSSIBLE METHODS OF SPACECRAFT PROPULSION

of the Church of the Golden Cross, Fresno, California, he tells us this about certain of his native planetary spaceships :—

'We also have a ninety-feet and 100-passenger circular vehicle which is a larger version of the turreted umbrella type of passenger ship. This spacecraft carries no robots and is strictly a passenger or freight carrier. The usual crew is three or six people, depending on the distance to cover.

'For short trips there is a pilot, co-pilot and stewardess. On longer trips, a pilot, co-pilot, cook, stewardess, a relief pilot, relief stewardess and sometimes an extra person to " fill in " where needed. The intermediate ships are much larger and are literally flying cities.

'There are two sizes of these in the Solar System of Sirius. Our smaller ones are three miles long and the larger ones five miles long. Both are dirigible in shape and each has its own distinguishing style. The three-mile-long ship is powered by four sets of four collector rings and propulsion sphere units, with another set of auxilliary rings in various places on the ship.

'This spaceship has storage for 180 of the sixty-feet saucers, as Earth people call them. They are stored in two vertical cylindrical areas of ninety vehicles each. These stored saucers face an open flight deck or area in a circular manner, which is literally the hatchway to the outside into space.

'A maximum crew is 5,000, with a passenger capacity of 20,000 to 40,000 people. Also on board are the sensing devices and the magnetic defence beams, always carried on these ships in addition to the ones on the stored flying craft.

'The five-mile-long ship is also called an intermediate ship and is a larger version of the three-mile-long craft. These dirigible type ships are powered by six units of four collector rings and a propulsion sphere. The crew may number up to 20,000, including the full crews of the 360 craft of the sixty-feet variety.

'These saucers are stacked in silos of 100 each. In addition to this, there is room for one-and-a-half million passengers. These ships are often used for evacuating planets or solar systems before an expansion, to populate planets, or to haul freight, animals, insects and vegetation to new planets before a migration of people who are placed there.

'Then we have the giant ten-mile-long arks. These are also dirigible shaped vehicles and carry a crew of 50,000. They will accommodate 1,200 of the sixty-feet craft and approximately 20 million people.

Some of these arks are equipped to carry the three-mile-long ships, but this is not considered practical.

'Flying one of these arks is far different from any other type ship. Because of its size, it takes twelve to twenty very busy people. There are pilots' compartments in the nose, on the right and left centre sections and in the tail fins.

'The steering is done at both ends, sometimes separately. The right and left pilots can institute a sideways motion, if necessary. Communication between these centres is by thought transfer, so all know what each knows. This eliminates the need for massive amounts of electric gear.

'Everything in these arks is controlled from the nose post command, yet each station will react in the proper manner, as and when necessary. These arks are powerful ships and can manoeuvre as nimbly as the smaller craft. Since everything is magnetically locked in position to the ships, inertia has no effect, even on the people.

'Sudden changes of direction for even the largest ships are possible at any speed. The defence magnetic beam is used by all our vehicles and is a variation of the levitating beam employed to load the ships. The most powerful, of course, is on the ten-mile-long ark.

'This can be sent like a light in a narrow stream, or broadcast as a wide circle on the target. Or it can be focused to a pin-point or twisted into a crooked, parallel beam that will avoid obstructions and still reach its target.

'This beam can be used to heat, chill, disintegrate, freeze, fissionize, alter frequency levels, kill, burn, alter thought patterns, anaesthetize, monitor, crystallize, levitate, nullify the magnetic fields, heal living tissue, revitalize and restore energy in living organizms, generate electrical and magnetic force fields.

'It has all these capabilities and more. This beam is a very powerful force and most certainly not one to be facing as its target. All the spaceships are very powerful vehicles—and all that power can be directed into the magnetic beams if necessary.

'For instance, enough power can be discharged through one of the unmanned three-feet robots in one 5,000th part of a second to operate electrically the whole State of California for twenty-four hours. The beams of the larger ships are even more powerful than that.

'Because of this fantastic power, incomprehensible speeds are possible. According to the computers on these ships, 10 billion miles

UFO PROPHECY

POSSIBLE METHODS OF SPACECRAFT PROPULSION

per second are possible now. Most vehicles " top out " at eight billion, 500 thousand miles per second.

'At these terrific speeds, dimensional changes do take place. There is no sense of time or age. This speed has broken into an area of timelessness. The all-over speed rate is computed at the end of the journey. These speeds place even the most distant galaxies within easy reach.

'The trip to Orion from the planet Sirius 2 used to take 1,500 years. Now it is accomplished in one-and-a-quarter days. Many, many people have ventured to numerous distant places not heretofore readily accessible, and have returned while the home planet is still as they remember it.'

Diophanes concludes that unenlightened Man on Earth would not have the God-given wisdom to control such power. However, he ends : ' When Man has elevated himself to where he has learned to live and walk in the ways of God, the Divine Creator, then he will receive this power and all that goes with it.'

Fact or fancy ? On the face of it, absolutely incredible and unworthy of serious consideration, even by lowly and degenerate Man of Earth. Yet there could be a modicum of truth in extravagant premises. Compare them with a chapter in *The Warminster Mystery*, dealing with observed descents of small discs from large ' space stations ' or arks.

Also in my last book were details of the vertical build-up of these space ' children ' in circular array against the wall linings of ' mothers,' and one can but wonder . . . The apparent rapid changing of shape and form, at speed, is compatible, too, with dimensional shifts and alterations referred to above.

Let the scientist dwell on the exciting probabilities that would leap into being if Man, instead of simply being able to split the atom, could create atoms . . . Supposing flying saucers have no moving or mechanical parts like blades, or a centrifugal gallery, or jet impetus.

Suppose that nothing is done by mechanics as such, but that they utilize non-gravity and subtle high frequency magnetizm : in essence, that it is all a matter and question of polarities ? Imagine the use of a combination of quartz crystal and an ' ideo-motor ' principle of superconscious thought and mental vibrations. A semi-material, semi-physical alliance of this nature would obviously strike the realist as a more remote likelihood than power forces so far enumerated.

Never forget, however, that the whole Universe is in a state of continual change, a flux of perpetual evolution. So, therefore, is Man,

UFO PROPHECY

no matter what stage he may have arrived at already by transcending previous barriers to progress. All matter has its birth in the mind or spirit.

The world cannot stand still and its intelligentsia are forever breaking into new dimensions and through old obstructions. We on Earth have perhaps only begun our journey into the complexities and triumphs of Tomorrow. We are still treading infantile paths towards adolescence, nowhere near real adulthood in evolvement as yet.

Fresh ideas that are valid and valuable cannot afford a static period in which to get bogged down by lengthy preoccupation. They must be thrusting onward and outward and therefore intrinsically futuristic, judged by the average levels and criteria of civilization or consciousness, pushing towards further hurdles in the challenge to Life. New concepts of atomic structure and composition, creation by Man of power prototypes to lift him from his moderate status in the Universe at present, must be more than idle dreams of the future...

THE LAMENT OF MORNING

Gabriel's hair is a straight mystery falling,
Looking among the pale apples of Dawn
For something resembling a miracle.

Two rivers of light streaming without target,
Brushing the cold upstanding tides of grass
Where, reproduced in mirrors of crystal dew,
The long saturnine face of the grasshopper
Agitates through alabaster teeth ; whispers
With his ancient whisper the secret of his bones :
That he is the echoed pattern of the first leaves.

The morning rain's thin sadness falls on Gabriel's hair,
On Gabriel's hair the lament of morning begins ...

CHAPTER NINE

UFOs not Bourgeois Journalist Fabrications

It was officially announced in December of 1967 that UFOs have become the subject of serious study in the Soviet Union. Recent sightings of such objects appear to have compelled the Russians to abandon their former opinion that such phenomena are the fabrications of 'bourgeois journalists' and Western paranoia.

Reports on the subject have been published in the USSR and a special committee established to study the flying saucers. No possible reason for the objects, even that they may originate from other planets, is being ruled out in the survey. Dr. F. Y. Ziegel, a scientist engaged in this study, has refused to dismiss flying saucers as figments of the imagination.

'This view is very convenient, as it demands no intellectual effort and kills off the problem at birth,' he wrote in a recent article. He tends to believe that the spacecraft are some previously unknown natural phenomena—just as radioactivity was unknown seventy-five years ago. On this premise, he argues that any possible explanation deserves consideration, even the possibility that saucers are manned by intelligent visitors from Outer Space.

'This is an extreme theory,' he declared in his article, 'but since the problem of the unidentified flying object is not yet solved, varied and even extreme views are tenable.' Apparently, the new Soviet interest has been particularly centred on a UFO seen over Bulgaria in November.

It initially appeared as a silver blue disc, then changed to a pale blue trapezoid which glowed like a neon lamp. Bulgarian scientists, who saw it, said that it could not be an aircraft or an Earth satellite, two explanations often given for such sightings.

The disc-trapezoid hung over Sofia, the Bulgarian capital, at sunset. Observers watched it through telescopes. They averred it had a halo of green light and gave off a spark-like radiation from its apex. The object was as inexplicable as an earlier sighting in Bulgaria last April, when a triangular object hovered over a village for forty-five minutes, and a series of Soviet sightings which up to then had not been officially reported in the Soviet press.

But the Soviet flying saucers, including what was described as a sickle-shaped object that flew over the Black Sea in the summer of 1967, have been numerous enough, and sufficiently mysterious, to lead to the creation of a special committee to investigate the phenomena fully.

Professor Ziegel lectures on astronomy at the Moscow Planetarium, in addition to conducting courses on higher mathematics at the Moscow Aviation Institute. Last April he published an article on UFOs in *Smena*, the magazine of the Communist youth movement. The group of which he is a member has 200 reports of sightings on file. Preliminary analyses suggest a number of important conclusions, he affirms.

Most characteristic type of UFO sighting in Russia is defined by Ziegel as ' A luminous orange coloured crescent flying with its outward bend forward. Its surface is only a little duller than that of the moon.' The horns of the crescent throw out jets, sometimes with sparks. The outer contour of the crescent is sharp and the inner contour blurred and wavy.

A bright, flaming disc preceded by a crescent is sometimes observed. Occasionally the crescent is preceded and flanked by what look like first magnitude stars that keep at a constant distance from the crescent. In certain cases, Professor Ziegel reports, the crescent dwindles into a disc or dot.

One of these objects, sighted in the Ukraine last September, was reported to have executed a manoeuvre when approached by a plane. Astronomers in Kazan, according to Ziegel, set the diameter of the crescents they observed at 500 to 600 metres, about 1,640 to 1,840 feet, and their speed at about five kilometres, or 3.1 miles, per second.

He also notes that the classifications of observed objects in the Soviet Union fit into observed patterns in the West. Calling for ' a joint effort of all the scientists of the world ' to determine the precise nature of UFOs, Ziegel alludes to difficulties experienced by those like himself who take UFO sighting reports seriously.

' Unfortunately, certain scientists, both in the Soviet Union and in the United States, deny the very existence of the problem instead

UFO PROPHECY

UFOS NOT BOURGEOIS JOURNALIST FABRICATIONS

of helping to solve it,' he alleges. Such frank references to internal scientific controversies are infrequent in the Soviet Union.

In December last, the view expounded by Professor Ziegel was carried an important stage further when a retired Air Force general in the USSR announced on television that an official commission has been formed to study sighting reports.

However, some of the edge of this 'victory' was rubbed off by later reports that the officer, Major-General Porfiry A. Stolyarov, had spoken prematurely and that the commission, which he was supposed to head, had not yet come into existence—and might not do so in such permanent and official form.

A well-known Soviet aviator, Akkuratov, says: 'International scientific co-operation in the solution of this problem would long have become a reality had not sensationalizm and irresponsible anti-scientific assertions as regards the "flying saucers" interfered with it. But just as astronomy defeated astrology, the scientific truth will prevail in the UFO problem as well, we are sure.'

Professor Ziegel asserts that the main task is to organize systematic study of the phenomena from astronomical and meteorological observatories. It will then probably become possible to determine whether the objects are of protoplasmic origin or come from another planet, he continues.

'The second hypothesis merits serious consideration, to my mind,' he stresses. The UFO phenomenon is a challenge to Mankind, he feels, 'and it is the duty of scientists to take up this challenge, to disclose the nature of the UFO and to establish the scientific truth.' The Russian moves follow the example of the United States.

Public clamour in the USA led to a hearing on UFOs by the House Armed Services Committee in April 1966. The American Air Force contracted with the University of Colorado to conduct an independent and impartial investigation. This has a formidable array of consulting laboratories and specialists at its disposal, in hopes of coming upon concrete evidence.

A fragment of metal could be tested to see if it carries the radiation material acquired in space. Photographs obtained by various meteor-monitoring networks can be analyzed to provide objective information on size, speed and direction. Discoloured material at an alleged landing site could be studied for evidence of an exotic or conventional propellant.

UFO PROPHECY

Photographs purporting to be of UFOs have been examined by photo interpretation laboratories and, in spite of scientific scepticizm regarding UFOs, there is a perceptible shift in attitude. At the meeting of the International Astronomical Union in Prague last summer, an informal meeting on the subject was held.

One participant, a professor at Massachusetts Institute of Technology, criticized scientists for invariable ridiculing of unidentified flying object reports. This only serves to alienate the public from science, he took pains to point out.

These encouraging factors are reassuring to us mere 'amateurs,' who have only seen hundreds of UFOs as opposed to reading about their convulsive capers and coy convolutions on the global front. Yet I have a strong feeling that, whatever channels of investigation are employed, final truths will emerge the same at the end of the exhausting hunt.

The non-scientific approach may be as exact and precise in unravelling the mystery as the scientific, in the last analysis. The spiritual is interwoven, conclusively to my humble reckoning, with the physical, in the overall enigma. There is no single glib and facile explanation that covers the enormous congregation of bewildering facets and aspects of UFO manifestation.

It is imperative that more must be learned concerning the identity of our visitors from outer regions of the Universe. Whether they are basically friendly or hostile, positive or negative in influence, is a cardinal question that must be resolved whenever one is given opportunities by apparently non-communicative denizens of other worlds who show themselves but fleetingly, ghosts that flitter into the shadows, shy violets that refuse to bloom.

The hotly contested realms of physical contact and its feasibility, telepathic rapport and other media of establishing UFO truths, must not be intolerably bypassed in the search. Here, much depends on witness reliability and integrity. There could easily be spiritual overtones that dominate rather than constitute an integral part of UFO appearances.

The open mind will gather light and illumination; the closed mind will amass only the moss of negative stagnation. Unexplored dimensions and unexperienced senses that dwell in the sleeping consciousness of a macrocosm and a microcosm must be awakened in us before final answers are available.

UFO PROPHECY

UFOS NOT BOURGEOIS JOURNALIST FABRICATIONS

Here is a quaint facet of the mystery... For about six weeks in early 1966, when the planet Jupiter was very prominent in the heavens above Cradle Hill at Warminster, we were perplexed by two unlisted 'stars' that were equidistant from the planet, Jupiter comprising the topmost apex of a triangle in their company.

The flat yellow orbs we termed 'pinion' or 'anchor' stars, because whenever a UFO came over that particular span of sky at night it habitually encircled one or other of the two base stars. It was so consistent, this aerial practice, night after night, that I made an effort to confirm it when spending a weekend at the Chelmsford home of my parents, Thomas and Jane, in Essex.

For six hours I kept diligent watch from a high point at Danbury, a nearby village. I saw only one satellite in that period. But here is the astounding revelation in miniature that struck me: Jupiter was still in the sky, of course, but there were no pinion or anchor stars below it forming a triangle, as there were over Warminster.

When I arrived back, I immediately contacted my team mates. Yes, they reported, the peculiar base 'stars' were still present at night. A number of astronomers and UFO enthusiasts belonging to BUFORA will corroborate that these stars were actual, seen by them and unmarked on any star map.

After six weeks of dimly glowing over our noted hill, the yellow orbs suddenly flared into unmatchable brilliance one early May night—and rolled away to disappear farther aloft in an elegant sweeping motion, just as though we had been imagining it all... Deduction? They were space stations organized by our visitors for a special purpose.

'We have made your town a base for our operations,' said Aenstrian callers in *The Warminster Mystery*. Remember? We did not infer, from this, that the base was in fact an aerial one rather than established on terra firma. Although it needs little thought to decide that, as and when they wished to visit Earth, they most certainly came down around our town for essential tasks from their stationary space stations in the heavens above.

A boldly headlined story in the January 13th 1968 issue of the Bristol *Evening Post* evoked memory of unworldly extracts from my last book, almost too outlandish for the rational mind to grasp, let alone understand. Titled 'A Ghost Crash Baffles Police,' the news item brought back memories of strange 'accidents' around Warminster.

'Police at Cirencester today called off a search for a man believed

UFO PROPHECY

to have been injured in a road accident, and admitted " We are baffled." For, after two searches lasting about four hours, there was no sign of the crash victim.

' Police said that Mr. Arthur Gibbs, of The Old Vicarage, Coombe Bissett, Salisbury, was driving along the Cirencester to Cricklade road last night when he thought he struck a pedestrian near the Royal Air Force Station at South Cerney.

' He was " overtaking a car when he felt a bump and saw a pedestrian," said Chief Inspector Alfred Harris. Mr. Gibbs made a thorough search of the area, but without success, and then called the police. The car wing mirror was twisted and there was a dent at the top of the offside door of his own vehicle.

' Chief Inspector Harris said " It is all very mysterious—and it is definite that Mr. Gibbs struck something." ' (Author : Or ' someone' who is not as we are at this stage of human development on Earth ?)

In its issue of Saturday January 27th 1968, the Southampton *Southern Evening Echo* featured an odd news story on its back page, ' Found by Roadside—Unknown, he Moves on.' There may be a perfectly normal explanation such as temporary loss of memory, yet here again the circumstances tally very well with revelations in *The Warminster Mystery*.

The story reads : ' The man found unconscious by the side of the Andover to Ludgershall road, last night, discharged himself from the Royal Hampshire County Hospital, Winchester, later this morning, still without saying who he was.

' When he was found, police efforts failed to identify him. Aged between 25 and 30, he was found lying by the side of the road near One Hundred Acre Corner. He was first taken to Andover War Memorial Hospital, where a doctor found he had no visible injuries.

' He regained consciousness for about an hour, but police were unable to communicate with him, so he was moved to the Winchester hospital. The only possessions found on him were a comb, a handkerchief and one penny. In a description given by Andover police he was said to be slim, 5ft. 4ins. tall, with dark brown hair and grey eyes.

' He was wearing blue jeans, wellington boots, a double-breasted blue-checked jacket, a red and black checked shirt, a pink, green, blue and white bobble hat and a yellow scarf. He also had a brass ring on the second finger of his right hand.' That is the report in the *Echo*, and

UFO PROPHECY

UFOS NOT BOURGEOIS JOURNALIST FABRICATIONS

whoever he was the man must certainly have been a 'colourful' character.

Returning to the possible propulsion methods employed by UFOs, Derek C. Samson, of NICAP, editor of *NICAP Chronicles* in Britain, has published conclusions of his organization that some flying discs are constructed by Man on Earth. From knowledge I have, I would not disagree with this assumption, although I assure him and other sincere research students that these are not the shining spheroids that fly regularly over Cradle Hill, Warminster.

Derek told me: 'Our recent investigations have uncovered certain facts to prove that a good percentage of small flying discs observed all over the world are Man-made, and are the products of amateur groups. These amateur scientific investigators lead the professionals in this field of technical research.

'One of these groups has been producing working prototype discs since 1951, "playing by ear" without seeing UFO books or photographs until 1967. Scientists or technicians can only produce workable electromagnetic propulsion systems if they realize the trap set for those who try to explain how or why an ionized drive works.

'Separated fragments have been explained and demonstrated during the past two-hundred years whilst the secret has been examined. The wider perspective has been too simple, too obvious. Why? An explanation may be found in certain modern developments.

'In recent years, governments of major countries have encouraged their scientists to build and operate craft propelled by electric magnetic drives. Many fragments of details can be found in the numerous UFO books published, one example being the works of Leonard Cramp, complete with illustrations.

'Scientists have worked secretly and separately, all on the same projects, the same principles, and from the same textbook information. Their work has produced uncollated fragments, they have all been sidetracked, equally in secret and in exactly the same way because:

'(a) All our experiments are monitored, and adjusted to work constructively; (b) all government departments wanted an ultimate weapon of destruction from electromagnetic propulsion experiments; (c) there are no secrets, only things we hide from ourselves. We limit ourselves for our own protection—that is the safeguard on ultimate weapons. And (d) no scientist has a clear picture of the ultimate in life, or death.

UFO PROPHECY

' Wider horizons of discovery are arranged by ourselves for ourselves, as part of a programme of current space development, specifically. Technical details of electromagnetic propulsion systems are included. Amateur experimentors can produce a flying shape disc or cigar operated by electromagnetic propulsion if technical facts are collated from different sources; and if the right combinations of components are incorporated with a shell which has a balanced proportion.'

Mr. Samson went on to say that five photographs were taken of a flying object over Passaic in New Jersey, USA, as published in a magazine in August of 1966. They showed a Man-made disc in flight. Most of these have high domes and can be likened to a Mexican hat.

He continued: ' NICAP investigators know of three amateur builders in England. Each one is working on a different principle, these being: colour, latent energy and ionization. We shall continue to keep their names secret until they wish otherwise.

' One thing is certain for the future research of UFOs. A greater study of shape, speed, size and detail is needed to determine which are made by Man and which are not.' So we learn that the experimentation department of NICAP now engages itself with collection of data concerning unusual magnetic fields that can be attributed to the following :—

Ionization, colour, sound, spiral vortex, etc. They point out that it is quite possible that some of the drives employed by spacecraft are extremely simple; in fact, so simple that we have bypassed them in our haste to harness the atom.

All things are based on Nature, so perhaps it is Nature that Man ought to be studying more closely and minutely for essential clues. Telepathy also comes under sympathetic survey by NICAP members in Britain. Experiments have been carried out, I understand.

Already, crews of long-range, atom-powered submarines are being taught the rudiments of this type of communication, which would truly have been scorned as useless before the last war. Mental telepathy cannot be picked up by the use of radio scanners.

Therefore, it would obviously be an ideal and valuable means of relaying messages and information during times of war. If employed for this inane object, for warlike aims, will such experimentation and training ever succeed, fully? Personally, I very much doubt it. Doubtless, David would agree with me here.

It was no Earth-made machine that caused considerable discomfort

UFO PROPHECY

UFOS NOT BOURGEOIS JOURNALIST FABRICATIONS

to businessman Leonard Pike when he was motoring to Frome from Warminster on an early September night in 1967. He told my co-observer Sybil Champion that the interior of his car became unbearably hot and his ears were shattered by the almost deafening buzzing of millions of bees.

It filled the inside of the vehicle, bemused his senses, heat growing more intense all the while, at that notorious spot on the road near Cley Hill, Corsley. The sheer agony of a double phenomenon terrified him. His motor started to cough and whimper, shuddering in the few yards it took before his brake clamped hard. He jumped out of the car, which shook as though travelling a bumpy byway, although its engine was dead.

Gazing up, he beheld a large white circular object spinning overhead. It weaved in a jerky motion from side to side directly over the car. Sound tore at his eardrums. The craft banked slightly, then went into an upward spiralling movement, did a figure of eight, balanced on its rim before becoming temporarily elliptic, then rolled away.

It hurt Mr. Pike's eyes to keep vision on the twisting and turning spheroid. It eventually sped towards Cley Hill, remaining stationary over the smaller peak for about forty seconds before darting away to the North and out of sight.

The motorist lit a cigarette from a match flickering in palsied fingers, clambered aboard his car and pressed the ignition switch hopefully. Greatly relieved when the engine purred into instant life, he continued homeward without further incident, bleakly wondering what had hit him, and why, in those few minutes of aerial battering.

The heat, the weird humming, the stopping of his motor—these features are consistent with dozens of cases similar in nature around the Warminster area. Again—do these odd happenings denote hostility or merely a means of shocking a fresh victim into realization that extraterrestrial forces are at work in our atmosphere, whether we choose to welcome them or not?

UFO PROPHECY

THE VISITOR

He was standing as a compliment to the trees,
The beautiful youth with the Moon still chiming in his hands.
The stars have faded and the airs of Earth
Suffuse him in a carapace of light.

Above the river bank the kites of Summer
Pull clouds and children by the hand;
Brandish their silken verse in banners
Of birds arrowed in leisured flight.

The youth with the beautiful face
Has dropped through mist to the morning,
Where the bushy fields dream of wild horses
And sleep to their hummocked knees in purple marsh.

He has written the wind and taken the scene like a mirror,
But the forest cannot translate where its ground
Is illustrated by his feet; for they have used as bridges
The stepping stones of planets and burning Suns;
And only the consumed atmosphere can tell
He is the Author of another place.

CHAPTER TEN

Reconstruction of Ancient Grid System?

Almost imperceptibly as yet, the magnetic poles of our Earth may be shifting in readiness for an event of the future engineered by crews of alien spacecraft and carefully designed by even higher intelligences. There has already been a detectable 'wobble' of the Earth from its axial equilibrium, the balance temporarily affected by a slight tilting that caused no lasting damage, presumably.

One cannot emphasise how catastrophic the results would be if, as probably happened in one previous civilization, all ice and snow at the South Pole suddenly melted completely. Major cities of the world would be submerged and crushed by massive tidal waves as water influxes increased dramatically to make all oceans rise by over 200 feet.

This prospect, according to experts, is remote for millions of years, but such prospects frighten by their possibility under given or changed conditions. My interest was aroused by a letter from fellow author Maurice Neal, living at Worthing, Sussex.

He used to be the chief investigations officer to the Government of Ghana and gave details of four reported sightings of UFOs in that country. These he directed his attention to as a responsible government official, on the practical side, pointing out:

'I have also followed the mystical and visionary path for many years, which is not as strange as it may seem. Perhaps because we are trained observers, we have an interest in the normal and the paranormal; and the retired chief of police in Ghana, and the retired director general of police in Turkey, share with me similar interests.

'I could tell you of things relative to UFOs that are concerned with both fields of inquiry. One is that I believe our brethren from Outer Space are rebuilding a grid system that existed in pre-Biblical times, and that the Pyramids and Stonehenge are both part of it.

'The grid aerials are being activated as construction is taking place and this will result in changes in the magnetic field of Earth, which even now is very close to a position of 75 degrees 18 minutes latitude and 97 degrees 30 minutes longtitude.

'This indicates that the North Magnetic Pole has shifted and work is proceeding to bring about the completion of the Southern Magnetic Pole, which will also be at 75.18 latitude and 82.30 longtitude—and ultimately the Northern Pole will complete its movement.'

This is information I had already gleaned, in essence, from a mysterious 'caller' back in May of 1967, described later in this work. So I was more than normally intrigued by this letter from the author of 'Ju-Ju in my Life,' who wrote to me on December 12th 1967 and continued:

'You probably heard there is much UFO activity in this area recently. One case arousing especial interest was that of a flying saucer landing on a road near here. Two lorries approaching from opposite directions were stopped because of the UFOs magnetic field.

'I believe I have seen on two occasions visitors from Outer Space; one in East Africa in 1948 and the other last year. I am of the opinion that they can materialize and dematerialize at will. Your appendix on Aenstria in *The Warminster Mystery* I do not think is in the realm of phantasy at all.

'Had I been in your position I would have introduced myself to the "stranger" whom you saw walking on the other side of the street, for therein lies the hope of our world. Our scientists in the main are not governed by moral principles and are "obsessed" in the pursuit of knowledge without regard to ultimate effects.

'They have "lifted up" a curtain on the Cosmic Stage before they were governed by principles of goodwill and spiritual well being to their fellows; and it would seem that the situation is now almost out of hand. I believe even more strongly that we have reached the end of the Old Age (Pisces), which was concerned with great activity on the water plane of expression, and have now commenced the New Aquarian Age whose expression will be in Space in its "outer" form, while on its "inner" it will be concerned with the mind—and finally the soul of humanity.'

An artist friend at Ravensbourne College of Art and Design in Bromley thinks: 'The submerged psyche of the Warminster populace may contain undreamt of treasures. Contemporary dream researchers now realise that dreams are far, far more than incoherent residue of memory.

UFO PROPHECY

RECONSTRUCTION OF ANCIENT GRID SYSTEM?

'It seems to me that a formidable "anchor-man" project is required to correlate the many diversified fields of study, when each seems to hold a part of the answer. 'If only they could come together!' he enthuses. This man has seen four 'indisputable' UFOs in his young life.

'The most outstanding of my sightings took place in May this year. It was about 8.15 p.m. and I was working late at the college. I was on the fourth floor, checking tones of paint at a window, when I was aware of a very bright light over Bromley, which lies about a mile North of the college.

'This light was a fiery red and perfectly rectangular, in a clear patch of sky, the sun setting about a third of the horizon away. I called the attention of other students to the spectacle and about two dozen of us observed the Thing for about five minutes. Then, gradually, it began to dissolve.

'It assumed the fiery silhouette of a robed figure with its arms outstretched; then resolved into a luminescent pink cloud and disappeared. We found out later,' he reported, ' that the Thing had been sighted all over the Bromley area, and a short time before our sighting there had been some 200 reports of an orange object flying low over the Thames, lighting up the water beneath it.'

Then my young friend makes the following admission: ' During March to December of 1966 I, and other serious artists, were engaged in the taking of mind-changing chemicals. Since then I have ceased taking any sort of drug, but am associated with psychologists and research workers both here, in New York and Sweden, who are studying mind-change, dreams and unusual phenomena such as UFOs.

'Our work and our personal revelations, which we "pool" as frequently as possible, have been leading us into a direct understanding of the teachings of various mystics and of various esoteric religious organizations. Have you heard of the work of a German scientist called Doctor Lohr?

'He has been carrying out experiments with the "prayer marathon" on growing plants. This is a continual prayer, or one-pointed meditation, hour in, hour out, one or more people all praying for the same aim and object. This method reputably cannot fail.

'You have made preliminary contact with Warminster UFOs by use of flashlights. What about trying a prayer-circle or meditation-ring at Cradle Hill? A psychic beacon, as it were. After all, we "talk" aircraft down, so perhaps we should " pray " UFOs down ?

'A belief in a God is not necessary to the activity, only a belief in the possibility of its success. Have you had any dreams concerning UFOs and—particularly—dreams in which you have contacted extra-terrestrials ? Do you know if there have been UFO dreams experienced by your colleagues or anyone else in the Warminster district ? '

Hoping I did not regard such questions as flippant, the artist revealed that a friend of his, Irving Sleser, Ph.D., of New York, has been working on the most advanced dream research projects in America. ' If only Western society paid as much attention to its " sleeping " life as its " waking " life, we might find that the UFOs have been spelling out their messages to us in direct mind-to-mind revelations,' he urges.

Frankly, I have never broached the subject of dreams to my many Warminster witnesses of spacecraft in flight. However, I made an original discovery, quite by chance and perhaps closely allied with the remote control of sleeping mental energy, while talking with some attestors long after their individual experiences.

Usually months after I had taken their evidence in shorthand, with no prompting from me whatsoever, they confided that their lives have altered in subtle ways, emotionally and spiritually. One witness who was initially scared stiff at loud sound vibrations that rocked her bedroom walls put it this way, typical of how other victims have been affected in a long term sense :

' Before hearing those awful noises I just could not care less about my neighbours and their troubles. I did not give any conscious thought to them! One has enough to contend with in life without worrying over what happens to the rest of the world.

' I have always felt it is up to myself to look after my own interests and overcome personal trials and tribulations as best I can. Hang the rest—it is up to them! That was once my attitude to life and other people. I have changed. Since hearing the Thing, I realise how different I have become in so many respects.

' Without thinking, I look for opportunities to help those less fortunate than myself, nowadays. If a friend or neighbour is ill, or has a house with ailing children, I pop in and volunteer to do her shopping or washing chores. What is more, I do it cheerfully, without thought of thanks or reward.

' It is a wonderful feeling, really—like being born again. I find, too, that I listen much more carefully to the opinions of other people.

UFO PROPHECY

RECONSTRUCTION OF ANCIENT GRID SYSTEM ?

Formerly I considered it a waste of time listening to the views of others —and I used to like getting my own way in an argument, anyhow.

' I often shouted the views of another person down, convinced she was wrong and I right—which is a bad habit. When you first interviewed me in August of 1965 I did not know you were writing a book. But certain extracts from your last chapter on the Aenstrians had instant response from me.

' I must say they have changed my thinking and made me a better citizen in consequence. I feel sure that is so—although I cannot speak for others who have heard or seen these craft.' Eighteen local witnesses have made similar confidences to me, quite unasked for, long after original testimony re UFOs was taken.

To avoid embarrassing them, I must omit names on this occasion, yet surely this is an important truth that must connect with inherent friendliness of our visitors. The majority must be beneficial in influence. It is one further small clue to fill an empty space in the jigsaw puzzle.

It proves that, whatever the eventual mission of alien spaceships and Outer Space denizens may be in our atmosphere, it cannot be wholly destructive or evil. Our UFO friends are capable of reshaping our thought patterns by media unknown and invisible to us.

Providing the alteration remains towards a favourable end, who are we to stop that influence penetrating deep within our subconscious selves, to the very essence and enrichment of our souls, echoing inside the chambers of minds quickened to respond ?

From the emotional to the practical, here are some findings by my young collaborator from Burnham-on-Sea, Somerset, Douglas Chaundy, additional to his interesting discovery that constellations of the Northern sky are copied by long barrows on Salisbury Plain, dotting the terrain around Warminster.

Douglas wrote to me on August 28th 1967, after I had addressed a large assembly of Ufologists at Caxton Hall in London, presenting findings that go much deeper and must have great significance. Many people are aware of the celebrated White Horses cut into the chalk of hills in Britain.

My Somerset friend wrote : ' The remaining White Horses of Wiltshire, together with the Uffington white horse and Stonehenge, form a very intricate pattern that is very interesting, particularly when one considers them to have been built by people of allegedly light intelligence.

UFO PROPHECY

SOME LOCATION LINES

- UFFINGTON WHITE HORSE
- BROAD HINTON WHITE HORSE
- MANTON WHITE HORSE
- PEWSEY WHITE HORSE
- CHERHILL WHITE HORSE 6½
- ALTON BARNES WHITE HORSE
- WESTBURY WHITE HORSE
- STONEHENGE

II ISOSCELES TRIANGLE

6½

5½

5½

I 45° TRIANGLE

UFO PROPHECY

RECONSTRUCTION OF ANCIENT GRID SYSTEM?

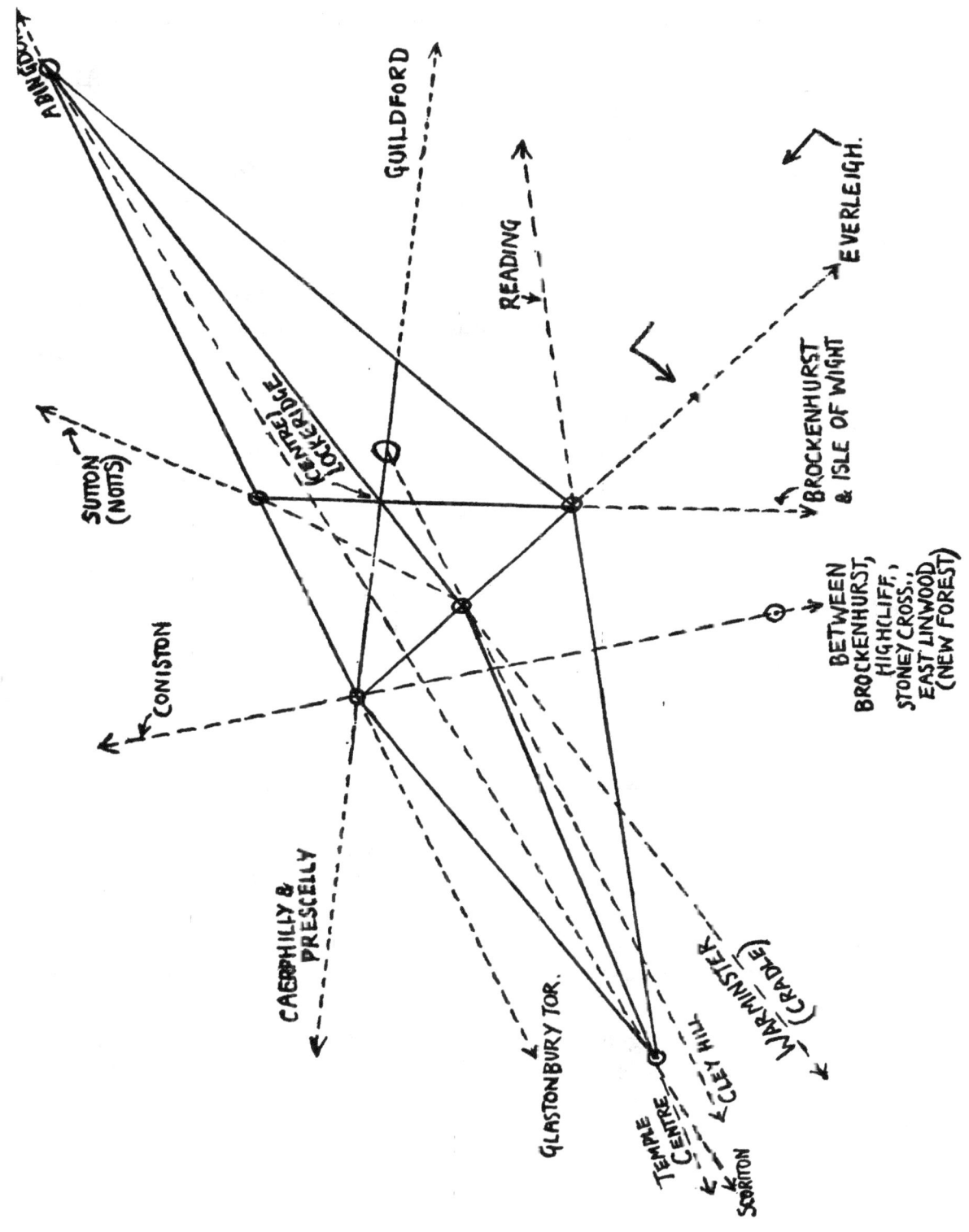

UFO PROPHECY

'The central line of the pattern is formed by the white horses at Cherhill, Alton Barnes and Pewsey, which are directly in line with each other and also exactly the same distance—Cherhill to Alton Barnes and Alton Barnes to Pewsey.

'On the Eastern side of the line there is formed an Isosceles Triangle of perfect dimensions. The Western side of the line forms a forty-five degrees angle of perfect dimensions, also. The two patterns are explained by the diagrams enclosed.' (See illustrations).

'These two triangles are interesting by themselves; but are far more interesting when they are joined by the connecting line (the central line). The most interesting part of all, however, is what happens from the moment these triangles are connected to produce one complete pattern.

'As you can see, on the diagrams there are lines showing the outline of the triangles and the interior of them. Here is the amazing thing: If these various lines are continued, and extended from the triangles to certain localities in England, we arrive at specific points that have been visited by extraterrestrial craft.

'These are not simply plain sightings, but in every case except one or two they turn out to be actual LANDING locations, starting from the white horses that are used. 1.—WARMINSTER (Cradle Hill-Battlesbury)—extended from the line that goes through Uffington and Alton Barnes.

'2.—CLEY HILL—from the line that runs through Manton and Alton Barnes. 3.—CONISTON—from the line that runs through Stonehenge and Cherhill. 4.—SCORITON—from the line running through Uffington and Westbury.

'5.—SUTTON, Nottinghamshire—from the line running through Alton Barnes and Broad Hinton. 6.—READING—from the line running through Westbury and Pewsey. 7.—CAERPHILLY, South Wales—(1909) from the line that runs through Manton and Cherhill. 8.—NEW FOREST—from the line that runs through Cherhill and Stonehenge.

'These are sighting areas that only tell part of the story. There are so many more—sightings and landings from near Guildford, at Tottenham, at Stonehenge, at Abingdon, near Oxford, etc. Apart from the sightings, there are lines that run to sundry other interesting places.

'Four lines go to the Glastonbury Temple of the Stars, among

RECONSTRUCTION OF ANCIENT GRID SYSTEM?

which is one that goes to the Tor itself, another that runs to the Zodiac centre at Butleigh. There is a line that goes to Everleigh, also to East Linwood, both mentioned in Eileen Buckle's *Scoriton Mystery*. (Publishers, Neville Spearman).

'There is also a line going to the Prescelly Hills, the origination of part of the fabulous Stonehenge. The New Forest line I have mentioned proceeds both to the location of the new July 5th activity between Brockenhurst and Highcliffe and to Stoney Cross.

'You will notice that the white horse at Manton, also called the Marlborough White Horse, seems to be in the wrong place. It should be, according to the remainder of the coherent pattern, at a point in the Savernake Forest. However, if this white horse HAD been in the Forest, it would have made the findings entirely wrong.

'By its being at the present location it is possible to arrive at locations which would otherwise have been missed. Another strange thing is the fact that the only other white horses which are in Wiltshire have been left to deteriorate; only the white horses in the pattern have survived and are being regularly looked after and tended.

'The relevant and overriding question must be posed: Why are the interplanetary craft employing these obvious and prominent landmarks as direction finders? And what is so special about the places where they land and where they stay for months or years on end, as is the case in the Warminster area?

'In your book, you express the point that it was revealed to you that there is a UFO base only a few miles from Warminster—and the peculiar triangle or pyramid shaped impressions left in rear of two leaping UFOs in a photograph mean something profound. I seriously suggest that it could be within the Triangle Pattern!

'It seems that the extraterrestrials could conceivably have their beginning FROM the triangle ... I am sure that what I have found cannot be dismissed as sheer coincidence, for the simple fact that it happens so many times. I have found no fewer than seventeen lines, involving many sightings, and I am still finding them,' he assured me.

Essentially, Douglas is a realist, like me; yet his view that the pyramid impressions on the UFO photograph 'mean something profound' concurs with mine, exactly. The strong spiritual corollary to the physical properties of UFO manifestations is confirmed in various ways, as explained anon.

In a quietly thoughtful letter to me, Cyril F. Armes of Leigh-on-Sea in Essex wrote on March 6th this year (1968): 'I have read *The Warminster Mystery* and feel that at least one of the channels for TRUTH about our visitors is in safe hands.

'I feel certain you realise the importance of the work you have undertaken in recording the events taking place. "Truth will out" as we all know, but misplaced zeal is often responsible for distorted reports—and even fiction.

'There is a great longing for Unity, Peace and Brotherhood among men of all nations. It is emerging, it is pouring forth from the Son of man, and the world is gradually finding its identity in God. Organized religion is failing, as is man's government. Man is seeking a direct communion with the Harmony of the Universe. He is finding it.

'In the consumer society, everyone can have what he wants, but it does no good for his Soul. The very material abundance makes him realise the special need for a real foundation in life, a Spiritual rock to anchor on to. Freedom is a Soul experience and is available in the deepest dungeons of man's experience.

'Truth is a feeling, an instinct as natural as breathing. Attempted suppression brings a reaction akin to sealing a volcano, an unwise course for any. Universal Truth is the Light which dissolves all fear of the unknown, revealing the presence of God in all experience.

'I trust that you will be a channel for God's Truth in the work you are doing, revealing worlds beyond ours, worlds governed by the Universal Brotherhood of Love in God; to be an example to us and possibly help us find our true identity. I am sure only good will flow from contact with the visitors.'

I thank Mr. Armes for his undeserved tributes. A humble UFO investigator could never live up to such high precepts, for I admit ashamedly that the truth of a Supreme Deity and Spirit of Creation was far from my consciousness until August of 1967. That was when surprises galore beset me...

'Space people ARE with us. I have MET them,' is the claim of Carson McCormick, of Belfast, Northern Ireland, who in late summer of 1967 penned the following: 'Their appearance, their activities, together with one's spiritual perception, confirms this—but each person must await confirmation for themselves.

'I will relate just one story on the subject. A wise and learned man whom I met was sitting reading one evening when he became aware of a man sitting in the chair opposite, dressed as a conventional spaceman.

UFO PROPHECY

RECONSTRUCTION OF ANCIENT GRID SYSTEM?

My friend seemed to dismiss this apparent illusion on this first occasion.

'But it reappeared two days later and inaugurated a conversation which has continued and developed intermittently since that. The gist of the confrontation is this : The spaceman said " I am a space visitor from Venus. What are you going to do about it ? "

'My friend asked him what he meant and the space visitor said " You do not believe me, do you ? " Anyhow, to cut a long story short, my friend had to admit that the strangely dressed visitor, who had obviously materialized, was real.

'From then on, the gentleman has returned to tutor our friend in paraphysical matters. From my own awareness I am going to say that, until recently, human beings had to wait until they were at least thirty years of age before they could become spiritually born.

'But now, in this New Age rushing in upon us, I find that the children being born are doing so both physically and spiritually ; and that to all appearances they are not Earth children at all. Venus seems to be their homeland and they are much more evolved than their parents.

'In fact, they do not belong to their parents. The parent is only the custodian in Christ's name. Even the Communist countries know this, although they do not call the cosmic consciousness " Christ." But " a rose by any other name would smell the same. '

'I have witnessed the unusually clever activities of such children. There was one who actually said to me, " I came from Venus. I remember being there." Yet older ones will not confide to disbelieving minds. Why should they ?

'We are being " taken over " by another planet. Their people are here and they are raising such humans as are suitable to their level of consciousness. And the others—well, I will not say it, but it is all in the Bible . . .

'It is possible that the events foretold may come as a blinding flash changing every man, woman and child, or they may only be recognized by those who are spiritually mature ; but all the signs ("you can tell the signs of the weather ; you have not learnt to tell the signs of the times, yet ") are pointing to a spiritual breakthrough, the production of a new situation in human nature or else a second Sodom and Gomorrah.'

It is surprising how many times, along slippery paths navigated by the conscientious UFO investigator to get at shining truth, spiritual considerations display themselves. They come from a good fifty per cent of all people who visit Cradle Hill to see genuine UFOs.

These people are firmly of the belief that the flying chariots constitute part of a Divine plan necessary to save our Earth and people from maximum effects of severe catastrophes in the near future—or, in simplest terms, herald the promised second coming of the Christ King.

What saddens me, assuming their prognostications could prove right, is : Most of that fifty per cent are convinced that only a selected few, relatively, of the native population of our planet will be saved. The remainder are doomed because of their abject refusal to seek full enlightenment at this momentous time.

It is all clearly stated in Holy Writ, they point out. No one dares to defy or deny the will of God. Yet too often the all-pervading assurance that the Highest Deity of the Universe never destroys one of His creations, human or otherwise, is never mentioned.

That is a pity, because it is the greatest and most comforting beacon of hope to Man on his long journey towards sure redemption. The answer to the whole UFO enigma could indeed be wedged within the context of things spiritual, in future happenings on our planet. But I would hate to join the pessimistic band of the doleful Prophets of Gloom !

The dawning of a New Age should be a golden opportunity to look forward to immensely better conditions of Life appertaining to all : not a singularly unhappy event which is bound to tear out the hearts of Mankind as well as the bowels of his planet !

CHAPTER ELEVEN

Watch-Stopping, Space Scripts and Sounds

Wrist watches have been affected by strong vibrational emanations from overhead when UFO activity is at its height. Mine has often ceased to tick, stopping for an hour or so before returning to normal, when alien spaceships have been gyrating closer than usual above Cradle Hill at night.

Incidentally, for the statistician, we experience UFO presences at lower than 600 yards altitude and 880 yards distance from us, on average, once in every thirty nights they are seen. Allowing for improbability of sightings in bad weather periods, this works out at seven good close-ups or veritable landings per year during our two-year stint of night sky observation.

The town of Berkhamsted suffered in signal manner in this watch and clock stopping malfunctioning. Under the headline ' Enough to Stop a Clock—Several of Them ' and the sub-heading ' The Mystery Baffles Owners and Experts,' the *Gazette* which flourishes in the county told the following story:

The great watch-stopping mystery still remains unsolved. Since it was reported in the *Gazette* a fortnight ago that a number of people in the district discovered that their watches and clocks stopped for about an hour during the night of September 9th and 10th, 1967, details have been received of other people who have had similar experiences.

Mr. Peter Ward, of ' Monaco,' London Road, Berkhamsted, who compiled the information, told our reporter that he had, up to the present moment, heard from nine people whose stories seem to coincide. Mr. Gilbert, a motor engineer in Berkhamsted High Street, said on Tuesday:

' I wound up my watch, a good Swiss non-magnetic model, on Saturday, the 9th, but when I was playing tennis the following morning

I discovered that my watch was an hour-and-a-quarter slower than anyone else's.'

A merchant seaman, Mr. Brian Warrington, of Piccotts End, Hemel Hempstead, who is at present on a ship bound for Australia, told Mr. Ward that his expensive Omega manual-wind watch, which had never stopped before, also lost an hour during that night.

Mrs. Barbara Smith, a housewife, who lives at 29 Swing Gate Lane, Berkhamsted, reported that her watch, 'a perfectly reliable Accurist,' had also lost time. 'I wound it before going to bed,' she said, 'but on Sunday morning when I woke up it was exactly one hour slow.'

A Potten End builder, Mr. E. W. Rayment, had the unusual experience of both his watch and bedside clock losing an hour. 'I noticed both the watch and clock had lost an hour after I finished watching "Your Witness" on BBC TV,' he said.

One of Mr. Rayment's employees, Mr. John Booth of Dunbar Cottage, Back Row, Potten End, described how his wife Kathleen's watch had stopped altogether on the Saturday night at about 8 p.m. 'We fiddled about with it for around an hour trying to get it to go again, but without success.

'However, the following morning,' he went on, 'the watch started to work again without anyone touching it, and my wife has had no trouble with it since.' Each of the individuals interviewed could offer no explanation why the watches had lost time on the Saturday night and were convinced it was not due to lack of winding.

The Head of Technical Services of the Chronomatic Branch at the Ministry of Defence Navy Department's observatory at Hurstmonceux, near Eastbourne, Mr. W. P. Roseman, was informed of the unusual happenings on Tuesday. Said Mr. Roseman: 'We have hundreds of clocks and watches here at the observatory and none of them lost time during that night.'

A spokesman for the Science Research Council based at the observatory was also asked to comment about the strange phenomena and said that 'nothing like this has ever been reported before.' However, neither could give a cause for the watches losing an hour, all at approximately the same time.

Some jokers have suggested, added the news report, that the watches had formed their own unofficial union and went on a 'go slow.' Joking apart, no one has come up with a plausible reason for the watches

UFO PROPHECY

WATCH-STOPPING, SPACE SCRIPTS AND SOUNDS

'rebelling' and it looks as if the matter will 'gradually unwind.' Or will it?

Peter Ward, mentioned in the story, came up to Cradle Hill to see UFOs later in 1967. He confided to me that a number of Berkhamsted people heard odd humming sounds on that Saturday night, not connecting these with the stopping of watch and clock mechanizms. In fact, three people there actually saw a peculiar aerial shape in the sky.

I am not being irrelevant or facetious at this juncture, but may there have been a clue here about Earth 'time' running short? When the reader reaches my chapter on Karne, my unearthly visitor in May of 1967, such a bizarre series of time-changing incidents would seem to fit in with warnings he gave me at my front door.

Now let us press on to another aspect, about whose relevance I cannot yet be certain... Confidential documents that define and deal with the speech and writing forms of some of our visitors from Outer Space have recently come, unbidden and unexpectedly, into my hands.

Naturally, as I was permitted only brief glances at the volume of written material and a short hearing of special tape recordings, I would not brashly assert with any degree of finality that this influx of the feasible was absolutely genuine and incontestable.

One would have to study them more minutely, at undivided leisure, to prove undoubted authenticity. Neither would I dismiss such items of evidence lightly, as of no consequence or bearing on a facet of the UFO mystery; for they were brought for my cursory inspection by a charming Norfolk man with honest blue eyes, humble approach, disarming candour and integrity sparking his personality.

Apparently, exceptional gifts have been bestowed upon him by virtue of his lineal descent. His forbears were decidedly exotic people. Among his ancient ancestors was the daughter of a Sioux Red Indian chief. She lived as squaw and brave, wife and hunter, with a being from another planet 'many moons ago'—to use the picturesque language of the Indian.

The fact that my surprise caller can converse freely in more than one Indian tongue, yet has never ventured as far as North America, impressed me. Byron, as I shall term my bearer of linguistic tidings from other worlds, has already contacted a number of influential people associated with the governments of our Earth.

Because of the frustrating 'official' attitude to UFOs, I cannot quote names of persons involved. Suffice to state that they are men highly qualified in their respective branches of scientific research. Some are engaged in secret activities of important governmental departments in Britain and Europe.

After receipt of a magnetic tape and a specimen of Venusian script from Byron for examination, a philological expert went into raptures over their contents. A master of language studies, he is also a distinguished astronomer and astro-physicist. Here is an extract from his reply to Byron:

'I have studied these documents most carefully and I must say right from the start that they seem to be most extraordinarily interesting. There have, of course, been several reports during recent years about contacts being made with visitors from one of the nearby planets; but this is the first occasion on which, to my knowledge, the visitors have allowed themselves to be recorded so intimately.

'A few points about the various documents: (a) The tapes: semantically and morphologically speaking, these tape samples of speech are adequate for making some assessment of the psycho-physiological mechanism of the Venusian sound organs.'

The government expert continues: 'These appear to be characterized by a considerable flexibility of the larynx and epiglottis, plus a slightly harder velum than we are used to thinking of normally.

'Sound production is diphasic: this means that the two lungs are accurately out of phase with one another, thus enabling the creature to speak for a long time without taking breath; and this also leads to an extreme rapidity of transmission. This fact alone proves a point I shall raise in a moment.

'(b) The script: this is quite uncharacteristic of anything found on Earth except possibly the Sacred Boggah Script of the Abluti Indians of Paraguay, before the Jesuit missionaries entered the country and introduced the modern West-European way of writing.

'As near as one can tell from the prevailing direction and thickness of the strokes, the present script is written with some sort of hard and sharp instrument, possibly a pen, held between two or three semi-prehensile members which are somewhat similar to our fingers.

'From an application of Reinmann Phoneme analysis techniques —first stage, naturally—it can be concluded with fair certainty that the creatures in question possess a large hand, possibly with all thumbs, and it seems likely that they are accustomed to a fairly low gravity.

'This leads me to the question of their origin. The only creatures

WATCH-STOPPING, SPACE SCRIPTS AND SOUNDS

possessing these faculties of flexible larynx and epiglottis, hard velum, five-thumbed hands, and living normally on a world of low gravity, are most certainly the Krxyzcs who, according to all research on the subject, originate on the Planet Kruger 60b.

'The fact is incontrovertibly proven by the rapidity and prolonged nature of their speech, which has been received a number of times on the new radio-telescopes being erected for quite different purposes. Although it is often believed that they come from Venus, this is merely their base.

'They can tolerate the high gravity but could not do without the warmth so necessary to them, not to mention the CO_2. In fact, by the medium of Wuhlmic Energy, we have been able to listen in to their conversations. To all intents and purposes they are colonizing the Solar System; all the unoccupied planets, that is.

'We do not as yet understand their purpose, although we are fairly sure that they are not hostile. The most promising theory seems to be that they wish to perform some sort of scientific experiments in sociology, once they have mastered the purely technological problems of living on an alien world.'

A Master of Arts in the Interplanetary Philological Institute wrote to Byron to point out 'some slight misunderstanding as to the origin of these creatures, whom we have identified by their writing as Krxyzcs.' The Planet Kruger 60b is their home, he stressed, the second planet out from the star known in the Institute catalogues as Kruger 60.

He continued: 'Its distance is not great as far as stellar distances go, and by means of an application of para-Einsteinian time-warping techniques the Krxyzcs are able to make the journey here in reasonable time. This is especially convenient for them, since they are very short-lived compared with Earth men.'

The executive member of the Institute said that the most important point is: It is they and they alone who are at present inhabiting the planets of our Solar System, Earth excepted; and the suggestion that these planets have indigenous inhabitants is quite erroneous.

To Byron the writer emphasized (although Byron does not necessarily agree with all Institute findings and interpretations): 'This may surprise you, since you have obtained samples of writing from various planets which obviously differ from each other most markedly.

'Your idea that the last of these was from Saturn was no doubt prompted by the occurrence of the symbol, ⊖ which does admittedly bear a striking resemblance to the appearance of that planet.

'But you must realise that any native Saturnians would never have seen their planet from the outside, and therefore could never have intended to represent it in their alphabet. This ideogram in the form of a drawing of Saturn proves that it must have been done by someone seeing Saturn from outside. The only persons who could have done so are none other than the Krxyzcs.

'You may possibly object that this does not explain the differences in the scripts. Well, Krxyzc writing varies in different parts of their planet just as Terran writing all over the Earth. It is only to be expected that differences will occur.

'Your manuscripts are therefore most valuable, because they enable us to make a direct comparison of the various Krxyzc dialects and alphabets, which has never before been possible. At least, we in the Institute have not previously come across any examples of directly comparable work.'

From evidence that the Interplanetary Philological Institute have collected from members throughout the world, they have now compiled a Krxyzc alphabet that represents the most commonly spoken dialect of the Krxyzc peoples.

The senior officer welcomed information from Byron on the intentions of the Krxyzcs 'regarding our home the Earth' as 'most stimulating.' A later chapter describes these messages from our space visitors, via Karne the Aenstrian, whose gleaming chariots flash across our skies with the grace of airborne gazelles.

Adds the scientist: 'One cannot really blame them for feeling somewhat nervous about trying to land on Earth during the present troublous times. It is up to all of us to do all that lies within our power to make the world a friendlier place for Krxyzcs to live in.'

An expert in astrophilology claimed that Krxyzcs have four thumbs and not five, as deduced by the first doctor, together with 'two finger-like members, which for some reason they hold in the extended position when talking to Earth men. We did not know of their power to make themselves invisible.'

Way back in 1958 a German professor said: 'The intricacies of the Venusian tongue are not yet fully solved, but at least our researches have enabled us to make a real start in this important work, which will do so much to foster interplanetary good fellowship.

UFO PROPHECY

WATCH-STOPPING, SPACE SCRIPTS AND SOUNDS

'It is a pity that so far, at least, none of the leading universities will collaborate with us. No doubt the time will come. What we really need is a sort of Rosetta Stone which will clear up all problems once and for all.'

Later, having estimated at first hand the value of contributions made by Byron to the science of philology, the professor enthused that all were wonderful tapes. One was then being inspected at Cambridge, another being re-examined by a professor of linguistics at Birmingham.

'It seems to me there is an affinity between Venusian and ancient Atlantean, which is not really surprising,' the German expert announced. He was appreciative of a forecast made by Byron in the same year, 1958. This was distinctly unique even if, through no fault of his own, it failed to materialize.

There should have been a spacecraft landing on Earth in the summer of 1958. This was a confident prediction made to the Institute in plenty of time by Byron. Something went awry—but not over his prophecy. He was given the information by space friends in person, so knew they spoke truth.

Here is what a scientist had to say about this apparent 'failure' to Byron, some months afterwards: 'We have had definite information that a craft was dispatched to us a short time ago and that it was to have come by way of the Moon.

'Unfortunately, it suffered a terrible accident and crashed upon the lunar surface. The special fuel it uses was scattered over the ground in a red patch. This is what was observed as the 'volcano on the Moon' that has been so much talked about in the newspapers recently.

'By great good fortune, none of the space beings was hurt in this disaster,' he reported. They had soon after been picked up by a relief spacecraft. Another German expert in the philological field contacted my new friend Byron and pointed out:

'The only specimens of Atlantean writing known to me are those given by Roglub, whose authenticity is unquestionable. But the specimens are, as you know, very battered—and the photo reductions are not easy to decipher. They are, however, markedly similar to the examples given by you.

'It is clear that your work is an important advance, and you have improved very much upon my own work; largely, I have no doubt, because I depend entirely on scientific aids.' (The German, incidentally felt there was 'close affinity' between Venusian and Martian tongues).

Byron agrees with this, generally, yet is sure they are differing types of being in the physical sense. The Venusian dwellers are far more friendly to Earth people than those who have colonized Mars. The latter have no desire to harm denizens of Earth, especially civilians.

They recognize that ' we are all children of the Supreme Intelligence of the Universe.' Even so, they badly wish to wreak havoc with military installations in nuclear power-crazed countries on Earth. Only prompt aerial preventive action by Venusians has so far stalled an all-out attack.

This might have been carried out with deadly heatray weapons on the centre of Salisbury Plain, not too distant from Warminster, where space people know there are dangerous devices being employed in battle exercises. They have threatened a gigantic display of mass destruction as a demonstration of protest against all at fault in Earth reckoning and experimentation.

A Mariner Mars survey allegedly precipitated this vengeful attitude of mind they still possess. Because of this, relations between Martians and Venusians have cooled considerably over the past year or so. Any demonstration embarked upon by the space being 'rebels,' however, would be directed against military might and not civilians.

Morally, spiritually, culturally, almost all have very high standards which are rigidly adhered to; yet there is a mischievous minority tempted to sin against a strict code of honour, said Byron. Their exploits when near to Earth probably account for 'hostile actions' claimed by victims in Brazil and the USA particularly.

Byron said he had to warn me of these dangers, which come from craft that are ruby red in colour. That was how to distinguish them at height. Funnily enough, although I have seen many crimson air chariots over Cradle Hill and experienced only one antagonistic force field from a near landing, Bob Strong has never succeeded in capturing a single red-bodied UFO on film, even from extremely close range. It may be sheer coincidence.

A blind musician friend of mine, Philip Rodgers of Grindleford in Yorkshire, has many inexplicable recordings on tape of beautiful space music and lilting airs. He is sanguine these emanated from passing spaceships direct on to his machine, this taking reception on 'playback' rather than 'record.' Strange, yet true.

UFO PROPHECY

WATCH-STOPPING, SPACE SCRIPTS AND SOUNDS

Philip, one of the top five recorder instrument players in the world and a teacher of music, was with me at Cradle Hill on an August night in 1966 when an amazing yet amusing landing of a small 'robot light' took place in a cornfield near the white gates. Eileen Buckle was a witness, too.

Foolishly I was sending a series of 'SOS' messages to a hovering UFO, with a bulldog torch; Philip was playing our aerial 'guests' a piece of music by Mozart; Eileen was attempting, eyes closed, to gain telepathic rapport with those on board the craft. It then blacked out.

There was silence for a few seconds, until a small disc no larger than a soup plate and similarly shaped, with a glowing aura or halo at its edges, came whistling down to the gate. It scythed through the corn in rear of us with a peculiar warbling note that belonged to no known bird, just missing physical contact with Philip's recorder.

Honey, Philip's lovely dog and guide, gave vent to a low growl that was not wholly of displeasure, we thought. I chased the 'brain beacon' up the rough trackway and field of wheat, but it followed the example of the carrier craft above and blacked out. The warbling notes issuing from the miniature disc were recorded by Philip's machine.

As we stood by the gate, both Philip and I felt moisture as of a fine rain drizzle touching our cheeks. We remarked on it, later, when joined by Warminster businessmen David Mitchell and John Kinzett. Yet there was no rain—it was a starry night blessed by summer warmth and crispness of sky detail. Those wet cheeks have always puzzled us...

As is evident from Philip's tapes, space people love to laugh, sing and play practical though harmless jokes. I cannot question his innate sincerity and can personally vouch for much that his machine has unwittingly recorded of material and voices from worlds other than our own.

Molly Thompson is another person gifted in her liaison with space friends, in the musical sense. She has sung space songs by popular request in many sectors of the world, inspired by melodies lazily drifting through the ether and captured by her ready consciousness of their presence.

There are probably others who have thus been 'contacted' by spacecraft entities who swish noiselessly overhead and are anxious to communicate per vibrationary patterns that concur with our concepts. One astrophilologist echoed thoughts that must surely predominate

UFO PROPHECY

in hearts and minds of all UFO believers when he wrote to Byron, wistfully:

'In the hurly-burly of modern life, lived as it is in the shadow of the H-bomb, very few of us poor mortals have the time to sit in quiet meditation of things—and I fear that the road ahead may be stormy. We can only hope that the beings in spacecraft realise that we mean them no harm and are merely desirous of settling our own affairs peacefully!'

Religious or not, we can all echo a sincere 'Amen' to those sentiments... Now for a recent countryside cameo with an odd difference, two reliable witnesses involved, discounting a dog.

A letter headed 'Spirit Visitor?' in *Western Gazette* (Yeovil) of April 12th 1968, from Mrs. Eileen Palmer, of Skerrymore, East Knoyle, Salisbury, Wiltshire, reads: 'Monday following on Palm Sunday, being such a glorious day, I begged my husband to take me and our dog Toby for a car-picnic, instead of doing the usual dreary Monday washing day. We visited Beckington Church and found the carved marble wall memorial to the poet Samuel Dangel (1619) placed there in memory of her beloved tutor by Lady Anne Clifford, Countess of Pembroke.

'We ate our lunch by Edington Priory Church (1351-61) and watched the workmen preparing the bell tower for the rehanging of the bells. What a joy to know that they will soon ring out again after many years of silence. On our homeward drive through West Lavington and Shrewton, the dog became restless and barked, so we looked for a wide grass verge to pull up. This we both spotted just before the B.3083 joins the A.303 at Winterbourne Stoke.

'There was a man in a snuff brown coat sitting by a five-barred gate, but when we pulled in he had vanished. I cried out, "Where is the man?" and my husband answered, "I saw him, too!"

'Nothing but open country on either side, so he must have been a spirit visitor from another generation. Perhaps some of your readers have seen him, too?'

(Author: Shrewton is very close to Chitterne, mentioned many times in local UFO sightings, and not too far from Stonehenge).

UFO PROPHECY

CHAPTER TWELVE

Interstellar Visitors Furtive and Secretive?

Readers of my last book, *The Warminster Mystery*, have pointed out that a recurring description from witnesses likens the flying saucer to a human eye, invariably a huge and all-seeing eye. It may be of relevance to recall the Egyptian story of Creation, which tells us that it all started with a giant eye floating on the surface of the water.

It may well be that the pattern of Man has evolved through all creation—not biologically so, but like an artist or a musician would do a repeat, as it were, with subtle variations on a theme until pitch and perfection are reached, after trial and error.

It is somewhat in accord with a group of super artists and craftsmen experimenting with living tissue rather than with paper, paint, stone or wood. Not only are they IN religion, but are the very REASON for it, perhaps. These superb craftsmen are not only capable of monitoring thought impulses and mental progressions of the less enlightened, but may be the cause of certain energies springing to life.

These may flourish in inspiration presented freely to Man in the form of mathematical creation, musical composition, chemical research, etc., to advance a backward civilization to the required spiritual and cultural momentum that almost keeps abreast of their own unfaltering steps in advancing stages of life.

There is purpose behind the UFO manifestations which we find great difficulty in understanding or determining if measured by the yardstick of Earth concepts alone. Many may have wondered at the irreverence of the term ' Thing ' that was frequently used, in my last book, for one or more inexplicable flying objects.

Yet in the distant past in Brazil they were called ' Cosa,' which is Spanish for Thing. And a new translation from a recently discovered papyrus from the tomb of Thutmose, 1504-1450 BC, reveals that the ' Thing ' appellation is nothing new. It was employed by the Egyptian troops and their commanders.

UFO PROPHECY

Pharaoh and his Army apparently all saw UFOs on numerous occasions. Pharaoh ordered that an account of it all should be 'written in the annals of the House of Life so that it can be remembered for ever.' Afterwards, we learn, 'it rained fishes and volatiles,' whatever that may mean.

Alexander and his soldiers saw 'Things,' also, it is recorded in historical documentation. Furthermore, we find mention of Pharaoh Pepi I in an ancient book on theology which tells us that the entrance of the Great Pyramid points directly to the Pole Star, for the Gods were supposed to 'inhabit that region of the sky.'

The Pharaohs of that period did not 'die' in the conventional sense, but 'chose to leave' this world and journey afar with the Gods. It is for this reason that the pyramids were provided with vents for entrances and exits, because in essence the pyramid was intended to be an indestructible home for the Gods to use on return trips to Earth.

A psalm on the departure of Pepi I intones: 'O men and Gods. Your arms under King Pepi! Raise ye him, lift ye him to the sky. To the sky! To the great seat among the Gods!' And another records: 'This King Pepi dies not. Have ye said that he would die? He dies not. This King Pepi lives for ever...'

To all accounts and purposes, therefore, he went off in company with the Gods in the direction of the East, up a golden ladder in a fiery chariot. He certainly has no tomb. Up until this time, they were all expected to go that way—but, since, things and conditions have deteriorated and changed, one must assume.

Stonehenge and the Great Pyramid could well be centres of power —not only in the direct physical or electromagnetic context, but also in the arcane or esoteric sense. On Lord Bath's Longleat Estate at Warminster is a beauty spot venerated by the name of Heaven's Gate; at nearby Botany Farm is a feature known as Jacob's Ladder. Significant names which, Biblically, denote the 'taking off' point for the cherished and hoped-for 'goal' at 'death' and the means—the golden ladder—by which one ascends to the space vehicle taking the departed there...

It is foretold that 'in the last days of the Earth' the lion shall lie down with the lamb, thereafter eating grass with the sheep. Curiously, lions roam on one side of a high fence in an enclosure at Longleat— and sheep champ grass in a nearby field of a farmer who leases land from Lord Bath.

UFO PROPHECY

INTERSTELLAR VISITORS FURTIVE AND SECRETIVE?

It perhaps only remains to be seen which lambing season is going to be the vital one in years to come, for the Holy prediction is feasible under these particular circumstances that currently apply at Warminster. If one is entirely swayed by the religious and spiritual angles of UFO magic, this would adequately explain why our town has been the centre of so many appearances of alien craft.

The true symbolizm of the lion, incidentally, is not generally known today. It was certainly known to selected initiates in the long ago. It is difficult to present a detailed explanation, but suffice it to say that in the very beginning the Lion signified the Power of Divine Truth. The Celestial Lion has the responsibility for protection of the Divine Secret and preservation of the Hidden Truth. He epitomizes spiritual power, in fact.

The initiates were termed Lions. Christ was sometimes referred to as the Lion of Judah. Solomon was depicted and portrayed as a lion and references to these kingly beasts are frequently to be found in a study of the ancient wisdom. They are the Vigilantes who always guard important, sacred or secret places.

They are often symbolic of people having great spiritual power and knowledge. The Lion was to guard against the phases of transition corresponding with different states of consciousness in relation to various Earth times. One often sees, in library or study, the popular back-to-back lions of the ancient East, commonly used as ornamental bookends.

This was not their prime function, of course, in design and elaboration. One represents Yesterday, looking benignly West. The other watchfully guards Tomorrow and gazes to the East. The past is buried and forgotten; the future is bright with promise after pitfalls have been negotiated.

Lions are also intrinsically connected with the Sun. This is often portrayed with the spiky 'mane' of a lion for 'rays,' and the lion betokens the Great Heart. The 'body' of the Sphinx is leonine and the 'head' is manlike, expressing the potential progress of Man from animal status to eventual godlike perfection.

From what we deem to be our pinnacle of present day enlightenment, we are inclined to revile and condemn the primitive natives of our planet, those pagans and heathens—in our falsely exalted opinion—who worship the Sun. If only we knew full truth in all its glowing facets, we should cease to upbraid these 'less civilized' brothers and sisters.

The Sun is the living and vibrant power extraordinary, the radiant and matchless energy, of the Supreme Deity in our own Solar System. It is the generous giver of light, heat and life, which should gratefully and gracefully be acknowledged by Man. I shall return to this theme later.

Many letters I received after publication of *The Warminster Mystery* were intelligently phrased, curious and fact-seeking, most of them complimentary. In a few instances, minor criticizms were made of the appendix that dealt with phone calls I had from denizens of the cantel Aenstria. Opinion was fairly equally divided: the calls were genuine, or I had suffered a monumental leg pull.

Here are extracts from a typical letter from interested reader G. D. Croft, of Crowthorne, in Berkshire, reaching me on March 2nd 1968: ' Setting aside the end part of the book, which I am reluctant to accept, except of course as another aimless and purposeless example of the religious pseudo-mysticizm so frequently seen to mar honest reportage, there can be no doubt that at Warminster we have heard of some definite " evidence " upon which sensibly reasoned theories can be based.

' To do this, one must necessarily ask certain pertinent questions. Above all others there is the vexing problem of why interstellar visitors should choose to be furtive and secretive, and of course their odd channels of communication we are asked to accept that they employ.

' The latter I dismiss. It is too easy to assume the guise of being a Saviour or Messiah for the benefit of humanity, but which is in reality a manifestation of paranoid tendencies that in strictly clinical terms can be seen to be rooted in other matters above—or beyond—the problems of extraterrestrial life.

' The real issue is the discrepancy—an obvious one—between a civilized creature with science enough to span a galaxy and an apparent total ignorance of our social structure, anthropologic antecedents, and so forth. It follows that where there is no communication, it is not for lack of means, but because such an action is not desirable or considered of no real significance.

' Owing to present day trends in world affairs, I think it a fair comment to say that in the light of historical research and records, despite all our intellectual information and emotional reactions, we are

INTERSTELLAR VISITORS FURTIVE AND SECRETIVE?

unable to compromise in any way with war. War is at bottom the self-destruction of race.

'It needs little enlargement or argument to fathom out the reason why our hereditary instincts for self-survival are time and again overridden by an urge to destroy our own specie—as well as the lesser creatures of this planet, to whit: the Dodo, passenger pigeon and so forth.

'Such contradictions in basic behaviour patterns are not found in the realm of animals. It is one peculiar to Man, and this may give you cause to wonder why I bring it up here in connection with your book. There are very good reasons indeed. There have been various sightings and phenomena, some of which cannot easily be explained away as natural phenomena.

'Very well. It would appear, then, that we can settle down to an analysis of the whys and wherefores of it all. It would be ridiculous to assume that because certain writers dance from cold fact to fantasy, we must abandon in entirety their suggestions.

'One writer, Leslie, suggests an earlier and more advanced civilization, though much of his evidence is inaccurate or doctored to suit demand. There are certain reasons for believing that some evidence does exist for earlier visits by extraterrestrial creatures; some recent, others very ancient.

'The purpose of these visits has not yet been rationally explained. Here is a new—or should I say different?—line of reasoning . . . Scientific thought is analytical, for without analysis there is no incentive for research. Part of scientific procedure assumes that, at some stage, reasoning must pass from pure analysis into synthesis (creation), which is secondary to but complemented by analysis.

'Logically, our planet provides for any other planetary visitors a gold mine of new information, ideas, races, fauna and flora, for the suggestion that other worlds are identical to ours would be in line with Man's most drastic complaint; that peculiar monomania which leads us to assume that we are the only intelligent creatures in the Universe, inviolable and answerable only to God, which image is representative of any other intelligence outside Earth (and must therefore be Divine because only Man exists otherwise).

'But a race capable of crossing galaxies, perhaps through time and space, would have passed beyond the parochial limits of localized exploration. Here I am suggesting that planets themselves would become living laboratories. Scientists at Passadena are already talking in these terms, hence the irradiation of Mars probes so as not to upset any existing ecology here.

'Your interplanetary visitors talk like heroes from a science fiction novel of the 1930's. They talk to a reporter with no lines of communication, no power, no authority in judicial or military matters, Explorers from earliest times have sought out the seats of power for their conversation, for obvious reasons . . .

'But let me postulate that the creatures do not want any lines of communication, that they are here not to bring Messianic messages of obvious import (any fool knows what a hydrogen bomb could do to London) but merely to monitor this planet?

'Why monitor a planet? Perhaps Earth has some special interest—and here we can turn to Charles Fort and James Churchward and others for a glimpse of the reasons for this. True, there are gaps in the evolutionary scheme we find hard to explain, the most obvious one being the existence of primates clearly rooted in common stock, yet which have for some reason not marched with Homo Sapiens towards physical development.

'Parallels to this phenomenon must be looked for in the laboratory and not in the sky. Botulinus virus is artificially bred at Porton Down, yet the parent virus continues to breed in its usual fashion inside the human alimentary canal and duodenal tract.

'Other deliberately muted virus strains—and some not so deliberate—have been let loose by accident, a case of Neumonic plague for example in 1959. What is significant is that common germs have largely been replaced by strains now considered pathologic to human systems, but once only freak mutants.

'Let us consider the sudden emergence of Homo Sapiens in the same extraordinary light. In less than 500 million years we have had two Ice Ages, which have obliterated from this planet the sabre-toothed tiger, mammoth, mastodon and woolly rhinoceros, to name a few obsolete animals.

'However, where it should have eradicated the ill-equipped tortoise, this creature survived. So did Man. In less than fifty years, with the use of the centifruge, biochemists have synthesized viruses and altered germs to order. Our knowledge of DNA gives us the threshold to creating living molecules of the protean order.

'In another fifty years, at the same rate of progress, we shall be able to produce to order androids, totally artificial men and women growth,

UFO PROPHECY

INTERSTELLAR VISITORS FURTIVE AND SECRETIVE?

in vats. A race which can cross the stars could conceivably radically alter the genetic makeup of a specie of biped and sit back to await developments.

'To do so would not be a short-term project, so some sort of temporary base or camp would be necessary. Hence the legends of Mu, Atlantis, Pan and so on. The product still retains a dim ancestral memory of its " maker " in a most literal sense!

'This then would also give us an insight into the peculiar religious element associated by many with the UFO business; and the odd assumption that a flying saucer can be associated with theology in some way. There is a necessity here to apply the knowledge of psychology to this vexing matter.

'We should admit that perhaps Jung was right when he observed that saucer-spotters are those who, as a result of the emergence of the thermo-nuclear bomb, had developed anxiety neurosis.

'I can collate this letter to relate to Warminster, for the necessities of applied science would oblige our hypothetical visitors to match data. Data does not alter because of time factors, unless it is inaccurate. Our progress towards self-destruction is not a matter of religion but of necessity.

'The researcher with his botulinus might wish to experiment with a rat, but he would not be expected to converse with it, no matter how intelligent it was; and on completion the rat would be consigned to the incinerator. Similarly, any specie made " different " by deliberate biochemistry would, in the nature of things, not be expected to survive.

'But a super-scientist with moral views may not relish the task of eradication, and would build that task into the creature itself. It would be a self-destroying mechanizm which would never fail itself, no matter how much reasoning or rationalization was applied to it. Thus the ethical issue is neatly sidestepped and only time becomes a significant factor.

'Warminster is only a measuring ground for given stimuli and measurable reactions to them. I do not think for a moment that the affairs at Warminster are over. On the contrary, we can expect more. Reading between the lines, what have you given us?

'Not much more than a fear stimulus . . .What of greed, cupidity, destructiveness, prejudice, hatred, love, sex? No—the probing continues.' A hard-hitting letter from a man with scientific knowledge, obviously. I welcome anything that provokes thought, constructively.

UFO PROPHECY

However, I reiterate: The final decision on what constitutes truth about UFOs and their crews must be made by the individual seeker and assessor. Conclusions must be formed on the basis of how many useful ladder rungs in personal experience and contact with UFO aspects, at first hand, have been climbed in the search.

As a serious investigator and author, I have to decide which influences entering my life are constructive, positive and beneficial in impact and worth; also those which are destructive, negative and valueless or harmful. I am terribly conscious of enormous responsibility, as my final chapters show only too plainly.

Whatever conclusions I have drawn will not satisfy everyone: no matter how painstaking my work of discovery, I invite some ridicule and perhaps condemnation of my analyses, given after careful thought. The reader will note that my mind has been made up. Perhaps I shall at least have fulfilled one useful purpose; that of causing people on Earth today to begin thinking, seriously, for themselves about the greatest mystery of Life—Life itself and what it all means . . .

Let us make a preliminary search, here, for some of the most simple of these mysteries and what they imply. Let us assume that around various suns in the entire firmanent are planets where are taught the continuing lessons of life and purpose in differing degrees. No one Man has universal knowledge; each Man is our teacher; and some have far more than others because they search with greater sincerity and diligence.

If we are willing to suppose that Venus is inhabited by beings capable of existence in intense light radiation or heat, in a duality of form—physical and spiritual—we learn that a child is there taught to remember its past carnations and so profit by past mistakes.

Once it has been schooled to arrive at a clear picture of past incarnations, it is ready to embark on the sciences and study of other subjects. Masters on such a planet teach the essential fact that—before anything can be learned—the Venusian child must know the art of 'tuning in' to cosmic consciousness via the primary source of Wisdom.

This source is not another Venusian but that which we on Earth call God. To attempt to understand physics, mathematics, or indeed any other science in its fullest and truest aspects, the first rule is that the mind of the child must be trained to contact this highest source, which is All-Wisdom.

Geometry, languages, biology, etc., these come at a very much later

UFO PROPHECY

INTERSTELLAR VISITORS FURTIVE AND SECRETIVE?

stage in the education of a young person under the guidance of a Master; and never before he or she has firmly grasped the significance of the Divine, from whom the beauty of Nature is inseparable. The reverse procedure applies on Earth.

Here, we stuff the minds of children full of scientific subjects before mental channels are trained properly to accept the idea of the existence of the Creator. All this would, one must imagine, produce on advanced planets ideals and perfect societies.

This is not entirely the case, I am given to understand, since—although these societies are so far and away above our own in all respects—they are nevertheless in a constant state of evolving. Therefore, there is inequality of brilliance and spirituality, mentality and morality, there as well as here.

However, the least evolved Venusian might be said to resemble a Man of the stature of a Leonardo da Vinci, without his weaknesses. Where there are failures on Venus to go beyond anything more than a shadowy concept of the Divine, God, the Immortality of the Soul, the education of a failure proceeds no further into the sciences, but he or she is trained as a servant. Servant: One who serves others—so wrongfully despised or looked down upon here on Earth.

The form of education for a Venus child is on a par with initiation for a mature Earth adult into the Hidden Mysteries, as were taught certain advanced minds in the temples of ancient Lemuria, Atlantis, Egypt, Greece and India. Interplanetary dwellers are sure in knowledge that reincarnation is not theoretical myth but established fact.

At this present time, few people will comprehend that our Moon is the planetary 'twin' of Earth, that the Moon is the male twin and Earth the female. Looking farther skyward we can study the Martian satellites of Phobus and Deimos. Phobus is not an artifact of Mars, but is definitely used by the inhabitants of the planet (as Byron says, these may not be indigenous) in a scientific way.

Phobus is extremely rich in minerals for its size, compared with the Moon. It is almost wholly composed of minerals. Were all the present untouched mineral deposits of Earth lumped together, they would barely total the amount of minerals on Phobus.

Mars is an industrial planet, thousands of spacecraft turned out regularly from its workshops for interplanetary brethren and their own employment.

Phobus is literally covered with Martian scientific apparatus, the landscape liberally sprinkled with a mass of shining, metallic objects, buildings, factories, even landing strips. Once, Phobus was part of the second satellite, Deimos, but the whole small Deimos-Phobus planet split in twain many eons ago.

The reader may well ask where I get my information, at this stage. Later chapters, dealing with very unusual ' people ' I have met (but not, I hasten to add, directly from alien spaceships) present some of the answers. I would be the last person to pack a load of rubbish and nonsense into a book that is dedicated to propagating facts as near as they can be determined.

We shall return, in due course, to other exciting possibilities that exist in connection with neighbouring planets which Man has already reached with scientific recording instruments, if not in an actual physical capacity.

CHAPTER THIRTEEN

Constructed According to Cosmic Principles

Chasing every clue, large or small, leading to cosmic truths, I met a serious young man whose ideas about his particular role in the future destiny of Man on Earth are unique and devastating. He is a quiet and likeable person, shy yet frank. Honestly, I could not credit what he told me.

After hearing of predictions he was making to groups of youngsters in a neighbouring town in Wiltshire, I interviewed him on July 18th and August 3rd of 1967. I shall name him Matthew. I classified him as a crank extraordinary, the type of misguided person whose entry into the Ufological field brings the whole subject into disrepute.

However, he gave me names of people I could freely contact at a Midlands University to check his story. Because of his medical history, I did not do so, but in fairness to the reader, perhaps as a warning against encouraging the crank element, I now present details he gave me.

The reader might find his disclosures of sufficient interest, although disquieting, to stir thoughts; while disagreeing—with me—over specific points made in a strange narrative. Matthew had never seen a UFO in his life until coming to Cradle Hill over August bank holiday weekend.

'I already know they exist, I know who mans them, so I do not hanker for visual confirmation,' was his first reaction to my sympathetic invitation. Here is the complete version of his story. Bob and Sybil, incidentally, refused to accept him as a regular member of our modest team:

'My mission on this planet commenced in November 1964, when I was at a university in the Midlands. It will be completed by Christmas of 1967—that is, after three years of involvement. In May of 1965 I was forcibly removed from the university by the authorities and placed in the city hospital to receive "treatment" for a so-called "mental illness."

'This lasted for four months, until the end of September 1965. I returned to university in October 1966 and this May, 1967, the same thing occurred again. This time, a Dr. Creighton came to visit me on May 24th. He told me that I had a transcendental mind.

'This is a mind capable of utilizing Cosmic or Divine truths, and he further warned me that I had no right to exist as such in the 20th century. He also knew that I had demonstrated my powers to fellow students. For example, I had:

'Abilities to materialize and dematerialize physical bodies, boil water and chalk with my hands alone, the mental attributes of being able to see into the past and future, read the mind of anyone, also exert control over the physical invironment.

'As far as this doctor and his associates were concerned, I was a Cosmic being. As such, I was an alien who had to be "stopped" by some means. I told them, however, that they could do what they liked, the decision being theirs entirely.

'I informed them that the treatment they had given me in hospital the previous May for four months, included drug dosages, brainwashing, occupational and group therapy, electro-convulsive treatment, could not work on such a being as I.

'So I was descended upon on May 25th 1967 at the university city and taken to a hospital nearby for "compulsory treatment." The student body at the university was extremely annoyed; so were the sociology department and my friends doing research in chemistry, physics, philosophy and mathematics.

'But unfortunately, none of them possessed the power and authority to free me from hospital. Sadly, the doctors, specialists and nurses at the city hospital did not realise that any treatment prescribed, whether physical or mental, would affect not only my own body and mind but have repercussions throughout the world.

'This is because my body is also in tune with Cosmic forces that are in control of all physical objects throughout the Universe, and so of the planet Earth also. They gave me drug treatment for nine days, endeavouring to conquer this Cosmic entity.

'The drug effect was reversed and accentuated my state of body and mind to such a degree that I could bring newspapers from beyond time and space. For instance, I read a local newspaper on the Thursday before it was due to be issued on the following Sunday.

'On the seventh day of "treatment," they realised that it was not

UFO PROPHECY

CONSTRUCTED ACCORDING TO COSMIC PRINCIPLES

producing the expected results. They therefore compulsorily passed an electric current through my mind in unawareness of what they were desecrating. This instantaneously led to the war in the Middle East between Syria, Israel and Egypt. At the same time I noticed that I was affecting time and space itself, so that time was being speeded up tremendously.

'I left hospital on the ninth day and my student friends got me to London. This was for safety. As soon as I left the Midlands city, a twenty-eight day detention order was placed on me. I now had the added problem of the medical authorities of the city, the university authorities and the police on my tail.

'For eighteen days I lay low in London, discovering that I did not require any sleep whatsoever—and also that, while my friends had eight or nine hours of sleep, I was awake and for me only about a half-an-hour had elapsed. This raised certain difficulties.

'I had synchronized my time with that of this planet and all forms living on it, and have done so, in consequence of which Earth time has indeed been shortened as your caller Karne said in May.' (Author: See chapter 16).

'I saw an American clinical psychiatrist in London, who informed me that I was not mentally ill or insane at all, but was " a very corrosive element in society." This psychiatrist knew a doctor at University College Hospital who would be friendly towards me.

'So from June 19th until July 8th, a period of three weeks, I was in hospital in London. Thus the Midlands city medical authorities are now satisfied that I have received " treatment " they wished to give, whereas in fact I have had none at all.

'I will now tell you the connection between my friends from the other planets, myself and yourselves at Warminster; and also the significance of the ancient monument of Stonehenge. At the dawn of the first advanced civilization on this planet, there was only one system of knowledge of all things, based upon Cosmic laws.

'The knowledge was brought here by advanced beings of the other planets in our Solar System, under the unerring guidance of Divine will. The present civilization is the third in the series, the last two having destroyed themselves.

'Stonehenge, the Pyramids, the ancient cities of Central and South America erected by the Aztecs, Toltecs, Incas and many other enlightened races, the Hanging Gardens of Babylon, plus a great number of the ancient temples and monasteries distributed throughout the world, are constructed according to Cosmic principles.

' Stonehenge is in essence a "prehistoric computer" erected for sacred occasions, and was used to compute the times of future events on a Cosmic scale. Such monuments and edifices are directly in line with the four primary Cosmic forces which act in the North, East, South and Westerly directions.

' Thus, when the present civilization draws to a close, these forces will be activated; and anything not constructed according to such Cosmic laws will be razed to the ground. When the members of the first and second civilizations began to create divisions among themselves—that is, between races, creeds, colours and the inevitable lust for power and domination over their fellows—so separate societies and nations arose. This led to conflict and wars.

' Initially, beings of the other planets landed here to provide guidance and wisdom, learned from long and sometimes painful experience, for their erring brothers and sisters. But as time progressed, this was no longer possible because of the aggressive spirit shown against them.

' They came in infinite love and peace and were turned away. Then resort was taken to the method of reincarnation. Throughout the world, from the North American Indians, the Aztecs of Mexico, the Incas and sundry other tribes of South America, to the Cretans, Etruscans and races of Asia and Polynesia, comes the legend of the White God or Great White Spirit.

' Few realise that Jesus Christ has been incarnated many times on this Earth planet, in an endeavour to teach Cosmic truths and guide the people of the world towards unity. His last incarnation was in the year 37 BC, towards the conclusion of a 2,000-year Universal cycle.

' His crucifixion came at the close of that cycle. The majority of people imagine that the actual date now is 1,967 years after His birth, whereas in fact it would have been 1,967 years after His death. There has been interference with the time-space dimension leading to the addition of 33 years, so that it is now nearly the end of the next cycle.

' It is almost 2,000 AD—and that is very significant in Cosmic calculations. Before 1,000 BC, Italy was settled by a race of people called the Etruscans. They were very advanced, but unfortunately—in the time of Jesus—the Romans, Israelites and Gauls all wanted this kingdom for themselves.

' In an effort to unite the Israelites and Etruscans, Jesus married

UFO PROPHECY

CONSTRUCTED ACCORDING TO COSMIC PRINCIPLES

Ursena and became the leader of the Etruscans. Ursena was a raven-haired beauty of that tribe. In spite of which, the Israelites and Romans independently wanted the wealth and power that the Etruscans possessed.

'The Jews loathed the Romans but eventually decided that Jesus would be tried for " political " offences before the Roman authorities. The Jews had to agree to this, lest they be persecuted and destroyed themselves. So Christ was crucified.

'At the same time the majority of the members of the Etruscan civilization were massacred, together with Ursena, for supporting Jesus to the end. The Etruscans who survived, few in number, were forcibly absorbed into the Roman stock by intermarriage.

'Rome took her art and science from the Etruscans, together with their social, religious and political customs and institutions. The 33 years of mass destruction of the Etruscans, also of the Jewish sects who supported Jesus (for example, the mass murder of the Essenes at Maseda) were then erased from history, the largest portion of Jesus' teaching obliterated from the view of Man afterwards.

'An evil curse was placed upon the long-lost burial city of the Etruscans, which is verily a most sacred place. The long line of Roman popes decided to call themselves " infallible," so that they could maintain their power and authority in the Roman Catholic world and their influence upon future events.

'Jesus prophesied that, upon His death, He would return 2,000 years hence, then rule the Earth for a further 2,000 years. It is only natural, therefore, that they should conceal the truth in order to maintain their power and dominion, so that no one would be able to discover what really happened.

'It also explains their extremist actions 2,000 years ago . . . In early November of 1964 Ursena appeared in flesh and blood at the home of Mario Signorelli, an Italian music teacher who lives in the village of Viterbo, some 30 miles North of Rome. She led him to the Caves of Riello and showed him around them.

'In reality, these are not caves at all, but underground streets leading into the heart of the burial city of the ill-fated Etruscans. She told Mario that she had died over 2,000 years ago and had been reincarnated to meet a man who had also been reincarnated on Earth—Jesus Christ —and that she had loved him with all her soul; but that they could not find eternal peace in death together.

UFO PROPHECY

' There will indeed be a Third World War—the biblical Armageddon—but it will involve intense race riots, violent earthquakes, floods and antagonizm between the minority of individuals who head the governments of the world and the vast majority who are subject to such rule.

' Already the British civil defence units and air forces are on the alert, knowing that Mao Tse-Tung will in all probability try to start a nuclear war by antagonizing America and Russia, who are naturally willing to retaliate.

' In Britain, only one in five individuals will be able to gain protection in the event of such disastrous destruction: there may be violence erupting between the majority of the British population, police and government, when this hour finally dawns.

' People from the other planets cannot interfere in the affairs of Earth, just as I cannot, and indeed no one else can, due to the application of Universal law. The world will not come to a physical end this year, but many thousands of individuals are likely to die in the process of near-future events.

' When Jesus reigns, many of those who die will be reincarnated. When Karne says that if you both meet again it will not be in your present form, he means that it will be in another physical form, when both of you are reincarnated and take on more perfect human bodies, whether you meet again on this planet or on another in the future.

' The great thinkers of the Western world today utilize their individual faculty of reason in order to construct theories, ideologies, concepts and hypotheses in which their observed facts fit. The intellectuals (Einstein is a case in point) approached this in their work, yet relying more fully on the Universal faculty of the intellect to resolve problems.

' The majority of human beings in the Western civilizations utilize reason, which basically provides relative truth. Speaking for myself, I do not use reason at all; only the intellect to which I have identified myself completely.

' Such purely intellectual knowledge is Universal or Divine and emanates from the Supreme Intelligence, so is not a construction of the reasoning of Man. I participate directly and actively in Divine knowledge and as such am endowed with absolute truth.

' This intellectual knowledge proceeds not from belief or the process of reasoning, but from the infinite and Universal Truth that dominates all forms. As such, it is not the exclusive possession of any race, nation,

UFO PROPHECY

CONSTRUCTED ACCORDING TO COSMIC PRINCIPLES

civilization, group or individual, whether these be highly advanced or primitive as regards their stage of evolvement.

'My purpose is to remain here until this civilization has reached its end—then help those who remain to rebuild the civilization according to the Divine plan. The beings from other planets can then land, helping to restore the planet to "normal functions."

'The new civilization will be perfect, headed by Jesus and Ursena, with no wars, plagues, diseases, famines or "natural" catastrophes such as earthquakes, floods and tornadoes, etc. Peace will then reign at long last. This Earth is in the hands of the Supreme Intelligence himself.

'Therefore nothing can prevent the emergence of events which have to come about for the liberation and freedom of all from human bondage. Christ says that no one would know in what day and hour he would return to judge Mankind—not even " the Angels of Heaven, but my Father only."

'The Bible tells us, also: "Watch therefore: for ye know not what hour your Lord doth come. Therefore be ye also ready: for in such an hour as ye think not, the Son of Man cometh." Matthew 24, verse 22: "And except those days should be shortened, there should no flesh be saved: but for the elect's sake those days shall be shortened."

'I have already mentioned that I noticed a difference between my own conception of time and of that around me. Last May I perceived that "time" was being speeded up—to such an extent that the days are now in fact shorter. It is logical that the fourth dimension of space-time is being altered in some way, so that physical bodies of three dimensions that are placed in the fourth dimension have experienced a shortening of time-space.

'Karne, your visitor, knew this. It is predicted plainly in the Bible —and I noted the change in May this year. Regarding the working out of when Christ will return, as promised, I will elaborate the method I have used. Jehovah's Witnesses calculated that Jesus would return to found his kingdom in 1976.

'This was arrived at by multiplying the number of weeks in a Cosmic yearly cycle by the approximate age of the Divinely incarnated being (Christ) at death, that is: $52 \times 38 \simeq 1976$. There are other estimates to show that he may have died at the age of 37 years 6 months (that is: $52 \times 37.5 \simeq 1950$).

'A few weeks ago I learned about the girl called Ursena who visited an Italian music teacher at Viterbo. She took him to see the lost burial city of the Etruscans in early November 1964, which is two years and eight months ago from the present month of July 1967.

'I already knew about the sacred symbols used by ancient priesthoods all over the world to decipher the meanings of given words. Upon checking the letters U-R-S-E-N-A against the corresponding numerals 2118195141, and writing down the hidden meaning of the numerals one to ten, " God's Daughter " was the answer.

' " U " is the feminine pronoun in the Hindu language as well. I was also told that several people had independently discovered the meaning for themselves, one month before I did. Knowing that the most sacred symbols to the ancients was 10, and that three appears to have been a key figure in the life of Christ, I resolved to find the precise relationship, with 10 representing the Deity :

'Years of Christ's life $\{\overbrace{\underbrace{10 \mid 10 \mid 10}_{3 \times 10} \; 3 \mid \overbrace{4 \text{ or } 5} \mid 3 \mid}$

'Thus, for the first 30 years Christ was quiet, then he had a three-year ministry, and was crucified at $\simeq$ 38 years old, finally resurrected on the third day after death, being denied by Peter three times.

'If Ursena was indeed God's daughter, then it is probable that Jesus, wherever he may be, started this three-year mission in November 1964, when she appeared in Italy, which now leaves four months or so until the completion of that three-year mission.

'In this way, we arrive at about Christmas of 1967. If Christ was $\simeq$ 37 years 9 months at death, the recalculation is 37.83 x 52 = 1967+ (that is, towards the end of the commencement of the year 1967). War in the Middle East and a new civilization are certainly coming in the near future.'

That is what Matthew told me, sincerely, in two months of 1967. He gave me other revelations, weird and wonderful if true. Personally, although I was truly fascinated by his comments, which could be substantially viable in connection with spiritual evidence linking with main objectives of our UFO friends, I cannot fully share his convictions.

Arising from what Matthew says about the wife of Jesus, it is timely to recall a man of the church with peculiar notions concerning Christ. In the summer of 1967 he alleged that Christ may have had homosexual tendencies. This to him seemed likely because Christ had so little to do

UFO PROPHECY

CONSTRUCTED ACCORDING TO COSMIC PRINCIPLES

with females and preferred the company of men, judging from New Testament teachings.

I mention this, which created a furore of seething indignation from Christians in Britain when the sensational news story broke, simply because Matthew has offered us another and widely differing glimpse of the love life of the Messiah. It would be stunning, if factual...

Canon Hugh Montefiore, whose comments on Jesus and homosexuality made national headlines, was defended by the Bishop of Salisbury, the Right Rev. Joseph Fison, in his November Diocesan News of 1967 as follows: 'The view we take of his remarks depends on what is meant by the word homosexual.

'Heterosexual people can be depraved as well as homosexual, but neither need be. Affection is not sinful, but inordinate affection is always sinful, whether it is for someone of the other sex or of one's own, whether it involves promiscuity or perversion.

'Jesus had no use for it. There is not a hint that he ever gave way to it. Canon Montefiore did not mean that Jesus was a homosexual in any depraved sense of the word. He suggested—very improbably in my opinion—that Jesus did not marry because he had by nature a deeper love for men than for women.

'He was not denying Jesus' perfection. He was seeking to uphold it. But he was trying to show how greatly Jesus' ideas of perfection differed from those of the best Jews of his day. Jesus made a point of identifying himself with outsiders. He lived and died an outsider. Are we with him or not?'

The Bishop, who was Canon Montefiore's predecessor at Great St. Mary's, Cambridge, also referred to the Hippy 'flower girl' who was asked on TV what her experience was like and replied 'Paradise.' Asked the Bishop: 'Is that what flower people are after—Paradise Regained?

'If so, are they going about it the right way? Paradise can be regained, not by going back, by escape from life. The way is forward to the City of God, not back to the Garden of Eden. That does not mean escape from life, but a resolute facing up to life.

'Where does the blame for the present situation lie? With the young or the old? Probably with both. But, speaking as an elder, I think we have failed youth by not giving them any clear sign of the way forward. We have abandoned the pursuit and vision of true excellence and are content with at best an iridescent mediocrity.

UFO PROPHECY

'It is the perfection of Jesus and his excellence that youth needs to catch a glimpse of,' says the Bishop. Homosexuals, half-castes and pacifists, as well as Hippies, he points out, have all been in the news; and suggests that the Church can best reflect Jesus in its attitude towards outsiders.

Wars, rumours of wars, industrial unrest, political and racial assassinations, etc., make one thing obvious, now, to all save the dim-witted and insane: Man on Earth is desperately seeking a faith on which to cling, a prop against the materializm gone mad which a major section of his world currently suffers from in a purblind state. Weighing the impact and import of the following news item, from the Southampton *Southern Evening Echo* in February 1968, can there be any wonder that intelligent Man recoils from the blatant threats expressed?

'U.S. Claim Super Killer' says the headline, then goes on: 'Washington. A nuclear scientist revealed this week that America's latest planned nuclear weaponry—the multiple warhead missile—could imperil the lives of 60 million city dwellers in a single strike.

'Dr. Ralph Lapp, a nuclear physicist who worked on the original A-bomb project, described the system as the "ballistic six-shooter." He said only 45 intercontinental ballistic missiles would be needed in such an attack, because each could be equipped with up to six H-bomb warheads, capable of being dropped at intervals on 20 selected city targets while the carrier missiles remained in flight.

'Dr. Lapp's disclosures, by coincidence, followed the denial by the Pentagon of a *Washington Post* story that the United States are making a fundamental shift in the targeting of missiles—aiming at cities rather than military installations.' (Author: Charming!)

Crop circle discovered in July, 2016 near Cley Hill, a prominent hill to the west of Warminster in Wiltshire, England.
Photo courtesy Steve Wills

UFO PROPHECY

The Cley Hill crop circle, like others that have been discovered near Warminster, could possibly be associated with the mysterious UFO activity that has occurred over Wiltshire for decades.

CHAPTER FOURTEEN

Young Drug-Takers Groped and Grovelled

Bearing the headline 'UFO Riddle of Whirligig Damage to Farmers' Crops,' a leading news story in the *Sunday Express* of November 5th 1967 asked: 'What caused the damage in two farmers' barley fields in the Isle of Wight?' It then continued:

'For weeks, agricultural experts and five aeronautical scientists investigated the strange whirligig patterns left in crops flattened along a narrow strip three-quarters of a mile long. But now the scientists, led by Leonard Cramp, an aeronautical technician with the British Hovercraft Corporation, claim:

"It was, without doubt, the path of an unidentified flying object as it was coming in for a touchdown." Yet the farmers who own the three fields that were damaged, John Warne and Donald Thomas, are not impressed. They do not believe in flying saucers, but they are completely baffled.

'For they saw nothing, heard nothing, and admit they do not have a clue. Both sides agree on one point. Inquiries show there were no humans, cattle or mechanical farm gear which could have caused the damage, anywhere near the fields at the time. Nor was there any wind, storm or rain.

'Mr. Cramp said: "We checked out everything else it could have been and drew a complete blank. The children from the nearby school in the village of Whippingham denied playing in the fields." Mr. Warne, of Coburg Farm, Whippingham, said: "I have never seen anything like it.

"The ears of the barley were threshed bare, all the grains gone. I cannot explain it. It certainly was not the weather—but I cannot believe in flying saucers, either." Mr. Thomas, of Padmore Farm, agreed. So did a leading agricultural expert called in by Mr. Cramp.

'Then Mr. Cramp lined up his team for the field investigation. All are members of the British UFO Research Association. They work for aviation firms and are: Squadron-Leader Bob Cox, a technical author; Tom Pattinson, an electrical physicist; David Crewman, a rocket telemetry engineer; and John Feakins, a rocket telemetry and guidance engineer.

'The trail of damage appeared overnight in July. It began and ended with the scattered remains of a wood pigeon. Mr. Cramp said: "At 9 a.m. on July 10th children were just going into Whippingham village school. Two of the boys spotted a hovering object about 500 yards away.

"When they came out to play at 10.30 a.m. the object was still in the area. I questioned the children separately and in the presence of witnesses. Their accounts tally beyond question. The two boys who saw it first gave me an estimate of distance, size and height.

"I was able to work out that the craft was about 37 feet wide—bigger than a double decker bus. From the marks in the barley I figured it was no higher than 30 feet and travelling at about 40 miles an hour. We found the beginning of the barley damage within 40 yards of where the lads had seen the craft.

"It was there that we found the pigeon." The investigators examined and re-examined the trail of damage every day for six weeks. "It looked," said Mr. Cramp, "as if a mad thing had ploughed across the field. It was a deep trough in which the barley had been flattened to the ground in a continuous whirligig pattern.

"The trough, up to four yards wide, ran practically straight, except for carefully skirting a little hut. Every few yards there were little twisted central tufts of barley with broken and bare heads. The ground in the centre of these tufts was quite bare—as if stalks, roots and soil has been violently tugged out."

'The investigators took still and cine films of the trail and twice hired a plane to take aerial photographs. Now all the films and the results of the investigation are to be sent to the Ministry of Aviation. "Then," said Mr. Cramp, "perhaps we can have an official inquiry into the whole subject of UFOs at last."

Our neighbouring county of Hampshire and the Isle of Wight are fairly notorious for sightings of celestial chariots of fire. Seeing an unidentifiable flying object made so much impression on one Hampshire man that it gave him sleepless nights.

According to a *Southern Evening Echo* news story on December 1st 1967, headed 'Nightmares After UFO Sighting,' here is how one

UFO PROPHECY

YOUNG DRUG-TAKERS GROPED AND GROVELLED

witness reacted: 'It was the dreaming that prompted gardener Albert Marsh, of Itchen Abbas, near Winchester, to tell the *Echo* about a phenomenon which he admits terrified him.

'Mr. Marsh, known as "Alby" to his many friends, is employed as a gardener by Heating Controls Ltd., of Kings Worthy. It was at 2.40 p.m., with a clear sky overhead, when he first noticed a bright light high in the sky. "It was too high for a plane. I have seen enough of them to know," he told me.

'He added that it showed no vapour trail, nor was there any noise. He watched it hang motionless in the sky for some time. Then a cloud passed over it before it again appeared, shining just as brightly. To prove to himself that he was not imagining things, Mr. Marsh fetched two other employees from the company's workshops.

'Brian Cornish and Terry Martin saw the light, too. Later, Mr. Marsh said, another cloud passed over the light, which was strong enough to shine through. It was then that he admitted to being "terrified." He said the object, which up to then had comprised a single large light, developed a second, smaller light.

"Suddenly it began to plunge earthwards straight for me, it seemed," commented Mr. Marsh. He counted seven lights forming a rectangle, with the largest and brightest light at the front. At the end of its plunge it once again hung motionless in the sky.

"Eventually the object soared upwards again," explained Mr. Marsh, "and out of sight." The same newspaper published a front page story headed 'UFO Sighting at Gosport' on November 8th 1967 to the effect that:

Two Gosport police officers, WPC Edna Wielk and PC Tony Connell, were in a police car last night in Little Anglesey Road when they saw an unidentified flying object high in the sky near the submarine base at HMS Dolphin. WPC Wielk said:

'We thought at first it was a plane. There was definitely something there. It was red and white in colour. We got out of the car several times to make sure it was not an optical illusion. Altogether we had it under observation about five minutes.'

The previous night a local borough councillor, Ronald Kirkin, reported seeing a UFO at Lee-on-Solent. In the House of Commons the day before, the newspaper continued, Dr. Reginald Bennett, Conservative MP for Gosport and Fareham, asked the Secretary of State for Defence what organisation Her Majesty's Government has

UFO PROPHECY

for the analysis and valuation of reports of flying objects not identified as aircraft.

Mervyn Rees, Under Secretary, replied: 'The Ministry of Defence examines these reports in the light of their possible air defence implications and it obtains advice, as necessary, from Government and other scientific and technical organisations.

'The adequacy of our arrangements can be judged from the fact that between January 1st 1959 and September 30th 1967, some 625 reports were examined and 555 were found to have mundane explanations. The remaining 70 reports contained insufficient data for evaluation, but there was nothing to suggest that they related to incidents materially different in kind from those which were explained.'

On the surface, this appears a good, sound, non-alarmist response, illustrative of the 'official' attitude of course. Dig beneath the surface, however, and it is appreciated that these typical 'brush-off' explanations no longer satisfy many thousands of sane witnesses.

In the short space of fifteen months, I gathered almost as many eye-witness accounts of UFOs as the Government apparently had listed in the space of over eight years! Mine were all collected locally, over a seven-mile radius, too, whereas theirs are spread out through the whole of the United Kingdom, one assumes.

In its issue of November 6th 1967 the *Southern Evening Echo* told a back page story about a UFO that extinguished the lights of a lorry—an occurrence common to Warminster mechanical and electrical 'victims,' as told in my last book. Here is the *Echo* report:

Sighting of another unidentified flying object has been reported in the Fordingbridge-Ringwood area. This time the UFO was seen by a long distance lorry driver as he travelled along the main Salisbury-Bournemouth road at Ibsley late last night.

He immediately reported the object, which he claims landed in the road in front of him, to the police, but by the time officers arrived there was nothing to be seen. The lorry driver, Carl Farlow (25), of Hills Lane Drive, Madley, Dawley, Shropshire, told the police that as he was driving near the village of Ibsley at 11.30, he saw:

'A cigar-shaped object about twelve feet in length with a white dome underneath. It was travelling in the sky from the West and landed in the road in front of me.' Mr. Farlow says that, at the same time, a Jaguar car was travelling in the opposite direction.

The lights of both the lorry and the car failed and both vehicles

UFO PROPHECY

YOUNG DRUG-TAKERS GROPED AND GROVELLED

stopped, although the engine of the lorry continued running. After about two minutes the UFO, which Mr. Farlow says was showing green lights, became airborne again and flew off towards the East.

Then the lights of both lorry and car came on again. The lorry driver spoke to the driver of the car, who refused to give his name or call the police. He said he had been drinking. There was a UFO sighting near Fordingbridge about two weeks ago, when retired Royal Air Force Wing-Commander Eric Cox, of Hyde, and his wife reported seeing ' a flying cross ' in the sky.

The Christmas week issue of the *Westmorland Gazette* reported UFOs over Grayrigg and Milnthorpe : Unexpected visitors are not unusual at Christmas, says the newspaper, but the ' blinking red lights ' seen by several Westmorland people on Tuesday evening ' made them wonder who the next callers would be ! '

It was ' one of those strange unidentified flying objects ' which bewildered observers noted as it travelled Northwards from the Kent estuary, over Milnthorpe, Patton and Grayrigg, to disappear finally beyond Whinfell Beacon. Shortly before 9.30 p.m. Mrs. Mary Hyde, of Milnthorpe, saw lights of a strange aerialist coming from the direction of the Kent estuary, heading towards Kendal.

Children in Milnthorpe, who saw it, counted five red lights but heard no noise. Soon afterwards Mrs. R. Brassington, wife of the Vicar of Grayrigg, and her friend Miss M. Wootton, were driving through Oldfield Wood from Grayrigg to Kendal when they saw two lights in the sky, not far away from them.

One of the lights was small and pinkish in colour, the other—a bright orange—was flashing on and off. When Mrs. Brassington again caught sight of the lights, which appeared to have moved around the area in a semi-circle, she stopped the car and turned off the engine.

' It was certainly low and seemed to hover over one of the farms,' she told the *Gazette*. ' At first we thought it was a plane, but when I saw it the second time I was doubtful. There was a noise, but it certainly was not the noise made by an aeroplane.

' It was a sort of dull sound. I was not frightened at the time, but it becomes more frightening when I think of it now,' Later, Mr. T. Rowley, of Soulby Fold, near Kirkby Stephen, reported that as he drove along the Kendal to Tebay road he saw a formation of red lights in the sky.

The lights travelled North, halting and hovering over Whinfell

UFO PROPHECY

Beacon, then descended vertically on to the top of the fell. The report ends: 'Kendal police stated yesterday that PC G. Cox, of Grayrigg, searched Whinfell Beacon and had an excellent view of the area around, but saw nothing.'

An old age pensioner living near dense woodland, at a small village near Warminster and Frome, swears to a macabre sighting in early winter of 1967. Shunning publicity, simply because a friend scoffed at his fanciful story, he wishes to remain anonymous. He is a down-to-earth type, unflustered and not the imaginative person one would automatically suspect after listening to his amazing narrative.

He would tell me only bare facts, which aroused my curiosity to a burning degree, yet would not be drawn into elaborating beyond the following—so I respected his wishes: It was afternoon and he was quietly enjoying a pipeful of tobacco outside his tiny cottage, down by the gate at the end of his garden, which skirts the edge of a clearing through trees.

He is rather deaf and heard nothing as the UFO spun earthward over the tree belt. The simple life he leads is in close affinity with delights of Nature and the pastoral calm of the countryside. It overrides a poor educational background by that enriching factor.

The old man was not alarmed or surprised to see the craft land at the far side of the open space, swaying gently some four to six feet above the grass. It steadied to an even keel and two figures came from the rear, dropping to the ground and walking beneath the airship with lowered, helmeted heads.

The widower took the flying saucer to be 'some new-fangled contraption of the air force.' Still puffing serenely at his briar, he watched the two visitors walk with stiff gait and movements to a point some 35 yards to his left, some 60 yards from the silent craft. They went into the woodland, ignoring him.

Loving company in a lonely life, the witness started to make his way towards them. Getting closer, he noted more detail. They were fairly tall, wore dark grey and close-fitting clothing with a peculiar sheen, rounded helmets on their heads fashioned from black plastic, he thought. One was shaking his head from side to side as muffled tones of the other broke the stillness.

As the pensioner came to within the length of a cricket pitch, 22 yards, of them, one raised a gloved hand and—quick as a flash—both vanished. Now dumbstruck, the old fellow scratched his head, looked

YOUNG DRUG-TAKERS GROPED AND GROVELLED

towards the spacecraft—and gasped . . . A cloud of thick yellow smoke or vapour had surrounded and hidden it from view.

The old woodcutter told me seriously: 'Thinking it over later, it struck me that the men I saw must have rushed towards the aeroplane. My eyes are very sharp and do not miss much as a rule. I can see pretty well, even in the dark. I am sure I would have seen them move. Anyway, to begin with they were walking so slow, as though weighed down.

'Instead, they just faded into nothing as if they had become invisible. I don't believe in ghosts or any of that nonsense. It did not make sense to me at all—and still doesn't,' he added. All he was conscious of, at the end, was a flurry of movement in the middle of the mustard coloured mist.

'Through it, a light flew up from the grass and into the air. But I did not see any shape or outlines at all. I wondered if I had been dreaming—I am getting on for 80, you know—but my pipe was still alight and hot. I took a big puff at it and pressed it against my cheek to make sure I was awake.'

In a friendly overture, the old man had gone over to speak to the two unexpected 'airmen.' He would have invited them in for a cup of tea, the kettle on the boil on an old-fashioned gas ring at the time. They snubbed him, shocked his senses, so that he trembled at memory of his weird encounter while I was interviewing him some weeks afterwards.

Hostile or not? Who can tell with absolute certainty, when the 'visit' was of such a short, dramatic and utterly mystifying duration? I would be inclined to bracket it with the 'woman in the copse' episode, except that the intruders obviously spurned contact with the old man. Surely they did not fear him? The clue came when the woodcutter, asked whether he experienced any physical sensation at the time, confided:

'No, not then. When I had brewed a pot of tea, and was waiting for it to settle before pouring, I could feel my heart banging strongly like. Funny—it wasn't a heart attack or anything like that. My heart beat was powerful, for a change (I never notice it, usually), and yet it was beating at only about thirty a minute.'

To prevent delayed action shock, had the two visitors, or others aboard the craft, transmitted a ray towards the woodcutter which slowed his heart beats to avoid damage, collapse, even death? When running towards a UFO near Cradle Hill copse, one night, as it slithered from side to side close to the ground, I was stung by invisible rays and knocked off my feet.

Then the UFO climbed fast and high, I laughing ruefully as I gazed upward to follow its flight path. I felt my heart pumping with surging beat. My pulse rate was abnormally low. This corroborates the old man's story: so the UFO crews intend no harm to those who excitedly race towards them to gain knowledge. Instead, they ensure—while keeping people away from damaging force fields—that the main organs of Earth people are not poisoned by fear reaction, either . . .

As earlier incidents in this book amplify, one cannot dispute that a hostile and mischievous element does appear fairly firmly looped into the UFO network, however. To me it proves that a minority of space travellers are out to demonstrate to Earth people that they possess greater powers—including those for destruction, if the need should ever arise—than we have.

That UFO machines or crews have ever killed Earth denizens I would strongly refute. Most of the sensational and grossly distorted stories emanating from the USA, for example, are sheer poppycock and simply publicized, in the main, to net the tellers a small fortune and false fame.

Look closely at these outlandish accounts and you discover that, if any hostility or antagonism has occurred, it has invariably been instigated by Earth people and their innate fears of the unknown. Soldiers suffering burning or shock have first opened up on UFOs with machine guns or rifles; a stupid action.

The offenders must be put out of a fearful state, rendered *hors de combat*, by shock rays that stiffen muscular movements to inertia, slow down quickened heart beats to save organic damage to themselves. This is a mild warning that friendliness is the only approach to 'invaders' here for life-saving objectives at the heart of our planet.

As *The Warminster Mystery* (publishers, Neville Spearman) outlined, I suffered discomfort and niggling, electrically induced pain when a large airborne submarine was near in September 1965, affecting my eye, face and hand. An Army major had his car stopped, practically dead in its tracks, by downbeating soundwaves of violent pressure when journeying at 40 m.p.h.

The wife of a senior Royal Air Force pilot, living in Warminster, was stunned by sight and sound of an enormous UFO droning above a hilltop. A hospital matron was petrified by roof vibrations that flung

UFO PROPHECY

YOUNG DRUG-TAKERS GROPED AND GROVELLED

curtains and rail mountings from a Warminster bedroom window with unexpected savagery.

A number of heavy transport drivers had vehicles stopped by force fields of unearthly character, especially near Colloway Clump. Car headlights were smashed along the same stretch of road in June of 1966, Warminster Trades Councillor Richard Cox reported to me.

A young carpenter was pinned helpless under an aerial buffeting from a dish-shaped UFO on a lonely country road wrapped in thick mist. Yet no 'hostile' misbehaviour of these flying machines and crews caused lasting physical damage to anyone.

Taken on its own at surface value, each new facet or aspect of UFO findings conveys as much data as a tiny sliver of mortar that helps to cement bricks in a house of knowledge. When assembled in strength, however, their collective worth can be considerable to the questing mind.

Gradually, they lay a foundation or starting point for further exploration, so that a bridge is eventually built that narrows, if not completely spans, the gap between separate worlds and mutual understanding. Attempting to cope with the UFO enigma, we must force ourselves to cast adrift yardsticks used to measure ordinary phenomena, methods that merely mount molehills of the mundane.

We must rid ourselves for a fresh approach, be mentally born again as it were, to reach full comprehension of the Unknown. Guided by something much stronger than instinct, I feel sure this is essential. We chase shadows, we run along blind alleys, we try and compel the young to kow-tow to their elders—to respect a generation that has given them wars and racial hatred.

Our Cosmic friends must indeed possess and evince love far beyond our own hesitant and inconclusive standards, for we show so precious little we can give in return. Here is an odd facet which, at first sight, has nothing to do with flying friends from other worlds. Artist Gil Roberts, of Southampton, wrote to me at the end of 1967:

'We have quite a number of friends in the USA who know of our interest in UFOs. They sometimes send us cuttings about them and tell us of personal experiences. You may well meet one of our dearest next spring. He is an English poet who has spent most of his life over there.

'In fact, he has lived there since his 'teens—a wonderful poet and person who, as far as I know, is completely unknown in this country and yet has won literary awards and been the subject of documentary films over there. Although Eric's experience apparently had nothing whatever to do with UFOs, one of the visitors you told me about at Warminster brought his story to mind.

'I assure you that he is perfectly sane. It all sounds somewhat bizarre, even if quite simple . . . He lives at Big Sun amidst remote surroundings on the Pacific coastline.

'One day he was joined by a man, a real person who came and sat beside him on a rock—and the man was SHELLEY! And Shelley stayed for four days; in fact, our friend could not get rid of him. So I am mad to credit this? So Eric was pulling our legs? But he never dared to relate this story, before telling us, to anyone but his wife!'

No, Gil, I would not term that a crazy and unbelievable story. What would your reaction be if you met a person who can uncannily intercept your thoughts so quickly that he mouths what you were intending to say, word for word, a split second before the words issue from your vocal organs?

Or another who can materialize and dematerialize small objects, having physical substance, at will? Another who boils water by the mere touch of a finger tip? A fourth through whose sensitive hands streams of healing flow?

What impression would you immediately gain if, on a cold day, you suddenly pour with sweat as though stricken by a fever, feeling temporarily ill and dehydrated? Then the person with you pushes back his chair from a restaurant table and says sincerely, twinkle in his eye: 'I am so sorry. Please forgive me. I forgot to control my radiation.'

Or when coming under peculiar scrutiny from a person who, gazing around the area of your head and shoulders, warns you in friendly fashion to take things a trifle more easily for a few days, full of genuine concern for you?

When you naturally ask what he means, his prompt reply is: 'Your aura is the wrong colour and is slightly warped. It denotes you are suffering a certain amount of stress and strain at present, through over-working. Let up for a bit—take it easy for a spell. I can read your thoughts and unspoken questions, also.'

These are personal incidents and 'minor miracles' I have been involved in since my visit from Aenstrian Karne in May of 1967, described in a later chapter. They are most unusual people whom I

YOUNG DRUG-TAKERS GROPED AND GROVELLED

must, after careful thought and initial hesitation, classify as doubtfully of Earth extraction and therefore extraterrestrial.

Each claims to be a Cosmic entity dwelling on planet Earth, at this vital period of preparation, for reasons which will soon be apparent to everyone because of happenings in Zealand, Denmark. The Great White Brotherhood, Interplanetary Masters, Archangels and Angels or Angeloi figure in their speech. An extravagant claim? The reader must judge, later . . .

Expressions they employ are sometimes foreign to me in the widest sense of the word. I am no student of the Occult or the Holy Bible. They told me remarkable things concerning the terrific potential of Man in a fully enlightened and ennobled state free of weaknesses, including ability to project the mind to far distant realms.

Thus it could be used as a superconscious instrument to record Universal truths to store in the nine-tenths vacuum of his undeveloped, unused and deficient brain cells. One of my extraterrestrial callers is a scientist who specializes in chemical engineering, and production of heat energy, to all outward appearances.

Cosmically, he is an emissary and tester of human reactions, yet careful to hide his great knowledge and powers from the uninitiated. He gave me incredible evidence that drug-taking among our young people has calamitous results on the nervous system.

Conversely, certain drugs have a temporary effect of opening up the curtain of the subconscious, but only to a limited extent, so that glimpses of Cosmic consciousness and truth can be enjoyed. But these exhilarating experiences are but fleeting mental holds on levels of other worldly dimension. Exciting and falsely stimulating peeps into Cosmic vastnesses can be injurious to brain and nerve centres in the unsatisfying aftermath of the drug.

Sharp realisation that he is a Cosmic entity came to Mark in January of 1963, when he went to work as usual one morning with ' a sick headache.' During that day, three female and two male employees in the same office were taken ill. The girls suffered most. It was then that Mark knew he must learn to control his newly surging radiation power, for he was not of this Earth.

His fellow workers soon recovered from their dosage of unintended personal radiation. Mark is extra cautious nowadays to subdue and conserve radiation rays when near fellow humans. He is ever fearful that his 'identity' may be discovered, having special duties to perform in readiness for Mankind entering the New Age on Earth.

He related a fantastic story to prove that the drug LSD, in particular, overpowers minds of young takers unaware of its mind-changing, revealing yet damaging long-term effects. One night he took a stroll through a London heath clearing.

In the centre, a 'flower power' party and 'love-in' were in progress. The majority of backs of erotic youth were turned to him until he neared the revellers. Then each young person swung round, a half smile lighting every countenance, eyes ablaze. With no words spoken, the youngsters converged upon him.

Some groped and grovelled in a mad scramble to surround him, most on all fours in sheer animal frenzy. All looked upward at him, commenced to bow their heads to soil and grass. A few hands plucked avidly at his shoes and trousers. The experience taught him a swift lesson.

He raised hands in greeting to the assembly of drug-takers, walked sedately past; then broke into a run on the farther side of the clearing. He was scared at that moment and far more awed than the grovellers... 'They saw through me—they knew my vibrations are on a different level from theirs,' he told me sombrely.

'It happened, or almost happened, on a second occasion, too, near a tube station entrance. I rarely go out into parks and heathland, now. It is not only embarrassing, but far too dangerous because of the heightened perception of young people addicted to these hallucinatory drugs. I dare not risk exposure!'

If these modern day advanced chelas or disciples are to be believed, the end of our Earth as we know it, followed by the transformation to the Golden Era, will dawn between 1971 and 1975 at latest. I keep trying to shut that sobering possibility out of my mind. I must, for I am an absolute realist, hard-headed and uncompromising, still.

Perhaps none of the personal 'peculiarities' I have listed so far, exhibited for a purpose by my unusual 'visitors,' is anything beyond what many itinerant fakirs or yogis of the East can perform. These minor 'siddhis' or paranormal powers (such as ability to read aura signs, boil water at a touch, walk on fiery coals) are certainly not final proof that demonstrators are excessively wise, holy or advanced.

True mystics, indeed, tend to despise such demonstrations. Wrote the Sufi Saint, Ansari of Herat: 'Can you walk on water? You have

YOUNG DRUG-TAKERS GROPED AND GROVELLED

done no better than a straw. Can you fly in the air? You have done no better than a bluebottle. Conquer your heart—then you may become somebody.'

There is also the story of how the Buddha met an ascetic holy man who had spent twenty years in severe austerities and penances. The Buddha enquired what the yogi had gained by this long period expended in what virtually amounted to acute self-torture, this practising of self-denial.

The yogi replied that he could, as a result, cross the river walking on the water. 'You poor man,' replied the Buddha pityingly. 'The ferryman could have carried you across for a small coin!' These, as was explained to me by Dr. John Cleary-Baker, are interesting demonstrations but nothing more.

They are commonplace minor 'magics' which depend upon an ability—it may be conscious or subconscious—to control certain forces of the Astral Light. I would deny that 'pettifogging psychic tricks' have changed my realistic way of thinking. More profound reasons and considerations lead to my final conclusions, given in the last chapter . . .

UFO PROPHECY

CRADLE HILL

Near Cradle Hill the bucks burn green,
From fronded eyes the silver catkin leaps.
The scattered silence turns
And, in a deeper hush,
Sits on the startled trees
Like frozen nightingales.

The whale of night that sucks the darkness in
Chokes back a jonah cry and flings its stars :
The grass bends back in anguish
From the withered wind
And at its roots the mushroom pales.

O'er Cradle Hill the Moon revolves
And drops its shadow like an oval wing ;
The wise, consuming light
Its white, metallic smile.

What will there be to say, pray,
When the Man in the Moon steps out ?

CHAPTER FIFTEEN

Progression from Elementary Life Patterns

When I told Dr. John Cleary-Baker about the disturbing happening by the copse at Cradle Hill, in July of 1967, where Lydia was apparently 'cornered' and imperilled by a space being, he wondered whether an entity from another sector of the Universe was indeed responsible. After careful thought, he opined:

'It is not too surprising that Cradle Hill has, all of a sudden, developed a rather uncanny "atmosphere." The vibrations of UFOs sometimes "touch off" latent psychic forces in a given locality. This can lead to a temporary "haunting" or outbreak of poltergeist phenomena.

'There was a case of this in South Africa a few years ago. I have myself adverted to the possibility in one of my Editorials in the Journal. Cradle Hill probably has a rather powerful psychic potential. Bob Strong tells me that there was a highwayman hanged in the vicinity at one time.

'It is possible that the name "Cradle" refers to the iron, cagelike framework in which, in the 18th century, the bodies of executed criminals were hung and left as a warning to others. The rather intensive UFO activity in the Cradle Hill area could have awakened the dormant psychic forces of the place.

'For the time being,' he smiled, 'I would advise ladies to go and spend pennies along the hedgerow by the gate and not up in the copse!' (It was this friend from Weeke, near Winchester, who assured me that there is no such thing as the supernatural).

'The human soul, which survives death, is a natural thing and survives in Nature,' John explained. 'Everything which exists is a part of Nature and subject to natural laws. If one looks at things this way, one loses the sort of eerie, superstitious dread which can otherwise take hold of one at certain inexplicable happenings.'

He has been studying UFOs for seventeen years and psychic phenomena since his 'teens; 'and I am still going strong,' he added. In an article in the 'BUFORA Journal and Bulletin,' he pointed out: 'Three basic types of UFO phenomena have been reported from the Warminster area.

'Firstly, we have the occasional appearance of UFOs properly so-called, i.e. discoid and cylindrical objects, sometimes with the accompaniment of the now celebrated "Warminster Sound." I need hardly remind readers that such visitations are not of everyday occurrence, in this or any other locality.

'Secondly, there is the appearance of luminous, pulsating aerial objects (known as "pulsers" to local observers), which are a feature of the Warminster skies although not peculiar to them. Our own observers have reported "pulsers" on several occasions in Warminster Week.

'Thirdly, most common of all, are what may be called "UFO-lights," which may be mistaken for satellites until they stop in mid-career and hover, or alter course in a manner no satellite would or could do. These UFO-lights are probably similar to, or identical with, the "Foo-fighters" of World War Two.

'They and the pulsers may both plausibly be regarded as remote controlled scanning and recording devices of some kind, operated by those who control the UFOs. Scepticizm regarding Arthur Shuttlewood's claim to have witnessed several hundred UFOs, during his night watches, may be abated by the consideration that the majority of his sightings have been of these UFO-lights.

'I should like to go on record as stating that I, too, have seen some of them at Warminster. If Arthur's observations are to be dismissed as the fruit of ineptitude or falsehood, then let me be tarred with the same brush! Cradle Hill is unquestionably favoured with an abnormally high proportion of sightings of pulsers and UFO-lights.

'I am unable to account for this fact—for fact unquestionably it is—except to suggest that the hill is some kind of junction point between our own locale and that of the UFOs. The idea that UFOs are spacecraft operating solely in three dimensions is losing ground to more subtle conceptions.

'Time may play its part in the UFO enigma and almost certainly there is an "other dimensional" element involved in their operation. I will go "out on a limb" yet further and observe that, in my view,

UFO PROPHECY

PROGRESSION FROM ELEMENTARY LIFE PATTERNS

Cradle Hill is a focus of the positive and constructive aspect of UFO phenomena.

'Those who visit the hill are drawn back to it by some indefinable attraction. Cradle Hill is the demarcation line between private land and the wide area of Salisbury Plain appropriated to the use of the Military. Six miles or so from the hill is the deserted village of Imber-in-the-Down, evacuated in December of 1943 and abandoned to the tender mercies of the Army, which to date has declined flatly to return it to civilian control.

'It may well be that Imber will, in future, come to be regarded as a symbol of the war-torn age in which we live. Perhaps its battered dwellings and overgrown gardens will stand as a permanent monument to the folly, futility and ugliness of the agonized era in human relations which now is nearing its end.

'Bacteria at Porton, rockets at Larkhill and ruins at Imber ! If the UFO manifestations at Cradle Hill are indeed constructive and positive, would it not be hard to find an area in Britain more in need of such constructive influences ?

'May this be the clue to the Warminster complex of UFO phenomena ? Let me at least go on record as reaffirming that I do not anticipate an early ending of the UFO " flap " in this area,' adds Dr. Cleary-Baker. I will not comment on what the BUFORA Journal editor says about Warminster Week.

This found a large number of BUFORA members conscientiously engaged in constant day and night sky observation on high points around the town. I think the majority of these laudably curious-minded enthusiasts were satisfied with results, in spite of generally bad weather.

As the organiser-in-chief admitted : 'Certainly the number of sightings of unknown aerial objects was in excess of that which might be expected from an area of the country selected at random.' This unasked for credential backs the persistence of Warminster area UFO appearances, which I stressed at the Northern Conference of BUFORA at Bradford in September of 1966.

While there, I chatted with J. Leslie Otley, editor of *Orbit*, the journal of the Tyneside UFO Society. We agreed that a certain amount of mysticizm, bordering on the esoteric and arcane, exists in evidence so far uncovered.

It was *Orbit* which presented the following story, for example, bearing out the authenticity of the amazing story of the Plowmans

UFO PROPHECY

in my last book, *The Warminster Mystery*, and revelations of my phone calls from a trio of people from the cantel or planet Aenstria.

The story related how the outstanding part of the Space Convention held in October 1965 at Giant Rock Airport, USA, came when ex-Lieutenant Mel Noel addressed the 6,000 people on both days. He stated he was an ex-Air Force pilot, having left under a medical discharge in 1957.

There is a 10-year statute of limitations imposed on Air Force personnel, he explained, which does not permit them to talk publicly on any event involving them while serving. What he disclosed took place in 1954. He confided:

'I had to live with it stuck in my craw for over ten years; and now just have to tell people about it.' Ex-pilot Noel said they were flying North towards Canada over the State of Idaho in a formation of F-86 jet aircraft. This formation was flying at dusk at 38,000 feet altitude.

Suddenly, sixteen disc-shaped objects came from above and flew in a V-formation in front of them. The four F-86 pilots continued their flight, following the sixteen saucers, while they took pictures with their gun cameras as instructed by the Colonel then in command of the squadron.

Pilot Noel reported that the discs, in formation, flew at times from five to six times faster than their F-86 speed, which was 680 knots. The jets increased their speed rate to above Mach 1, the speed of sound, or 750 m.p.h. at sea level.

But the saucers flew circles around them. (We had our Warminster equivalent of this, as per my last book). He felt as though he was flying an old Wright biplane instead of a supersonic jet machine; and this continued for an estimated twelve minutes.

Mel Noel said that the saucers at one period flew close, only 1,000 feet from them, and affirmed they would then speed up, stop, reverse direction and perform manoeuvres impossible to achieve with conventional aircraft. When the conventional pilots landed, all film was removed from their gun cameras and sent to Washington DC.

A week-and-a-half later, while flying in the same area on another assignment, Mel attested that they were again accompanied by the strange saucer aeroforms. Then the Colonel instructed his men to switch to another radio channel. They did so.

Mel Noel says he heard the man in charge of the saucers speaking in slow English to their leader. When they landed after this flight, the

PROGRESSION FROM ELEMENTARY LIFE PATTERNS

pilots were ordered to fill out forms telling exactly what they had seen, yet say nothing of what they had heard over their radios.

Later, revealed the speaker, the Colonel told him of an arrangement made by the people in the UFOs to meet the senior officer in a specified room of a particular motel in Phoenix, Arizona, when he was flying out of Luke Air Force Base.

The Colonel said he was furnished an Air Force staff car by his superiors to drive to the motel. The Colonel went to the motel early. Soon, two men came to his door and he admitted them. They stressed that names were not important. The Colonel could call them Bill and Joe ...

They invited him to go with them, then drove their passenger beyond the outskirts of Phoenix into the desert, where a large saucer was parked. The Colonel said the lights on the car went out as they drove up near the spacecraft, without the light switch being turned off. (Shades of Warminster, here!)

As he and the two men approached the craft on foot, one of the escort handed him a disc and told him to hold it between his two hands. So they went aboard the saucer, where he found there were both males and females aboard the spaceship.

The Colonel was embarrassed when two glamorous women came into the 'room,' because he was doing what he called some 'progressive thinking' about the new arrivals—and soon discovered that they could read his thoughts! The females looked very young and he was startled when the spacecraft commander informed him that one was 78 years old, the other 146.

The commander, whom the Colonel described as of super-intelligence compared to humans, told him that the craft he was aboard was taken into a mothercraft for interplanetary travel. They told him there was once an atomic war between people occupying the Moon and people on Earth at that period.

(This may explain Sodom and Gamorrah of the Bible). The commander emphasised that reincarnation was a scientific fact to them. He said that one only re-embodies on Earth when one has failed to pass certain tests in his or her last lifetime.

The Colonel returned to flying duties with the Air Force a much-changed person, according to the Convention speaker. Ironically, he later vanished in a jet while flying over the Atlantic, and was never found. Mel Noel flatly stated that the Air Force knows where the saucers are from, they know why they are here on Earth, and that he believed the Air Force should reveal the true facts to the public.

The wife of the principal speaker was with him at the Convention. They have four children. Mr. Noel is trying to locate other Air Force pilots who have had similar experiences with flying saucers and who are now outside the 10-year statute of limitations, said the *Orbit* article, the editor crediting this astounding story to George Van Tessel's 'Proceedings,' Yucca Valley, California, USA.

Careful thought and precautionary checking must convince the most realistic person that the substance of this account is true in the main. It also serves to illustrate that craft and crews are used to moving in different dimensions from us. We are assuredly entering the fourth dimension on Earth, evidence is strongly indicating; so must prepare for shattering revelations before the end of 1972.

Now, more than ever, I feel certain that space visitors 'mean business' and can only trust in great faith that ultimate designs are peaceful and not hostile. . . . One possible reason for their 'invasion' of Earth was given to me by Arthur Bryant, who figured in Eileen Buckle's '*Scoriton Mystery*' (Neville Spearman).

Shortly before he died, in the 1967 summer, Arthur wrote: 'Is it not possible that, throughout the teeming billions who inhabit the Universe, the evolution of some has reached the stage where they are unable to remember their simple beginnings any more?

'Is it not possible that, by this inability, they are out-living their usefulness; and yet—somewhere out there—a spark still remains in a body, a ruler, a King (call it what you will) that knows stability and continuing existence can only be ensured by investigation? Do I make myself clear?

'The suggestion I have made in no way implies that they did in fact originate from this planet, but that they obviously realise that—after many visits, investigations, contacts, etc., on Earth—here indeed would be perhaps a more ideal place to begin to take up the simple threads again.

'The history of UFOs, so far as has been explained to me, has never at any time suggested that the occupants are what one would expect—"Supermen." They have been seen taking water from lakes, rivers and the sea, picking lavender in France—simple things that a child would do in some form or another.'

Arthur wondered if they have reached such an advanced stage,

UFO PROPHECY

PROGRESSION FROM ELEMENTARY LIFE PATTERNS

mentally and technologically, that they must start learning all over again or perish because their progress has left them with nothing to do physically, robots carrying out all tasks necessary for living. They have degenerated and need the stimuli Earth surveys give to keep life-saving interest aglow, finding weaker brethren to help.

Arthur wrote in another letter before he died: 'I am sure you are aware, as I am, that the average brain is naturally lazy and tends to take the line of least resistance. The mental world of the ordinary man consists of beliefs which he has accepted without questioning and to which he is firmly attached.

'He is instinctively hostile to anything which would upset the established order of his familiar world. A new idea, inconsistent with some of the beliefs that he holds, means the necessity of rearranging his mind, and this progress unfortunately is too laborious for some.

'I have been made constantly aware that a new approach must be made immediately if we are to receive an inheritance long overdue. I do not in any way suggest that we should disband, or abandon, various organisations that exist throughout our planet; but the true answer is that knowledge—and therefore civilization—are advanced by criticizm and negation as well as by constructive and positive discovery.'

Arthur Bryant claimed to have met three spacemen from an alien airship. My first actual physical contact with a person from another world beyond our own Solar System came under quite mundane circumstances, a mile-and-a-half from Cradle Hill—in fact, on my own doorstep!

There was nothing particularly exotic or glamorous about our encounter, which should have given me a tremendous thrill of pleasure and excitement, considering the many months our team have patiently waited on Cradle Hill for their landing and acknowledgment.

After it happened, however, I can only submit in retrospect that it was such an ordinary event as to be rendered extraordinary by that very factor. This is a paradox, so let me relate, truthfully and without any silly wish for notoriety, how it came about and what transpired. It is a simple story, devoid of frills or fancies.

There is no doubt in my mind, whatever, that my Sunday afternoon caller was not of planet Earth: my only anxiety is over the reality of what he told me in a series of disconnected warnings. Were they to be heeded in absolute seriousness, without question? Or was he deliberately fabricating information intended to lull suspicion and hostility against his people, when they land openly?

Two days after the publication date of *The Warminster Mystery*, released to the public on May 26th of 1967, I was working at home sorting out notes on a news event I had covered at midday. This, by the way, was Whit Sunday, and at dawn our team had come off an all-night skywatch on our celebrated Cradle Hill.

I managed to snatch a few hours sleep before attending the official foundation laying ceremony of a new out-patients' department at Warminster Hospital, conducted by the Marquis of Bath, patron of the appeal fund, the blessing given by the Vicar of Warminster, the Rev. John Freeman.

After lunch I was busy transcribing shorthand notes of Lord Bath's speech, writing the news item for five different newspapers to get it into the post that afternoon. Then, at 3.9 p.m. exactly, the telephone in the hall rang insistently.

A member of my family answered, a few moments later running in to tell me: ' It is one of those people from Aenstria again. He says his name is Karne. He says he must speak to you, as it is very important.'

As outlined in my last book, three persons purporting themselves to be space visitors from a cantel (planet) called Aenstria regularly rang me during a seven-week period in September and October 1965. Traellison was the female queen of the cantel, Caellsan the senior spacecraft commander, Selorik the English interpreter.

I labelled them ' hoaxers ' in my book and was soon to discover that this opinion had aroused their indignation. If their claims to be extra-terrestrial were not genuine, they were Earth people of high intelligence and accurate knowledge. Remember the warnings Traellison gave about dangers of drug-taking and peddling?

On the front page of *The People*, Sunday newspaper published in Britain, the following story appeared on January 14th 1968, headed ' LSD Boys Blinded ':—

' Six young American students at the Western Pennsylvania College have been permanently blinded by staring at the sun while under the influence of the drug LSD, it was revealed yesterday.' The importance of the Sun and damaging effects of LSD have been explained in part already, in this book.

The People newspaper furnishes one concrete example that evokes fresh thought application about the genuineness or otherwise of the

UFO PROPHECY

PROGRESSION FROM ELEMENTARY LIFE PATTERNS

Aenstrian caller. Another is afforded by studies of the effects of this hallucinogenic drug, which mirror a clear link between its use and changes in genes-carrying chromosomes, according to a report from the Medical Society of New York County.

This was released in January 1968 and warned that chromosomal abnormalities were found in some of the offspring of women who took LSD during pregnancy. Chromosomes are the rodlike containers of genes, the determinants of human characteristics.

The Society's sub-committee on drug abuse, who conducted a study on patients treated since the middle of 1965, said: "Thus the spectre of genetically induced damage in the progeny is raised.' The news came via Associated Press, appearing in English news organs on Monday, January 15th 1968.

The appendix in *The Warminster Mystery* gave frightening reminders that wrongful drug-taking and distribution can be prominent social and health hazards. This information came to me more than two years before the press release. Another Aenstrian warning concerned the importance of the protective belt or girdle around the Earth.

It must not be damaged, gouged or warped by insane nuclear experimentation by Man. If this happened, harmful rays from the suns would activate in water supplies and oceans during the planetary orbit and rotation, resulting in gross disfigurement, infant mutation in the womb, even death.

This particular warning reached me in early October 1965. Almost two years later, in June of 1967, American scientists revealed that some measure of concern was felt on discovery that the radiation belt known to us as Van Allen had suffered a minor breach. But, the report concluded complacently, this had been automatically rectified by the healing forces of Nature coming into play.

Might one humbly suggest, on behalf of the Aenstrians, that these powers of natural 'healing' were reinforced and implemented by timely assistance from watchful Outer Space friends, either Aenstrian or from other distant sky regions outside our ken?

They must have moved swiftly to counteract the threatened breakthrough of deadly rays into our immediate atmosphere. Yes—warnings had been proved correct by subsequent events, in several instances, I had noted. That our Sun is not growing colder, as our experts have adverted for years, was something the Aenstrians told me in September 1965.

UFO PROPHECY

And now—the return of the Aenstrians ? ' It is too good to be true,' whirred my mind as I bounded from my chair. Shorthand notes went flying ! I rushed from the room and leapt for the phone. The receiver crackled . . . Then I heard : ' Shuttlewood, this is Karne of Aenstria.

' We are disappointed that you persist in calling us hoaxers in your book, which we have read. You have faithfully reproduced much of that which was told you for the good of your peoples, and should know by this late hour that we speak only truth to you, for their sake and cantel Earth's.

' Another point that causes us dismay in your work is the reference to a telephone call box used by Traellison, Caellsan and Selorik, in Boreham Field. This information could alarm those who have habitations in that locality.

' You should not have revealed this, which is of no consequence and hardly secondary importance : only the many messages we issued to you for publications. As we emphasized, we speak truth : if you ignore this fact in future, it is probable we shall have to sever communication with you.

' When you fail us, in our work and yours as a purveyor of news, we hesistate to tell you more, but the situation is urgent now. You must copy our example and have complete trust in us, as we have had in you, or we shall know our trust was misplaced and we imagized the wrong person.'

His voice was taut, imperious, aggrieved, yet his English faultless. I was still unconvinced, wanting stronger proof. Moreover, I was tired and irritable through lack of sleep. With Bob and Sybil, I shared weariness of libellous comment over the integrity of our team and Warminster witnesses that had gained unmerited headlines in ill-informed magazines published by a certain group of ' armchair ' Ufologists begrudging our experience.

Thankfully, our former thin skins and sensitivity bore the brunt of these successfully. Nowadays, while still welcoming constructive criticizm, we ignore tirades of abuse. People must make up their minds as to whether we relate truth or falsehood. Our consciences are clear.

Leg-pulling we can stand ; mild disbelief is excusable ; but vicious attacks on character are unwarranted and totally unnecessary. Remember, pioneering in an unusual subject is often rebuked through ignorance : Galileo, Marconi, Stanley and Bell are perfect human examples of targets for public derision that misfired in the past. Envy

UFO PROPHECY

PROGRESSION FROM ELEMENTARY LIFE PATTERNS

and jealousy are terrible traits that show deficiency in Man.

Normally I am a calm and 'unflappable' person, tolerant and refusing to give way to outbursts of temperament under pressure. Now, in a nettled and needled state, I hurled bitter words at Karne: 'Look—if you Aenstrians had the guts and courage to come up to my flat in person, there to be interviewed properly, even if you wear horns on your heads I would have had no hesitation in calling you genuine.

'I would have put into my book my certainty that the calls were absolutely one-hundred per cent genuine. Any silly fool can make phone calls and tell a subscriber a lot of nonsense. How could you expect me to call you anything else but cranks and hoaxers? Personal contact is everything to a journalist.'

His cool answer was: 'As we told you many times, Shuttlewood, there are sound reasons why we cannot enter Earth cantel habitations. You must take everything we tell you literally; we know not falsehood and lies in our cantel of Aenstria.'

He continued with homilies of this sort for a while before I interrupted him angrily. Although usually placid by nature, I saw red! 'Excuses—excuses—that is all you people ever give me when I make a reasonable request. The sensible thing to do is come and see me personally, to answer my questions and give me your messages,' I retorted.

'I am a reporter of news, with a reputation at stake. I cannot afford to take anyone's word for anything, over the phone.' With that, I slammed down the receiver. White-faced and inwardly fuming. I settled back to work in the living room.

Within seconds of the call my doorbell rang. I told a member of my family to tell whoever was there that I was extremely busy; then altered this to say I was out and would the caller kindly return at 6 p.m.? The 'white lie' was forced because I was so far behind with my work.

The 'caller' shook his head and smiled gently, when told this. 'No—he is here, I know. He has just spoken with me. Tell him I must see him and that I have special warnings to present to him.' I was staggered when I learned this.

An Aenstrian, real and interplanetary, at my door? Never! It was far too good, too utterly fantastic, to be true...Our nearest public phone kiosk is next to the Town Hall, more than 140 yards from where

UFO PROPHECY

I live. Karne had negotiated that distance in no more than seven seconds flat, from the time I hung up on him.

No ordinary mortal can travel at that phenomenal speed! This thought was flickering through and gnawing at my mind as I ran downstairs, opened wide the door, which stood slightly ajar. What would my caller be like? What had he to tell me?

CHAPTER SIXTEEN

'Earth Time is Desperately Short' *Warning*

I beheld Karne of Aenstria, fully expecting him to be the same person who frequently haunts the pavement opposite my window, looking up incessantly with a sad-sweet smile on his face, as related in *The Warminster Mystery*. No—it was not he. This man was a good two inches above my own height of six feet.

His eyes, although blurred by thick spectacle lenses, impressed me straight away. They held my gaze riveted for several seconds. The glasses had silvery rims and sidepieces to long and slightly outthrust ears. The eyes were bright, a brilliant blue or grey-green, set wide in a long and narrow face.

I noted no trace of pupils at their centre, yet cannot be positive he had none. If he had, they were indiscernible to my penetrating scrutiny. I was on the watch for physical characteristics that vary from ours. Standing on the doorstep, a trifle irresolute, I judged his physical strength less than mine. I was bigger built and more powerful.

For a fleeting fraction of time I was tempted to lunge forward, grasp him tightly, usher him indoors, overpower him and ring the police. This would finally end all doubts as to whether Aenstrians are actual entities and not fakes. His hands, more than his eyes, dissuaded me from such action.

Slender, pointed fingers of his hands were meeting in a repeated movement in front of him as he stood there, immobile. He pressed them together as though making a personal power circle or circuit around him and between us. I find it difficult to convey in words, but as soon as the hostile thought flashed into my mind it froze.

It may sound stupid, yet I sensed that if he released controlled power I could become victim to a nasty accident: perhaps be frazzled to a cinder on the doorstep. There was no alteration in his serious expression, meanwhile. His eyes met mine squarely, frank and fearless, held and locked.

UFO PROPHECY

He glanced for a split second at a wafer-thin disc on his left wrist. I imagined it to be a watch, pale gold in colour. At that instant a warming glow filled me, intense, comforting, so that my frigid attitude thawed. My hand instinctively went out: he had no wish to shake it, so I withdrew, yet was not offended.

By now there was a shy smile lighting his countenance. Dozens of cars were lined-up over the road, carrying sightseers to the Longleat lions of Lord Bath and awaiting clearance of traffic congestion at the junction of Portway, where I live, with the main thoroughfare.

Several people I know walked past Karne on the nearside pavement. Each member of my family, mainly from curiosity, came downstairs and surveyed his tall figure. The only one he touched was four-year-old Daren, his hand flat on the boy's head while he blessed him in an alien tongue. My youngest child gave him a quick, confident smile.

Karne wore an ordinary gaberdine mackintosh coat, beige in colour. His brown boots—I initially thought them shoes until he eventually walked away—were about size ten. A muffler or silk neckerchief was wrapped close to his shirt collar, about which there was nothing distinctive. His thumbs were upbent and formed a triangle over touching finger tips.

Calmed and at ease, I said sincerely: ' So you have come at last? I must say I admire your courage and am glad, after all this time, to meet you.' He made a short bow, oddly polite, and replied simply ' Greetings to you, Shuttlewood. We bring great love and peace with us. You must learn fully to trust us, before it is too late. Your Earth time is desperately short.'

This momentarily worried me and has caused me anxiety since. Did he mean the end of our planet was near, imminent, or merely that the conception of time is different here than on Aenstria, his own native domain? I saved the question, noting other slight peculiarities that would pass unnoticed in a crowd.

His lips were a bluish tinge, rather like those of a patient suffering a weak heart or chronic asthma. On each cheekbone, high up, were similar blue blotches or contusions.

These features I saw subconsciously, concentrating on what he was telling me. When he spoke, or more exactly just before speaking, he drew in a deep breath with a low whistling sound that puckered his lips and mouth. Then, before taking another breath, his words tumbled out in a lengthy flow of sentences.

UFO PROPHECY

'EARTH TIME IS DESPERATELY SHORT' WARNING

Remember what I have written about his upraised thumbs, which is relevant, as explained later. Karne had a high and long forehead, not particularly wide. Two startling tufts of pure white hair were brushed back to either side from the front. At their terminus, they slanted slightly inward, one toward the other. His age I judged to be fifty-three.

Nevertheless, when he turned his head in profile, clearly observed when he prepared to depart, his head was then wide to my vision, the remainder of his hair iron-grey, satin smooth in texture despite the unruly frontal tufts. He assured me he had never seen or met me previously. That he recognized me immediately came from a special 'imagizing' process he later described.

The Aenstrian queen, Traellison, spacecraft commander Caellsan and English interpreter Selorik had returned to their cantel, said Karne. This is because none of his people can survive too much Earth atmospheric pressure and density difference for more than short periods. Two newly-formed 'minor cantels' are fairly close to Earth, he revealed, small space stations artificially formed, possibly by UFO crews of his own race, I gathered.

These will have a specific purpose if sudden emergencies occur on Earth due to the stupidity of Man in nuclear experimentation or warfare. (Author: Recall the false 'pinion' or 'anchor' stars at the base of Jupiter in early months of 1966, already described?)

Karne predicted that trouble would soon erupt in the Middle East. Some would mistake this as a sign of World War 3, which it would not prove to be. (War between Arabs and Jews broke out a few days later, in June 1967). Another prediction, cast-iron, was that there would be aerial manifestations in late October to make disbelievers sit up and take notice. Their significance would be spiritual.

I relayed this information to Anthony Brooke, former rajah muda of Sarawak, to Dr. John Cleary-Baker, Pat and Freddie Harding, Bob and Sybil. The 'flying crosses' witnessed by police and Royal Air Force personnel in the last week of that month, in Wiltshire and neighbouring counties as forecast by my Outer Space informant, were promptly ridiculed by the Ministry of Defence and Air Ministry.

They forget that, although you can fool some of the people some of the time, you cannot fool all of the people all of the time, even from the Ministry or Governmental standpoint!

All indications are that there will be a third World War on the

UFO PROPHECY

WARNINGS FROM FLYING FRIENDS

Earth cantel, said Karne. ' You cannot prevent it and we must not, for that would be contravention of Universal Law which decrees one cannot interfere with freewill and liberty of others in any galaxy.

' Nor may we actively seek to influence the affairs and vibrations of any other cantel,' he continued. ' We are not permitted to subjugate the wills of other brethren to our own, no matter how far they have strayed from the paths of Love, Light and Truth.'

Karne mentioned that the stability of the whole Universe depends upon magnetic balance. Even when what we term a supernova occurs, all people in habitable planets around that dying Sun system are warned well in advance, other homes awaiting them in similar type atmospheres elsewhere in their galaxy.

He wondered whether anyone had yet grasped the importance of the Aenstrian warnings, or reminders, that ' Remember—the light from the other suns affects us all.' He referred to ' another sun ' or ' a second sun,' although not elaborating on this theme. ' Man must learn to use his faculties,' he urged.

He gave the first intimation that the magnetic balance of Earth was disturbed by changes in and around the central gravity ball or inner core. Evidence of this would be seen in earthquakes and meteorological conditions, changing and fluctuating patterns of weather making forecasting more difficult. We were not to worry unduly—the situation was currently being controlled by interplanetary brethren and machines.

If restricted to conventional weapons, the next world conflict would not be impeded or stopped by his people, nor any other extraterrestrials at present standing by, alertly, for necessary saving and salvaging operations in an emergency that will arise after hostilities.

If nuclear weapons are employed, however, Outer Space travellers may adopt courses of action to shock and surprise those using them, Karne warned. Emphasizing that Biblical predictions must come true, the Earth planet has to be in a certain state at that crucial time, which lies within the next few years, he continued. Christ, the Alpha and Omega of our Solar System, will arrive not later than 1975 and possibly before the end of 1972.

Eager to get at truth over Earth time being in desperately short supply, Karne admitting that no Man knoweth the exact day and hour of the Second Coming, I asked him point blank—in view of woeful prophecies of those placing a wholly religious construction upon UFO

'EARTH TIME IS DESPERATELY SHORT' WARNING

appearances—if this meant our Earth would come to a close in a physical sense before Christmas of 1967.

'By the end of the twelfth month of this year, by your Earth time calibration, no,' he assured me. 'But the forthcoming years presage the death of your old civilization and the birth of a new and glorious age. Already many of your people are sensing a change within themselves, by peaceful usurping of their thought and behaviour patterns, by personal vibrations they now experience, have wondered at and are beginning to understand.'

On a personal note, he said I was 'pinpointed' by Aenstrians 'when of tender years in your native place.' (I spent my early life in Essex). He told me there had recently been an implementation of the 'imagizing' process I had then undergone. My image was imprinted by Aenstrian visitors because I had specific tasks in preparation for the dawning of the Golden Age and must be instantly recognizable to them; all Earth contactees have been imagized and photo-recorded on all planets engaged in this vast mission on Earth.

The end would come with great suddenness, he warned. Those who were fully prepared, who believed in UFOs—but, more important, in God and the Second Coming of Christ—would have much work to do in necessary re-construction. The overall impact upon the unready and disbelievers would be cataclyzmic in its physical, emotional and spiritual effects.

The old order would die. The new one taking its place would fit us to become members of the interplanetary brethren and sisterhood. Without a major upheaval the transition would be impossible, but only the Spirit of Universal Truth knew full details of how this will actually be accomplished.

Sons of Light from this and other galaxies are simply carrying out essential preparatory work before the magical moment of illumination when deficient Earth minds and souls will be enriched by new experience and awareness. He said many other things, which I mentally registered in the absence of a notebook, some of which appear towards the close of this earnest work.

I noticed that Karne sometimes had difficulty with his breathing. From time to time, as I shot questions at him during the nine-minute interview, he glanced at the pale gold disc on his wrist. He replied to certain queries immediately, shaking his head in the negative over others, after looking at his 'watch.'

UFO PROPHECY

One concerned the late George Adamski, I recollect. I asked if contacts alleged and related by Adamski were genuine; whether his photographs could be relied upon as authentic? 'We are not permitted to give you that information,' was his response. 'Adamski was not truly of your cantel—for the rest, you must look within for the answer.' (Pondering on this, subsequently, I concluded there was substantial truth in Adamski).

Repeatedly he stressed that Earth time, as we know it, is short: only the transmutation of human weaknesses and a change for the better in the thinking, conduct and moral code of Man could save our planet from darkness and doom in a spiritual sense whereby all souls are retarded instead of being elevated to higher planes and dimensions.

On evidence our visitors have uncovered about us thus far, during millenia of surveys and examinations in depth, this seemed most unlikely; yet they are dedicated to saving those who staunchly tread the right paths. The final decision rests with the Deity who is the Supreme and Divine Majesty of All Creation and Wisdom.

This I found rather conflicting, bearing in mind his earlier remarks regarding the dawning of a New Age; but he reiterated that this will come for those who combat dark forces continually warring against the finer instincts of Man, who—through progression from elementary life patterns—was created in the image of the One and Only.

'Man has the answers to all problems that beset him inside himself, plus the key to correct living and the great importance of love, if only he searches for Truth diligently,' said Karne. 'We speak truth as we know it,' he solemnly told me. 'Final truth, however, must come from His Divine Majesty, from Whom all Love and Wisdom flows in an unceasing stream of Light.'

When Karne prepared to leave, again giving a brief bow at departure, I could not resist an urge to show him a little of the brotherly love he exuded and advocated: a small reciprocal gesture. He would not shake hands, I remembered, so this was my way of bidding farewell in friendly fashion. I stepped forward and firmly grasped his left wrist and thumb.

Karne winced! I wondered why, assuming he disliked personal contact. My mind was busy with another visual mystery by then, however... On gripping his wrist and thumb, I looked at the pale gold disc. It was not a timepiece; simply a crystal and mother-of-pearl surface which glistened in colourful sheen and made no ticking sound.

UFO PROPHECY

'EARTH TIME IS DESPERATELY SHORT' WARNING

Karne used it frequently, as though seeking guidance about how much or how little he should expound on any subject thrown up by my eager questioning. Karne promised that I would meet other space travellers in the future, providing I did not continue terming them hoaxers.

In response to one question, he told me that if ever I met him again in coming years 'It will not be in this present form.' Which set me wondering anew . . . Had he, then, changed his form already in order to contact and visit me? Or was I to infer, in the wider sense, that we shall both be in a different mould or dimension of physical and spiritual structure when we renew acquaintance?

Before he waved farewell, to walk up Portway and towards the Cradle Hill direction, he turned stiffly as a soldier might under a 'right turn' command. Then it was that his left hand lifted in indication of *au revoir*. As he walked, I observed that his hands, fingers and thumbs remained in the same position by his sides as when he was completing the finger tip-pressing motion. The thumbs stuck outward, upraised, fingers together and curled inward.

From the waist up his bearing was smart, military, almost arrogantly proud. From the waist down, however, his movements were slow and deliberate. His legs seemed weighted, feet slightly dragging; yet to a casual onlooker he would have been dismissed as an old gardener type or old-fashioned and hard-worked farm labourer.

The greatest revelation of all was still to come . . . Next day, Whit-Monday afternoon, my 16-year-old son Graham was near the lake and pleasure grounds in Weymouth Street, Warminster. Jet aircraft were screaming overhead when Graham espied the 'stranger' standing on his own at the top end of the park.

He stood looking upward, shaking his head sadly from side to side. Not much is unusual about this behaviour, perhaps, in itself, but consider the following: ' I am sure it was him, Dad,' said Graham, rising excitement in his tones.

' Had he hurt his hand when he was here yesterday afternoon? ' I thought it an odd question from my son, assuring him that there were no marks of injury on Karne's limbs, so far as I knew. Then came the bombshell! 'That's funny, then, because he must have hurt himself somehow,' said Graham. 'He had a protective pink stall on his left thumb and a strip of bandaging up and around his left wrist.'

Why? I have often cogitated on this aspect. Obviously, when I grabbed him there at our parting the previous day, I must have injured his flesh. He could not stand the undue manual pressure I exerted, in addition to coping with our atmosphere, which is not the same as that of Aenstria, as he had pointed out.

But for an extraterrestrial to have complained of pain, in presence of an Earth mortal, would have been a sign of weakness . . . I then felt extremely sorry for this ordinary yet extraordinary being, who refused to enter my portals and courteously declined to shake hands.

You may think this a fantastic story within the framework of my broader story, more incredible and astounding than any fiction. I can but assure you that it is, as Karne would assert, strictly TRUE; and add that only the fantastic is feasible and plausible at the cosmic level of evolution to which these people have aspired.

Karne said I could publicly reveal his message in my next book, which I now do. No—I have no doubts about meeting extraterrestrial journeyers. I repeat: all that worries me is: Are they one hundred per cent truthful in what they say? Or are they deliberately 'pulling the wool' over our eyes and reasoning for an ulterior purpose? That most precious of commodities in life, Time, alone can prove.

Although I did not take verbatim notes during our interview, I can rely on memory pretty well to recapture certain things Karne talked of in those nine minutes. 'We have known your peoples from the long ago. Sadly, they have forgotten us,' was an intimation from Karne that we on Earth were on more than mere nodding terms with interstellar brethren in the dim, distant past, their presence illuminating the long dark corridors of our history until we switched out the light . . .

Einstein is naturally revered by most scientists on Earth. The controversial Relativity Theory is one which recognizes the impossibility of determining absolute motion, yet implies nothing travels faster than light. It therefore has the concept of a four dimensional space-time continuum. But the theory is, alas, false by the very fact that the great man of science on our planet limits dimensions to the small number of four.

If four, argue our friends from Outer Regions, then why not fourteen, twenty or even more dimensions? In the vast ocean of the Universe are manifold waves of discovery. Einstein could not prove otherwise, so consequently his theory is based on a wrong premise.

There is really no question of craft from other planets having to navigate tremendous distances in space, going from one planet to

'EARTH TIME IS DESPERATELY SHORT' WARNING

another; distances which we on Earth suppose to exist, distances we cannot comprehend, and at which our minds boggle when so little as a million light years is mentioned.

This question is one we posit because we have got time and space relationships all wrong, falsely calculated. When our physicists and astronomers attempt to measure the distance between Earth and Mars, for instance, they are doing so with intelligences that are as limited as the limitations of their physical frames.

I am not being disrespectful to them. When, and if, we can sensibly spread our vision outside all the limitations that our Earth mentalities impose upon us, we shall realise that seemingly enormous distances between the planets are an illusion and myth.

Indeed, if this were not so it would take space crews from—say—Venus a long while to travel in their chariots from that planet to ours, despite the speed of the shining spheres, and back again to Venus. Yet we are to understand that they do this not once but many times. Relativity itself, as expressed by Einstein in Earth concepts, is purely relative (forgive the pun) to a purely Earthbound, backward and materialistic notion of our place and stature in the immensity of the total Universe.

The idea that scientific concepts as we understand them today have a Universal application, literally, could only emanate from Earthly training and tradition. Our people of the present time are limited by sheer materializm in its most obvious aspects.

Interplanetary brethren have so far transcended such concepts, both in thought and action (e.g., space people who materialize as though from nowhere, together with their machines) that arbitrary and axiomatic postulates such as relativity and the Quantum Theory would never be taught in an advanced extraterrestrial kindergarten. We are not being mercilessly unkind, deliberately, to Earth science, in averring this.

The Quantum Theory supposes that radiation is emitted through space, not continuously but in separate proportions. Heaven knows what is meant by 'not continuously,' in view of the fact that all space is permeated with continuous radiations of one kind or another. These are emitted not only by the Sun of our own particular Cosmos and all planets in it, but by all known and unknown millions of stars and planets in the whole Universe.

'Remember—the light from the suns shines upon us all . . .' Radiations, vibratory powers and the influence of colour patterns,

UFO PROPHECY

are so scantily understood by Earth science that it is apparent more evolved aerial travellers—even if they ever entertained either of these two theories seriously—must surely have rejected it thousands of years ago as negative.

Only the positive factor counts with them. A space person would tell you that 'intellectual sympathy' is a meaningful expression. It is the medium of self transportation into the interior of a moving body or vehicle. It is synonymous with a form of mental or astral body projection whereby physical and material considerations are secondary.

Certain Earth people can achieve this incredible feat, so it would be stupid to presume that enlightened interplanetary voyagers, at so much higher a state of evolution, could not quite easily perform this. In effect, an 'other world' denizen can ostensibly 'vanish' 100 yards or more from a hovering spacecraft, after conversing with Man on Earth, then actually materialize inside a moving space vehicle.

It takes such an exceptional degree of evolution to do this that I would normally hesitate to write down such a revelation—to us, not them! Think back on the story of the old woodcutter near Frome and the two vanishing figures—there is visual proof.

Rapidly, we must learn the very opposite of the materialist thesis of jungle-Darwinizm which, however one appraises it, is a naked tooth and claw attitude that may sound plausible to the shallow thinker; but which obviously casts out no line of hope for the future development of Man as a being able to rise to his true spiritual stature in the sense of an ability to take a creative, positive and ennobled stand towards his fellows—and the titanic problems of the Earth as a whole in its current stage of evolution.

To their immense credit, a number of present day scientists are conscious of the fact that there is 'something wrong' and awfully awry with conventionally held ideas of evolution; yet they are unable to put their fingers on the error. One thing is worth emphasizing:

Real evolution is more in the nature of a never-ending spiritual quest in which the more advanced portion of the human race achieves a higher sense of responsibility, creative initiative, love of the Creator, love for the beauty of his world, resolution, justice and other qualities that have little to do with mere 'Churchianity.'

Descriptions of the last stages of evolution on Earth given by the great seers and prophets, of the future held out for Earth humans, or those among them who deserve such a future and strive for it, bear

'EARTH TIME IS DESPERATELY SHORT' WARNING

a very striking resemblance to the vastly superior civilizations of the more advanced and 'friendly' space people.

Upon reading these prophecies in an intelligent and imaginative way, one finds the resemblance so striking that the space people of friendly intent are practically a confirmation of those prophecies. They are also a refutation of the inordinately blind and muddled attitudes of the so-called 'thinkers' of the present age who understand nothing but brute force, however much they declare the contrary, and mere 'cleverness,' whereas the space people and evolved—not simply 'educated'—Earth people represent wisdom, which is a very different quality indeed.

It is worth underlining that the true concept of evolution as exemplified by the super-advanced spacemen does not come entirely 'out of the blue,' so to speak, in the sense of being total, sudden and unexpected; but that the seeds of future evolution, mental and spiritual greatness to be developed in the human race, exist already in the teaching and traditions of schools of wisdom open to all who genuinely seek truth.

'Look deep within yourself and the prayed-for inspiration of Light, Wisdom and Truth will be perpetually with you in your journeying through life,' Karne quietly assured me. 'It was always so, and always will be so. Time changes but truth does not.'

UFO PROPHECY

REFLECTIONS

How many know, oh ! morning star,
Of the secrets you hide out there ?
How many know, oh ! radiant star,
Of your people both wise and fair ?

Though you may seem so far and dead,
With a ghostly mantle round you ;
Upon your mountains angels tread
And drape a rainbow around you . . .

How many care, oh ! morning star,
For your valleys of hidden truth ?
How many crave for a joy-jammed jar
That is full of eternal youth ?

How many thrill, oh ! evening star,
To the dawn when true light will break ?
Can we be sure, oh ! evening star
That we shall all finally wake ?

Must we just dream, oh ! evening star,
How long you have been out there ?
What is your theme, oh ! evening star,
For us who, unknowingly, care ?

Sad ! Too few think of things outside
That influence our Earthly life :
Too many minds thoughts of love hide
Instead of suspicion and strife . . .

Travelling left and upwards. Trio of celestial chariots over Cradle Hill, taken by Bob Strong. Note surrounding force fields.

Between Chitterne and Tilshead, near Warminster, 2.45 p.m. Taken January 23rd, 1967. Original in colour. Photo by Bob Strong.

UFO PROPHECY

Above: September 3, 1967, Cradle Hill, Warminster. Typical egg-shape of "flying eye." Photo by Bob Strong.

Below: UFO over Cradle Hill, August 1967. Picture by Birmingham Contact U.K. group member Roger Blackwell.

CHAPTER SEVENTEEN

A Reprimand for Inadequate Understanding

Farming brothers Thomas and Stanley Crook, of Grately, near Andover, saw four mysterious flying objects on the morning of February 25th 1967. The hour was 6 a.m. and the brothers were out on farmland rounding up the cows for milking. Then:

A quartet of aerial objects, which they described as being 'the size of milk churn lids,' flew out of the clouds in an unusual formation. The objects were 'all lit up with a very bright light,' which went out as they turned in the sky before 'flashing on again, the objects reforming before flying away.'

The brothers were at opposite ends of the field when they espied the UFOs and compared notes on what they had seen when rejoining each other. The story merited headlines in the *Southern Evening Echo*, a fearless Southampton news organ.

Mystery in the sky... Somerset police received reports on March 30th 1967 about a strange object seen early in the day scorching the heavens. It was termed by one witness 'a very bright light with a long black shape suspended from it,' according to the Bristol *Evening Post*, another frank newspaper where UFO reportings is concerned.

It was noted flying ahead of her by a woman motorist as she neared the junction of the A38 road at East Brent from the Weston-super-Mare direction. Police who were contacted said they had had similar reports from as far away as Ilminster. Somerset and Hampshire are neighbouring counties to Wiltshire.

A farmer in the Brendon Hill district at the Western end of Somerset also reported seeing the mystery object. All these sightings were between 6.50 and 7.10 a.m. and 'the mystery fireball still remains a mystery,' related the Bristol newspaper.

A Nottingham friend and fellow Ufologist, Alex Kenyon, sent me this extract from the *Newark Advertiser* dated February 25th 1967: 'Whatever it was she saw in the sky on Sunday morning made a

UFO PROPHECY

Halloughton woman's 999 call cause a chase across Nottinghamshire roads by fire engines, police and a rescue tender, joined later by a spotter plane from nearby Hucknall airfield, but a search revealed nothing.

'Mrs. E. K. Green was looking out of the window of her South Rising home at about 10 a.m. when she saw a ball of fire in the sky. she said: "While I was watching, it seemed to change shape, like a glider, then crash into the ground and vanish. I did not hear any sound nor see any smoke."'

Two years ago, the news item continued, Mr. W. Phillips of Southwell, Notts., reported a kitelike object near Halloughton. Alex Kenyon added in a letter to me: 'Note—in 1965 three jets crashed onto nearby Calverton. I saw it happen.'

Another recent case of 'changing form . . .' Here is a brief news flash in the *Western Gazette*, published in Yeovil, Somerset, dated February 9th 1968 and headed 'Another Object From Outer Space?' The town of Frome is mentioned in the story—it is quite near the village where the old woodcutter was baffled by a spacecraft vanishing in yellow smoke, related in an earlier chapter.

'Mr. Terrence King accepted a lift at Frome in the early hours of Wednesday, while travelling from his home in Norwich to the West Country; and had been journeying in the lorry on the A361 road for "no more than twenty minutes" when he saw "a large object travelling a few feet above the ground."

'Said Mr. King: "At first I thought it was the moon. Then it came down nearly to ground level and its light clearly lit up the fields below it." He described the object as "huge and egg-shaped" and added: "As it got nearer to the ground, something seemed to come out of the top, until it was triangular.

"The driver thought it was a sputnik. We were both white and shaken up. It travelled along in clear view for more than a quarter-of-an-hour before disappearing." Frome police said later on Wednesday that they had heard nothing about unidentified flying objects, but Mr. Arthur Shuttlewood, head of the spotting team at nearby Warminster, said:

"Things were seen in Warminster on Tuesday night, so the report could be valid." He added: "The material I have been gathering over the past two years shows that the report is quite feasible."' On the night before the hitch-hiker's experience in company with the lorry

UFO PROPHECY

A REPRIMAND FOR INADEQUATE UNDERSTANDING

driver, our team saw a UFO altering shape from oval to triangular and back.

Hospital chef Rodney Mullins and a friend saw an identical craft at about 8.50 p.m., shortly before our sighting. Duality of form, therefore, applies to spaceships as well as occupants, one can deduce, whereas we formerly concluded that a fluctuating force field around craft merely gave that impression.

The triangle is frequently referred to in UFO reports and bears out the authenticity of our photography. It could be representative of the Great Pyramid, of an important land area locally, of the man-made colossus at Silbury in Wiltshire, or the supreme importance of the Holy Trinity at the present auspicious and revelationary period in the history of Man.

Apart from our own sighting tallies from Cradle Hill, I have received over 1,000 reports of UFO activity from enthusiasts in all parts of Britain in the past twenty months alone. Either the Air Ministry does not appreciate the extent of the phenomena, does not assiduously peruse all newspaper accounts of UFO sightings publicized, or rarely hears of things seen by hundreds of witnesses whose testimony is often valid.

As a team, our trio of investigators wonder whether our Government knows the truth about spacecraft, crews and their eventual designs : or is far more ignorant than we are . . . By helping us in practical fashion, they would have lost nothing and probably gained much, since the issuing of our earnest invitation to Denis Healey two years ago. We would not want their co-operation, now ; we may be verging on the curtain-falling stage of the final act in the greatest drama in history !

There was minor consternation a few years ago when the enigmatic Stone of Scone was taken, for a practical joke, from Westminster Abbey in London. The majority of people, on learning news of the stone vanishing, treated the whole escapade with an amused tolerance and detachment, quite unperturbed. A few throughout the world, possessed of certain knowledge as to its real history, were anxious over its disappearance.

The stone is featured in documented accounts of prophecies relating to the British nation ' from the Isles in the North-West.' This is where the prophet Jeremiah fled with the daughter of King Zedekiah ; and her lineal descendant sits on the British throne today and is crowned

UFO PROPHECY

with due ceremony on the Stone of Destiny at Westminster.

The ancient stone was brought there from Scotland, which is fairly common knowledge. However, it was actually conveyed there from Ireland, after Jeremiah transported the sacred relic from Jerusalem. This had been the original Pillow of Jacob or Pillar of the Covenant that the Supreme Deity made with Jacob when He changed his name to Israel: meaning 'Ruling with God.'

The several Lost Tribes of Israel were a maritime people who arrived in Britain after fleeing into the wilderness. They were wanderers who colonized and Christianized the whole world, as we have done in Britain—even to losing our first colony, the United States of America. It is fairly certain that the Virgin Mary was also of British stock.

She was kin to the Royal House of Britain and Caractacus, who made such a magnificent stand against the Romans in the first century AD, was related to her. One wonders whether perhaps she came from Wiltshire; even from the little town of Warminster? This part of Britain is the cradle of civilization.

It was her kin, Joseph of Arimathea, who brought Christ as a young man with him to Britain when he visited his tin mines in Cornwall and the Mendip Hills. Which is why, after the Crucifixion, Joseph returned with the three Marys, on his person one version of the fabulous Holy Grail.

The little phials of blood and tears, which he also carried, are still reputedly buried near Glastonbury. Here Joseph founded the first tiny wattle church on Tor Hill and in the grounds of the Abbey (built much later) grows the thorn tree planted from his stick, which always flowers on Christmas Day as celebrated in Britain.

Did you know, incidentally, that this is a misnomer? Shakespeare once used the term 'The Ides of March' in a play. He hit a Holy 'nail' on the head, according to my informants, even if inadvertently. Christ was actually born on March 15th, not December 25th, as an infant of Earth.

The small wooden cup or bowl, rather, comprising the original wine vessel at the Last Supper, is preserved most zealously in a country house called Nant Eos, not far from Aberystwyth in Cardiganshire, Wales. The same Powell family have held it in trust since the last of the seven monks (who brought it with them from Strata Florida Monastery, before it was destroyed by order of Henry VIII) died.

Mary Stuart-Reid, widow of a doctor, a visitor to Cradle Hill who

UFO PROPHECY

A REPRIMAND FOR INADEQUATE UNDERSTANDING

has seen our UFOs in action against the velvet cloak of the night sky, told me she has seen this precious wooden cup many times. Before that it was kept at Whitland Abbey, also destroyed, and came there from Glastonbury across the Severn Estuary, possibly when Glastonbury Abbey was razed and the monks fled first over the sea to Whitland, near Carmarthen.

It was subsequently thought safer to take it to mid-Wales, to Strata Florida, near Tregaron Marsh. There are medieval tiles in the cloisters there which depict a knight in armour holding a cup, a design Mrs. Stuart-Reid has never seen elsewhere.

The Welsh folk are extremely proud that the 'healing cup' is in their custody. But they will rarely speak of it; it is a taboo subject. The legend goes that, while it is in that country, all Welsh people will be protected; but if it should be lost, or taken away by 'evil men for gain,' disaster will surely fall.

The richly decorated silver chalice, made in Antioch to hold this tiny wooden cup with the replicas of the Apostles around it, is the Grail, still lost to human eyes somewhere in a cleft of the rocks. It may be North of Glastonbury or secreted somewhere in the Mendips, even at Cheddar Gorge.

'Birds have built their nests around it, but the eye of Man has not beheld it for hundreds of years.' It will be rediscovered when the time is right and minds of Men are ripened into maturity, its profound meaning understood, we learn.

Anthony Brooke, former Rajah Muda of Sarawak, whose views in part were given in *The Warminster Mystery*, is right when he asserts that events are taking place in all sectors of Earth which are of a remarkable nature. They test our faith and the tendency, however understandable it may be, to depend overmuch on the evidence of our five physical senses ' as if they were the yardstick for what alone may be regarded as true and real.

' In spite of the great knowledge modern science has brought us, we are surely glimpsing life imperfectly and incompletely so long as we remain slaves to what is called the scientific method, and to this alone. There are times when we need to place a greater trust in our own direct intuitive perceptions, especially when we are dealing with matters which escape the measurements of science as we know it today.'

Although this modern visionary was wrong in his calculation that

UFO PROPHECY

Christmas Day of 1967 would bring—in its entirety—the revelation of the Second Coming, this is a case where Man should not judge harshly, lest he be judged himself in the final reckoning.

Anthony Brooke miscalculated, yet there were sound reasons why what he had confidently been led to regard as the Big Day did not break at that particular period. Man was not mature enough at that time to accept the deep implications involved. More of this anon, for it is important.

What Brooke says makes sense set against the background of current world affairs: 'From now onwards we shall witness and participate in the most tremendous events of all human history. Although we must continue to live our lives in the light of our own individual understanding, I do believe that in the near future we shall find ourselves freely abandoning the trivialities and unessentials of our living to prepare and fortify ourselves, mentally and spiritually, for great Cosmic experiences which may come to us individually and collectively at any time.

'We are moving into a wondrous age and many of us will experience travel at the speed of thought... The Cosmic operation now upon us, in which all are called to take part, heralds unprecedented breakthroughs in understanding which are to lead us through the morass and darkness of our present time into the emergence of an overall heightened spiritual awareness.

'In this expanded consciousness, offered to all, we shall become cognisant of our Universal link in love with the entirety of the living creation of God throughout all the Universes. If this may seem a mind-crushing vision, let us remain in no illusion about the Cosmic character of events which lie at hand.

'The choice indeed lies between the shattering of outdated mental concepts—which have lost their meaning in the conditions of our present hour—and their transformation and expansion so as to enable our minds more truly to attune to pre-existing yet newly emerging truths.' Anthony Brooke believes that, in light of this heightening consciousness, which coming events are dramatically to intensify among the human race:

'We shall find ourselves becoming free from selfish and self-defensive attitudes that for ages past have been binding us in chains and blocking our forward path to unity. We are on the threshold of being moved swiftly and unfailingly into attitudes and qualities of living more truly

UFO PROPHECY

A REPRIMAND FOR INADEQUATE UNDERSTANDING

consistent with the fact that, under one Divine Creator, we are verily members of a single Brotherhood of Man—and of one essentially indivisible human race.

'No longer, through unconscious automatic living, can we continue our lives on Earth, nor even by more conscious and well intentioned (yet perhaps uninspired) activity on the part of so many of us who feel the need to translate into action our deeply felt concern for all that seems wrong in our human condition.

'Only by the wholehearted and unceasing offering of our hearts, our minds and our very souls to that point of Light which lies deep in the recesses of each one of us, shall we find the illumination to know beyond all doubt the part we are to play in the fulfilment of the true destiny of our race.' A destiny, he adds, giving 'a newness and a glory beyond the power of present language to describe.'

Forecasting that before long we shall find ourselves accepting Man as a Universal creature, existing throughout the galaxies of space, he points out: 'There should be little difficulty in accepting the idea that mind-to-mind contact between extraterrestrial entities and men of Earth is probable, now that we are widely beginning to accept the principle of telepathic exchange.

'If spacecraft from other planets are flying around inside our atmosphere, and I believe that they are, this would imply that the intelligences directing them have attained scientific and technological heights beyond our own. It is therefore unlikely that they would be less expert in the practice of telepathic communication, in relation to sensitives on our own planet, than are the Earth individuals in relation to one another.'

Flying saucers are an important link between the spiritual and material worlds and will prove to be a significant means of helping Man towards an understanding of the spiritual and universal oneness of all creation. It is of interest to recall what Lenin said to H. G. Wells, eminent historian, novelist and writer of science fiction, when the two men met in 1920 :—

'All human conceptions are on the scale of our planet. They are based on the pretension that the technical potential, although it will develop, will never exceed the terrestrial limit. If we succeed in establishing interplanetary communications, all our philosophical, moral and social views will have to be revised. In this case the technical potential, become limitless, would impose the end of the rule of violence as a means and method of progress.'

Coming from a man whom many in the West consider an extremist, a leading disciple and pioneer of Communist doctrine, those remarks of 48 years ago show shrewd sagacity and foresight only matched by the amazing predictions as to the future from the man to whom he was speaking!

Very much in line with information I have received from Cosmic entities are the views of the late Wilber B. Smith of Canada. He was a top-ranking scientist in the service of the Canadian Government. In addition, he was a sincere searcher for truth in connection with UFO machines and crews. Over ten years ago, on March 31st 1958, he told the Ottowa Flying Saucer Club:

'Our civilization here on Earth now is only one of many that have come and gone. This planet has been colonized many times by people from elsewhere, and our present human race are blood-brothers of these people. Is it any wonder that they are interested in us?

'To orthodox thinkers this may seem strange, but not nearly so strange as our orthodox ideas on evolution. The question might be asked: If these people are our brothers, and are interested in our welfare, why do they remain so aloof? The answer is available.

'There is a basic law of the Universe which grants each and every individual independence and freedom of choice, so that he may experience and learn from his experiences. No one has the right to interfere in the affairs of others—in fact, our ten commandments are directives against interference.

'If we disregard this law we must suffer the consequences, and a little thought will show that our present world state is directly attributable to violation of this principle. When we enter this life, we do so to participate in certain events, the sequence of which was established before our birth, and which if altered substantially would deprive us of experiences necessary to our development.

'We have built-in protection against altering substantially the sequence, in that we do not consciously know of them. But these people from outside have a much greater knowledge than we have, and have means of perceiving sequences which must not be changed.

'Therefore, while they have every desire in the world to help, and stand by ready, able and willing to do so, they are not permitted by Cosmic law to interfere. The dividing line between help and inter-as they do, and how it is that they can do things which to us are virtually impossible.

'The science and the performance check perfectly. Again, we have been told where our scientific ideas are wrong or inadequate and experiments have been suggested and carried out; and in every case the alien science has been vindicated.

'We may ask, if all this is known, why has it not been publicized? Why are not these matters being studied instead of atom bombs? The answer: It has been publicized. Books have been written and hundreds and thousands of copies sold.

'There are available many periodicals containing this material, which may be had for quite a nominal sum. Reports have been prepared by serious investigators and presented through the proper channels, but it is truly said that one can lead a horse to water, but one cannot make him drink!' (Author: How true!)

On both sides of the Atlantic, the first minute of the first hour of Christmas Day 1967 was foretold by Interplanetary Masters to be of momentous importance to our planet. This resulted in much mental and spiritual confusion in some minds when nothing visible or concrete happened.

The rumour had spread far and wide that the Second Coming was imminent on that day. That I did not fall into the deliberate 'trap' for the unwary was thanks to Karne, my Aenstrian caller, who forecast firmly that our planet would suffer no physical collapse at that time.

I felt desperately sorry, nevertheless, for Anthony Brooke and the Universal Link predictions, confidently given, which failed to materialize. In objective fairness, however, it must be pointed out that they were misled for a valid reason.

It was intended for them to propagate the 'rumours' referred to in the New Testament and unwittingly give the impression of 'false' Christs appearing before the true One, again according to Holy Writ. Each 'messenger' was in fact playing a predestined part in the Final Stages of a Divine Plan.

According to the level of evolution of the individual, assumptions of the import of Christmas Day 1967 were formulated. Two days prior to this date a Dutch contactee was afforded a further translation, as were other contactees, refuting destruction: but in his case the parable of the five wise and five foolish virgins was brought to the

UFO PROPHECY

A REPRIMAND FOR INADEQUATE UNDERSTANDING

attention, together with a reprimand at the inadequate understanding of the Christian Bible by Man.

Not one person with eyes to see and ears to hear can possibly eschew the prophecies of the Way shower Christ, within Matthew chapters 24 and 25. That there is but a short period of time left to Man to grasp every opportunity to evolve to the desired destination was again brought home to thinking Man with the reference to the thoughtless bridesmaids.

'Then the Kingdom of Heaven may be likened to ten bridesmaids who, having received their lamps, went out to meet the Bridegroom. And five of them were wise and five were foolish. Those who were foolish taking their lamps, took no oil with them; but the prudent ones took oil in their flasks, along with their lamps.' It is within the next paragraph that the secret of Christmas Day 1967 lies:

'While however the Bridegroom delayed, they all slumbered and slept.' Some of the assumptions expressed, as we have seen, were that the Messiah would return to Earth on that day. Yet the prophecies given to the Twelve tell us differently. The Bridegroom is now indeed 'delaying.'

An enlightened friend whom I shall call Thomas the Doubter (each time he looks at his hands he grimaces, claiming to be the present incarnation of one of the Twelve, known also as Didymus) told me: 'There are those who have passed sufficient tests in the transmutation of faults, the acceptance of every opportunity to assist others that the Masters who guide humanity unseen and unheard lay at our feet, to have stored up a considerable amount of oil in their flasks, thus entitling them to the final terrestrial reward of freedom from the wheel of rebirth.

'But,' he warned, 'there are those with the necessary potential who have not reached this stage. It is the foolish bridesmaids who have missed their opportunities, who have involved instead of evolved by kicking against the pricks of their own karma, who failed to accept gracefully all that came their way as their due, to whom the Masters are giving a further chance.

'Only by wise reflection and total honesty can we hope to learn what group we belong to—and when we have decided, we must act immediately!' he added. (Thomas came to Warminster on the morning of August 27th 1967, to carry out Holy 'recharging' or 'energizing' of specifically defined areas of prehistoric terrain, hills, ancient stones, tumuli, etc., within a twenty-five miles radius of Warminster. More appears about him, and other ' unusual ' Warminster visitors—some staying for long periods—later).

UFO PROPHECY

CHAPTER EIGHTEEN

Anatomy of a Holocaust—and 'Dying Fish'

During the first month of 1968 I was warned that 'the fish are dying.' Also that the date May 16th would be important in ways that ordinary people would not readily appreciate or recognize. My informant, Mark, rang me from London to convey this information, then asked me to use my own faculties to construe what was meant.

I translated the 'dying fish' as indicating that the Old or Piscean Age was entering its death throes and that the New or Aquarian Age was shortly to dawn, the precise transition point reached on May 16th. I was, moreover, urged to mark well the present climate and near future changes concurrent with magnetic field alterations of Earth, fierce forces emanating from the core of the planet heralding fresh earthquake or volcanic outbreaks.

The human conception of time itself is being transmuted in some subtle way, I was told. More and more people would become conscious of this, in varying degrees, with the impact of new and strange vibrations, as the months passed. In brief, one could liken this to a 'regulation' of the internal clock mechanizm built into each individual.

Its deeper or broader implications are that we are gradually shedding outworn skin and taking on new. Slowly but surely leaving behind the third dimension of life and being overhauled by the fourth, more prominent in some than in others, in effect. For some reason, this recalled a peculiar piece of literature I received a few months ago, entitled, 'Anatomy of a Holocaust,' in two parts.

The reader may well ask where this knowledge, true or false, springs from: but if it encourages healthy thought and controversy, it will serve a purpose. My last chapter shows my feelings about such warnings, in any event. Without intervening comment from me, here is Part One :—

'This is the story of Maldek, the number three planet in our Solar System sixty million years ago, through their doomsday down to ours

UFO PROPHECY

on the planet Earth, soon in the future. This explains the life of our Solar System and its effect upon planet Earth, then and now. D-Day minus five years : The Communists of the East part of the planet Maldek and the Faithists on the West side agree to dismantle all their multimegaton nuclear devices.

'Great spiritual awakening now engulfed the planet. The changes in the Communist nations manifest themselves, causing basic changes in nature of the civilization both of the Communist and Faithist countries. World-wide realisation of the perils of misuse of nuclear power demanded changes, resulting in the disarmament agreement.

'D-Day minus four years : The Communist system collapses under onslaught of a spiritually awakened populace. Democracy becomes a reality and individual freedom becomes the order of the day. The Faithists send advisers to the Communist countries and they are accepted with enthusiasm. Some reminders of Communism still remained there, but gradually these will disappear.

'D-Day minus three years : The whole world of Maldek is now united and a great celebration is planned. A week-long celebration becomes a reality. The whole planet celebrates and much happiness and joy exists. Traces of Communistic suspicion are gradually found to be disappearing.

'D-Day minus two years : This world is enjoying a period of prosperity unparalleled in its entire history. They receive their first contact with extraterrestrial people. Progress in this direction was slow at first because the people were reluctant to trust Wisdom of the Divine Creator and seek His advice.

'D-Day minus eighteen months : Minds of the people were turned away from nuclear testing and the undismantled nuclear weapons had been completely forgotten in a new wave of prosperity and abundance. Fake weapons of nuclear noise and fire, also smoke of the real ones, were now being developed for the forthcoming world celebration to mark the signing of the disarmament pact and the uniting of the people of the world.

'D-Day minus one year : Celebration plans proceeding as agreed upon. Fake nuclear weapons are fired halfway round the world to a designated target area, where the people are gathering to witness all the fire and noise of an avoided nuclear war.

'The people are delighted with the spectacle and planned more and greater displays. Prosperity continues : their contact with other

ANATOMY OF A HOLOCAUST—AND 'DYING FISH'

worlds was now firmly established and the first " trade " agreements between the worlds were discussed and projected.

' D-Day minus six months : Scientists mix-up in warheads occurs in the Communist country. This was unknown to the handlers of rockets and warheads, so fake heads accidentally stored with the real ones. Both were unmarked, so from outside casual appearance no difference was indicated to the workmen.

' The dismantling of live nuclear warheads was being now performed in the same area and under the same roof as the production of the fake warheads to be used in their celebrations. The shell casings of true warheads being dismantled were re-used for the fake warheads. Soon, loaded warheads were accidentally slipped through and placed with the fake ones.

' When sufficient rockets and warheads were constructed to produce a small and spectacular simulated nuclear attack, the production was halted and the mistake went unnoticed. Preparations were under way and being formulated to make this forthcoming celebration the biggest ever, for nuclear disarmament was not the only thing to be celebrated. The spiritual awakening was having a profound effect upon the people.

' D-Day minus three months : Enlightened beings from other worlds withdraw all monitoring devices off the planet in complete trust, leaving only minor unmanned robot coverage. These monitors reported that preparations were in full swing for the biggest celebration of all. Harvest also was in full swing. The preliminary harvesting indicated a bumper crop.

' D-Day minus one week : Rocket parts now transported to launching sites in both parts of the world. Assembly was begun at launch site. The bumper harvest was completed. Most beautiful crop of highest yield and quality ever recorded. The whole world of five billion people was making preparations to be in either of the two principal countries on this day of spectacular celebration.

' D-Day minus three days : Week long holiday to be proclaimed world-wide. Vast populations jam all forms of planetary transportation to be on time for the celebration. D-Day minus two days : Both Capital cities now swelled with incoming hordes of people from all over the planet.

' Karna, the Capital of the Faithist country, was a crescent shaped, sprawling complex with many small cities, towns and villages surrounding it, to the total of three-and-one-half billion people. The

UFO PROPHECY

ANATOMY OF A HOLOCAUST—AND 'DYING FISH'

'The first bomb fell late in the evening, Faithist time. Within thirty-two minutes, thirty-one nuclear devices fell on the country of the Faithists. They were patterned in such a way that they were overlapped for total destruction. The rockets were launched in groups, each group five seconds apart. At 10.30 the third group was prepared for launching. Two had fizzled out, so they remained on the pad.

'D-Day 10.32 p.m. Faithist time: Because of disturbances in the magnetic field of the planet caused by detonation of powerful nuclear devices, internal pressure suddenly built up until it blew the planet apart with a thunderous roar.

'When the monitor indicated a nuclear war was in progress, the nearest spaceship was twenty-seven minutes away. At the last five minutes of the life of the planet of Maldek, all who could be reached were evacuated by the space brothers.

'D-Day plus one: Reverberations and magnetic shockwaves caused by the explosion and loss of the planet upset the balance of the whole Solar System. Other solar systems sent ships and magnetic generators in an attempt to restore the magnetic field of the Solar System.

'D-Day plus one week: Magnetic shockwaves caused by the loss of the planet caused the central Sun to go into a pulsating and irregular action, resulting in its losing its grip on the remaining planets. Complete shifting of the planets and their orbits is now imminent.

'D-Day plus two weeks: The remnants of the two civilizations of the destroyed planet now firmly established on nearest planet. The planet Earth, number one in the Solar System, was nearest in orbit to Maldek. Therefore, it was the destination for remnants of civilization of the exploded planet. At that time, number one planet Earth was small and super tropical.

'Dense jungle covered most of the planet where giant lizards and flying reptiles abounded in endless numbers. Now the unstable pulsation in the central Sun caused pulsations of gravity of number one planet Earth. The people settled in caves temporarily until the Solar System settled down, but the system continued to convulse.

'Pulsations in the Sun grew stronger, causing the remaining planets to dance in their orbits. D-Day plus sixteen days: Evacuation of the whole Solar System ordered. Planet one Earth, convulsing under magnetic blasts of abnormal conditions of the central Sun. Earthquakes become the rule instead of the periodic phenomenon on planet one.

'Violent volcanoes sprout and grow in the most unlikely of places.

UFO PROPHECY

ANATOMY OF A HOLOCAUST—AND 'DYING FISH'

'The first bomb fell late in the evening, Faithist time. Within thirty-two minutes, thirty-one nuclear devices fell on the country of the Faithists. They were patterned in such a way that they were overlapped for total destruction. The rockets were launched in groups, each group five seconds apart. At 10.30 the third group was prepared for launching. Two had fizzled out, so they remained on the pad.

'D-Day 10.32 p.m. Faithist time: Because of disturbances in the magnetic field of the planet caused by detonation of powerful nuclear devices, internal pressure suddenly built up until it blew the planet apart with a thunderous roar.

'When the monitor indicated a nuclear war was in progress, the nearest spaceship was twenty-seven minutes away. At the last five minutes of the life of the planet of Maldek, all who could be reached were evacuated by the space brothers.

'D-Day plus one: Reverberations and magnetic shockwaves caused by the explosion and loss of the planet upset the balance of the whole Solar System. Other solar systems sent ships and magnetic generators in an attempt to restore the magnetic field of the Solar System.

'D-Day plus one week: Magnetic shockwaves caused by the loss of the planet caused the central Sun to go into a pulsating and irregular action, resulting in its losing its grip on the remaining planets. Complete shifting of the planets and their orbits is now imminent.

'D-Day plus two weeks: The remnants of the two civilizations of the destroyed planet now firmly established on nearest planet. The planet Earth, number one in the Solar System, was nearest in orbit to Maldek. Therefore, it was the destination for remnants of civilization of the exploded planet. At that time, number one planet Earth was small and super tropical.

'Dense jungle covered most of the planet where giant lizards and flying reptiles abounded in endless numbers. Now the unstable pulsation in the central Sun caused pulsations of gravity of number one planet Earth. The people settled in caves temporarily until the Solar System settled down, but the system continued to convulse.

'Pulsations in the Sun grew stronger, causing the remaining planets to dance in their orbits. D-Day plus sixteen days: Evacuation of the whole Solar System ordered. Planet one Earth, convulsing under magnetic blasts of abnormal conditions of the central Sun. Earthquakes become the rule instead of the periodic phenomenon on planet one.

'Violent volcanoes sprout and grow in the most unlikely of places.

UFO PROPHECY

Polar icecaps spawn giant icebergs because of the shaking of the crust. Icebergs move into the giant swamps that cover the planet. D-Day plus twenty days : Violent explosion in the central Sun shakes the entire Solar System. These events were clearly visible from the Solar System of Antares. The inhabitants placed upon Earth from Maldek were now taken to the Antares Solar System, while all efforts to stabilize the Sun failed.

' D-Day plus twenty-four days : Intact, unlaunched and unexploded missiles from planet three, the destroyed Maldek, fall on planets one, four and five. Their fuel tanks ignited, blasting large craters on impact. The warheads fail to detonate.

' The Solar System is abandoned as gigantic explosions plunge the central Sun into periods of alternate darkness and light. D-Day plus thirty days : The central Sun finally disintegrates in a tremendous explosion that sends flaming fragments across the entire magnetic field. The Master magnetic vortex is shaken but still functioning.

' The destruction of the Sun causes release of the planets temporarily, so most of them drift outward. Magnetic generators are moved into the vortex by the space people in an effort to stabilize and rebuild the Solar System. The Solar System—with its Sun—wanders in darkness, planets drifting slowly outward.

' The release of external pressure on planet one, Earth, results in major expansion of the crust, causing a polar change and dislodging of most of the features of the crust. All things not firmly a part of the crust are violently shaken free by inertial and supersonic winds.

' Dense clouds cover the planet, to condense into great snowfalls. Giant oceans form. Vast jungles of tall, towering trees topple into swamps. Animals and birds are thrown in every direction by supersonic winds, some blown into the shrieking blizzards, others hurled by inertia caused by the crust slowing in rotation brought about by the major expansion.

' Some of the outer planets, lacking momentum to go farther out, drifted inwards towards the struggling vortex. Others lost their satellites during their minor expansions, owing to the destruction of the central Sun. The central vortex slowly achieved a stable state, but before stability was established some planets drifted clear out of the Solar System and were taken into the Solar System of Antares.

' D-Day plus six months : The central magnetic vortex strengthened and again stabilized. A new Sun created and commenced

UFO PROPHECY

ANATOMY OF A HOLOCAUST—AND 'DYING FISH'

growing. The magnetic pressure and power was now sufficient to continue Solar power processes. Light again existed in the Solar System.

'The order of planets before the destruction of Maldek by nuclear war and after, as of today, is as follows: BEFORE—1 Earth, 2 Mars, 3 Maldek, 4 Uranus, 5 Venus, 6 Saturn, 7 Jupiter, 8 Xyglo, 9 Theus, 10 Korma, 11 Noran, 12 Goobet, 13 unnamed embryo.

'AFTER—1 Venus, 2 Earth, 3 Mars, 4 fragments of Maldek, 5 Jupiter, 6 Saturn, 7 Uranus, 8 unnamed embryo. END OF CIVILIZATION—1 Alpha, 2 Mercury, 3 Venus, 4 Earth, 5 Mars, 6 fragments of Maldek, 7 Jupiter, 8 Saturn, 9 Uranus, 10 Neptune, 11 Pluto, 12 Omega.

'D-Day plus one year: The Solar System now repopulated by people from Antares and many other solar systems. The system is stable and prospering. The last of the giant reptiles dies from insufficient magnetic balance on the planet Earth. Frequent earthquakes still shake the crust as stabilization is being accomplished.

Millions of people now migrate to the new Earth from other parts of the Galaxy, brought there by spaceships. Space travel and prosperity become standard ways of life on Earth. A new era of life begins for Earth and its great people sixty million years ago.'

The next chapter, from the same source, outlines Part Two of The Anatomy of a Holocaust. I wonder whether anything has struck the observant reader as most coincidental so far? Karne was my visitor from the planet Aenstria on May 28th of 1967, as explained in an earlier chapter.

We have just learned about the Capital city of Karna (similar) and I have discovered that another name for the planet Maldek (apart from Lucifer) was Aestrea (Aenstria? The mystery grows). Can it be possible that I was contacted by a spaceman from a 'dead' planet that lost its identity through a tragic misunderstanding and sequence of Cosmic events some 60 million years ago?

Another possibility is a connection between Aenstria and Antares; for it requires only simple juggling of the composition of the name, a rearrangement of its letters, to alter them from Antares into Anstrea, which is markedly similar to the planetary appellation I was always given by strange telephone callers in September and October of 1965; and of course by the unusual Karne.

The prospect is extremely sobering and not a little awesome, even

UFO PROPHECY

to a hardboiled newsman trying to uncover solemn UFO truths ...
Let us now proceed to Part Two of the Anatomy of a Holocaust.
We may be advancing into realms of knowledge that give a shrewd
and comprehensive pointer to the ultimate destiny of Man on Earth.

We may be able to snatch visionary fragments of his future and his
eventual state of pure evolution or evolvement, instead of involvement,
from the following extraterrestrial forecasting, that will present a
coherent picture when assembled by the rational and thinking mind.

UFO IN THE DOCK

Men drew all day, with eager speed,
   A new ship to produce;
A blueprint soon drawn up, complete
   For all the craftsmen's use.

Down in the yard things were prepared,
   The work was due to start;
The workers gathered round the berth
   To lay the first small part.

For many months they slaved away,
   Till all was nearly done;
The tension rose as final staves
   Were duly placed thereon.

Then something seemed to go awry—
   And all, bewildered, cowered:
For on the berth, for all to see,
   A flying saucer towered!

UFO PROPHECY

CHAPTER NINETEEN

The Dawning of the Golden Age of Man

' D-Day minus sixty million years: Conditions and explanations... The planet Earth is still in first orbital position in a tight, small Solar System of twelve complete planets and one just growing. Since they are small and orbit small, the period of rotation around the central Sun is much shorter than at the present time.

' The destruction of Meldek by nuclear war upset the whole of the system, causing the loss of five planets. Earth doubled its size during this time by unparalleled catastrophies that befell the surface features. The order of the planets in the Solar System shifted and reshuffled. The length of the orbits increased without exception.

' The rotation of the planets also slowed, so that the size of the Solar System doubled, with one more than half as many planets. The time of the destruction of Maldek, the years and days being shorter, was sixty million years ago; yet correlated into present length of time was only twenty-two million years ago.

' For two million years of true time, the planet Earth prospered and the people walked with God. D-Day minus fifty-four million years: The first civilization of Earth rejects God. Illness, poverty, starvation and premature deaths befell these people on our planet. Finally, the space people withdrew and abandoned the Earth.

' People then turned cannibal and retreated to caves in order to survive. Dwindling masses became anarchic and frightened with superstition and were disease ridden. Finally, God flooded the Earth and left it vacant for a long while. So from D-Day minus fifty-three million years ago to minus eighty thousand years ago:

' Small migrations from other solar systems are brought to Earth in an attempt to again colonize the planet. The retarded remnants of the first civilization destroyed each migratory wave by violent invasion and assimilation. D-Day minus eighty thousand years ago: The Solar System of Antares was destroyed by a vast fragment of a large dead planet being drawn into the central Sun by the vortex of that Sun.

'The fragment consisted mostly of hydrogen compounds. This triggered violent nuclear holocaust in the central Sun of Antares. Catastrophe had fortunately been foretold, so the entire Solar System was evacuated prior to destruction of the Sun.

'Flaming fragments of that Sun invaded the nearest solar system, scorching the third planet now called Mars, and created vortices that developed into new planets. The people of Antares were distributed throughout the nearest solar system.

'Millions came to Earth at this period. But the descendants of the first civilization weakened and ruined the people of the new migration. D-Day minus fifty-seven thousand, five hundred and twelve years: The entire planet Earth was again flooded. Then the second phase of the migration was prepared.

'D-Day minus fifty-four thousand years: Millions from other solar systems come to Earth once more and the civilization prospers and walks with God. Civilization is happy and its spiritual growth is phenomenal. Most of this civilization is concentrated upon one continent now called Atlantis.

'D-Day minus forty-five thousand years: This civilization finally rejects God. The continent sinks and is flooded by the sea. This civilization had prospered for nine hundred centuries of Earth time or four thousand actual years of time measured by the length of the present day.

'Here the planet Earth undergoes a polar change and a minor expansion. Power centres are built in Egypt. D-Day minus twenty thousand years: Planet Earth was revegetated and prepared for the next migration. The pyramid power in Egypt was activated. Advance explorations indicated that the Earth was ready for people.

'D-Day minus nineteen thousand and five hundred years: Major expansion and polar change delayed plans for repopulating Earth. D-Day minus thirteen thousand years: Polar change befalls Earth again. Minor migrations have occurred. These were evacuated prior to this last cataclyzm.

'The pyramids are destroyed by the polar change. These are rebuilt and freshly energized. Malfunctions develop, so the pyramids are dismantled and moved, rebuilt, tested but not activated. D-Day minus six thousand five hundred years: Another polar change has occurred.

UFO PROPHECY

THE DAWNING OF THE GOLDEN AGE OF MAN

'This time the planet Earth swiftly recovers and vast migrations from other planets arrive on Earth and set up a new civilization. On this occasion the few remnants of previous civilization welcome the newcomers, unite with them and become a part of them. Prosperity projected by God again comes to Earth.

'D-Day minus five thousand four hundred years: This civilization also rejects God and proceeds to obliterate all things associated with Him. Power in the pyramids is shut down. The pyramids begin to degenerate. Great rains befall the Earth and flood it.

'Some of this civilization is ordered to build a boat and load animals aboard before the heavy rains come. The boat builder was considered insane, yet harmless, by the people at large. Just as the boat was finished, the rains deluged. The entrance to the boat was sealed so that unenlightened people were kept out.

'D-Day minus five thousand years: The world Earth is again repopulated and the people for a time are once more prospering. Minor expansions indicated trouble later in the magnetic fields. The other migrations to Earth were closed when trouble showed in this new race of people.

'These had been from twelve tribes of highly evolved people of God. But they, too, decided that they did not need Him any longer so they gradually forgot the ways of the Divine Creator and proceeded to build a scientific materialistic world civilization.

'D-Day minus one thousand nine hundred and seventy-four years: A messenger from God incarnates upon the Earth from the planet Venus to lead these wayward people back to God. His message is not received and He is crucified. Within three days He returns from the dead to walk amongst the living dead.

'Earth history records this event. Some claim it was a hoax; others say that this Being never existed; still others say His deeds were done by another, three hundred years after His death. But the true records on Venus tell the right story. This Divine messenger was preceded by other messengers who taught the same thing.

'Only this One had the power of demonstrating—and a higher teaching that the others were not aware of and had not been taught. An era of darkness came to Earth after the death of this Divine messenger.' (Author: The vital date would seem to be 1974, so the remainder of this Anatomy of a Holocaust is slightly out. It is still bold reckoning, if true, by space people).

UFO PROPHECY

'D-Day minus fifty-eight years: Planet Earth is plunged into a world war. This provides a boost in Earth scientific achievements that continue after war ends. D-Day minus forty-three years: The economic systems of major democratic powers collapse.

'The effects are felt world-wide. Mankind has spiritually degenerated and scientifically advanced. Lean years lie ahead for the major democratic power. D-Day minus thirty-two years: The world is again plunged into global war, more devastating and deadly than any previous war. The entire world feels the result of conflict.

'Science makes a major advance during this time. D-Day minus twenty-seven years: Space people are alarmed and apprehensive as the world has its first nuclear detonation. D-Day minus twenty years: Flying saucers and other inter-planetary vehicles converge on Earth as the planet experiences its first nuclear fusion detonation.

'Alarm spreads throughout the Galaxy because people of Earth had the capacity to destroy the Solar System and throw the whole Galaxy out of balance. Rigid monitoring of Earth is begun. Further detonation prevented until the magnetic field of the Earth is stabilized. D-Day minus fourteen years: Messengers incarnated from other worlds are told of their pasts and of the future occurrences.

'Each in turn is notified and told of his or her present assignment and why they are on Earth. Uranus undergoes Holy tribulation. D-Day minus eight years (1966-67?): Abnormal weather emerges as Earth enters its last days. Magnetic frequency of vortex drives some to suicide. Others go insane. Flowers bloom out of season, trees lose leaves or go to seed out of season.

'D-Day minus six years: Weather becomes unpredictable and unstable. Many varieties of plants die. Small animals and some species of bird disappear entirely. Soon after, meat of meat-bearing animals becomes rancid and unfit to eat. The number of insects to sustain the human race fluctuates unpredictably, sometimes in hordes and sometimes not at all.' (Author: 1968-71?)

'World-wide Communism collapses under weight of desire of the individual to express and sustain free will. Communist world split by distrust and dissention. Threats of a nuclear war are diminished by internal troubles of the chief instigators.

'Interplanetary vehicles crowd the skies in ever-increasing numbers. An asteroid passes in close proximity of Earth, disrupting the magnetic field and causing darkness to engulf the Earth. Violent changes in the

THE DAWNING OF THE GOLDEN AGE OF MAN

weather are triggered by this happening, also earthquakes become common.

'Vast hordes of frogs, toads and insects are generated by the disruption of the magnetic field. The crust of the Earth is slowed in its rotation at this time, causing a polar alteration which disrupts surface features. Enlightened beings are lifted from the Earth at this period by flying saucers, physically.

'The final plan of evacuation is formulated also, at this time. D-Day minus three years: Diseases and plagues of insects, rats, mice, toads and frogs sweep across the face of the Earth as ever-increasing earthquakes rock the planet. The civilization has not recovered from the effects of the polar change.

'The world is in a state of confusion. Order exists only in isolated areas. The final evacuation takes place one year before D-Day. Following this evacuation, hordes of giant insects plague the people. Then in the Spring, one year before the last day, the plants do not become active but remain dormant.

'Throughout the long, hot summer, the people look out on to a dead world, frequented by terrible earthquakes, giant insect hordes, disease and large armies of rodents. The summer frequently is interrupted by freezing cold spells. Meteor showers pepper the Earth, some falling in populated areas.

'The governments of the world still had not recovered from the shock of the polar change. Chaos is the order and way of life on Earth. Large numbers of spaceships are seen everywhere. Then comes the day in the Spring when the whole world is silenced.

'The insects, birds, small animals and giant insects have all vanished overnight. The wind has stopped, no clouds are visible anywhere. All spaceships have departed. Then the fires begin spontaneously and quickly engulf the planet. The people that are left try to escape the flames—only to become on fire themselves.

'The civilization of Earth that had rejected God comes at last to its predicted fiery end. D-Day plus one week: The ashes of the Holy tribulation are still smouldering. Many places of Earth are too hot to approach. Nothing is left standing. All traces of a previous civilization are burned.

'Views of Earth will resemble views of Uranus fourteen years earlier or Sirius Six, twelve years earlier. All three holocausts followed a

UFO PROPHECY

Divine pattern. Evacuation proceeded as planned, the Master plan adopted to each individual planet.

'No mishaps recorded. Evacuees are taken to a place of safety in each case. D-Day plus one year: The first vegetation is brought to the new planet Earth to prepare it again for repopulation. D-Day plus twenty years: Large scale migration from the other worlds to Earth is well under way.

'The new, clean world of Earth is a beautiful place with a delightful climate. Only qualified souls are allowed to incarnate again upon the planet Earth. D-Day plus one thousand years: The planet Earth has enjoyed a thousand years of unrivalled prosperity.

'Plans are set up to continue this forever. Divine Wisdom is constantly requested and willingly given. The span of life for Man on Earth is no longer limited to a few short years, but covers many centuries now. Love is the way of life. Truth is the rule of life. Joy and happiness are the results of this way of life.

'This is truly the Golden Age of Man that all races strive for and many do not achieve, because of their own free will. Only God can bring this to pass, and only to qualified races. The final end of an unenlightened race is by God's fire.

'And this, then, is the Anatomy of a Holocaust.' If we dare to credit this prehistory, present history and future history as absolute truth, assuming that space friends vouching for it are not seeking cruelly to delude us, it appears that the end of planet Earth will come before the close of 1974.

I will make no personal observations at this stage, my last chapter presenting my honest opinions. One could easily spurn the foregoing as the imaginative and heartless prognosticating of a human-hating maniac... As a realist, I am inclined to do so and term it 'a lot of unmitigated rubbish.' However, there are other pressing considerations to consider, as the last pages of this book illustrate.

In the land of the blind, it is said, the one-eyed Man is King. May Heaven help us, at this critical juncture in Earth affairs, to start seeing in focus—straight, true, bang on the designed and desired target! I have already mentioned Thomas, who elucidated the essential comparison between the macrocosm, the great Universe and God manifesting through the Solar System, and the microcosm, Man regarded as the epitome of the Universe or macrocosm.

Under conditions of perfection, he insisted, these are synonymous,

UFO PROPHECY

THE DAWNING OF THE GOLDEN AGE OF MAN

no difference between the vast and eternal and the miniature or microscopic. The entire stellar geography of the Universe is duplicated by the atomic structures within Man. This I found difficult to understand.

Earth is known throughout the Universe as 'The Planet of Strengthening,' with the number of individual incarnations, alternating between male and female bodies or 'shells,' usually numbering thirty-three. Progression is applauded by the Interplanetary Masters. They prefer to see this rather than the retardment of a soul when slipping backward in retrogression.

'But God never destroys one of His children, who are legion,' Thomas assured me. Man could be so much closer to Universal truth and wisdom had he first learnt to split the atom within himself before doing it in a forceful 'outward' form that destroys precious life. Nature yielded one of her most zealously guarded secrets to Man—and he abused it in practical application.

Although Thomas exuded the calm confidence of certainty and inspiration in everything he said and did while at Warminster (he then went on, early this year, to 'safeguard' five Swiss mountains from threatening avalanches), he shuddered whenever he glanced down at his right hand. He claims he still feels the wounds of Christ, Holy blood indelible on his palm . . .

To report in extensive detail all he told me, as commanded to do by his Master, would fill another book for which—judging from human reaction to Divine teaching—there would be little demand. My last chapter, however, refers to important developments at Warminster that convinced me completely that the Will of God is behind UFO manifestations.

In the context of reincarnation as factual, 'As ye sow, so shall ye reap' becomes comprehensible in the karmic pattern of the individual; so does the reminder that 'the sins of the fathers are visited upon the children.' This makes sound sense when aligned with the continuous processes of regeneration and rebirth. In brief, it is Divinely decreed that each new-found physical vehicle for the long-suffering soul has debts to pay and arrears of errors and maladjustments to settle in each successive reincarnatory life cycle.

This ceases when there is no longer any need for the 'wheel of re-birth' to revolve any more. That is when perfection entitles the 'wearer' of the precious mantle to ascend into planetary regions where lessons of Universal life teach much more than the distorted visions of inner truth and inspiration Man aspires to on Earth.

When praying for guidance in a confused state, one should liken one's-self to the smallest grain of sand in a long foreshore, the humblest speck of dust in acres of newly ploughed land. 'Remember,' advised Thomas. 'For every step a Man takes towards a Master who holds truth in custody for God, the Master will cheerfully take two steps towards the honest seeker.'

'But,' he warned, 'when Light breaks in and illumines the mind of the inquirer, the Forces of Darkness are allowed in to try and wreak havoc with the spirit of the individual. These tests are all part of the tribulation of discipleship. Even the advanced chela is beset by these attacks. Be on your guard continually, therefore.'

While UFOs and their crews are busy on aerial and underground missions in preparation for the Second Coming, necessary for the absolute fault-free success of the great Cosmic Event (as already hinted at in changing of the magnetic field of Earth), modern disciples are doing work of tremendous importance simultaneously with these preparations.

'These tasks must be accomplished by us to sweep away footling chores from the auras of the Masters at this time,' Thomas confided. I can mention the following places 'energized' and 'reactivated' around Warminster, so they are rendered suitable for spacecraft to land at these predetermined points when the New Age is dawning :—

Glastonbury Tor, Silbury Hill (biggest and most mysterious man-made mound in Europe), Butleigh (where the zodiacal circle is centred), Stonehenge, Cadbury Castle and Hill (South Cadbury), Cradle Hill, Battlesbury, Teffont Magna, Chew Magna, Cley Hill, Heaven's Gate. There are points on the outskirts of Bristol and near Marlborough, too. Altogether, they number thirteen and are representative of Christ (Heaven's Gate) and his twelve Apostles or Disciples.

Apparently, 'holy charging' and recharging operations are going on at various centres in the world, the most marked being Borup, in the middle of the island known as Zealand, Denmark. Britain is the spiritual centre of the Second Coming, Warminster the hub around which all activity will revolve. The practical operating centre will be at Borup, where spiritual teaching has taken place.

These are extravagant and sweeping statements. Are they true beyond a shadow of doubt? Clues are given in my last chapter and

UFO PROPHECY

THE DAWNING OF THE GOLDEN AGE OF MAN

summing-up at the end of this work. Realising the heavy burden of my responsibility to relate truth to the public, I am at times bowed with sorrow. When a storm breaks, it is no use crying in a forlorn voice 'I told you so,' when too late to stop that destructive welter of the elements . . .

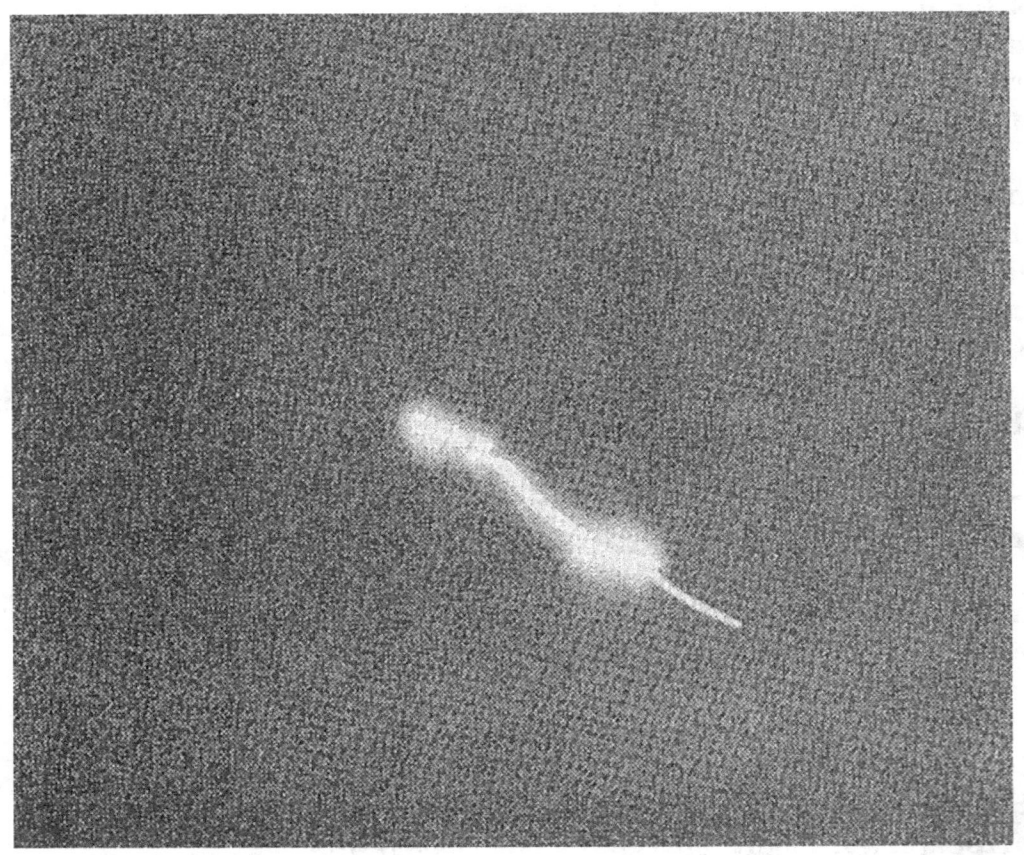

Warminster Dart

CHAPTER TWENTY

Interplanetary Existence 'Priceless Pearl'

An increasing number of Ufologists are finding that there may well be a profound connection between Biblical prophecies and UFO happenings over recent years, without having to join the ranks of extreme pessimists; those dispensers of gloomy and alarmist views about the impending breakup of Earth and dire personal consequences 'unless ye repent in time for salvation.'

To comprehend certain mysteries of Biblical occurrences, an understanding of the four primary Aspects of Interplanetary Masters is necessary, Thomas and Mark told me. No mere booklore can supply this vital information, which springs from the highest level of consciousness if one humbly seeks the golden altar cross of Truth.

The revelation can come swiftly or in slow dawning, depending on the utter earnestness of the seeker and humility in attitude. It can arrive in a blinding flash of inspiration if one is on a direct link with the Universal Spirit that transcends all. Or it can be conveyed in a more gradual and subtle fashion following contact with a being possessed of knowledge that at present eludes Man on Earth, forbidden yet to use the dormant nine-tenths of his mind.

In short, a being from an enlightened planet whose duty is to instruct those chosen as instruments of mediation. A study of the Occult brings preliminary knowledge to questing minds, providing the inquirers beware of the left-hand path leading to black magic and evil, keeping in patience and faith to narrow straits of the right-hand path in harmony with Sons of Light and Nature.

There is no middle road, no compromise, no halfway house for the lukewarm falterer along the highway of life. Halfway measures, half-hearted approaches, produce no lasting results to satisfy. Once a decision to seek full enlightenment is reached, it is all or nothing!

Where the current generation may be the last in the present life cycle on Earth for all, there is added urgency that Man, individually and collectively, must take advantage of every opportunity to transmute weakness and stiffen moral and spiritual fibre.

Individual experience may then make itself felt, so that the veils of confusion and doubt are torn asunder for some of the great mysteries of life and purpose, as ordained by the Masters, to become revealed, exposed and understood. In the unused portion of the brain of Man, sleeping yet waiting for the igniting of an unburnt wick in an oil lamp, are stored the secrets and treasures which enrich aware humanity —the living Holy Grail.

I have shunned everything that remotely savours of the mythical and illusionary, lacking shape or substance, in my work as a purveyor of news. I have therefore not placed undue faith in the esoteric, arcane, psychic and spiritual sources of information available as possible direction posts or stepping stones along the way.

A strict realist, I always suspected that mediums, spiritualists, mystics and clairvoyants are unreliable guides to shining Truth in its most compelling glow of conviction. Gimmickry and blatant sensationalizm that mark some seances and tumbler-pushing tabletop antics belong to the kindergarten of the immature. They may mildly amuse or strike a discordant note that shocks sensitivity.

Even genuine spiritual contacts with entities on another plane of consciousness or in a different dimension, disembodied or otherwise, rarely rise above purely personal trivia falling woefully short of Divine revelation. To be fair, the majority of such intermediaries are sincere in efforts to instil peace and comfort into bereaved and grieving people, when unpaid.

After recent vivid experiences of a paranormal type on Cradle Hill and in the sanctity of my own home (described in the last chapter), realising I shall continue a blind and unthinking fool if not grasping at every straw that helps build a nest of knowledge, my views have changed considerably, for there are avenues Man can sensibly explore to gain truth which do not conform to mundane channels of the conventional.

I had to learn the hard way, having tried every conceivable medium of scientific application and practical investigation in untangling the web of UFO perplexities confronting us. No one can be expected to take more than a vague, desultory interest in these spaceships unless one lands and yields itself and crew to thorough inspection.

Until a few months ago, when I met space people, I was unversed

UFO PROPHECY

INTERPLANETARY EXISTENCE 'PRICELESS PEARL'

in the workings of a Divine Plan that provides the only viable springboard for these aerial activities. I hate introspective thought, with its dangers of reliance on the subjective instead of objective. Yet the final answers are the same, no matter what media for determination are employed, if one is sincere.

So we learn that Interplanetary Masters, who ply the threads of reason and logic more expertly than a skilled embroiderer, under guidance and wisdom of the Supreme Intelligence of the Universe, do exist; and that their chelas, disciples or contactees on planet Earth number slightly in excess of 4,000 at present, from a world population of about 3,400 millions.

Most Earth contactees remain anonymous, fearing ridicule suffered by George Adamski, conscious of the fact that open confession of meeting beings from other planets will endanger their own lives and jobs—more important, jeopardize the safety of their new friends and a great mission now proceeding.

Who are these Masters? He who made them in the beginning made them male and female, or twin souls. George King gave this truth to Man originally; he must at least take credit for this, although I know little about the Aetherius Society he leads. So we learn that Aspect One is where the male and female Masters are conscious in the etheric body.

This structure can be detached from the other aspects at will. It is invisible beyond infra-red and ultra-violet, the limit of the non-clairvoyant vision of terrestrial Man. Aspect Two is where male and female Masters are conscious at all times in the physical, silicon-celled, interplanetary and ascended body.

This structure requires no food, water or sleep, our new-found communication with truth tells us. Immortality is their heritage. This is at first difficult to contemplate, let alone comprehend, for the majority of us are in the novice mould, souls still evolving towards a prized goal that may be, in Earth time conception, hundreds of years hence. More fortunate and progressed human elements must especially help backward brethren seeking Light today.

Aspect Three is where male and/or female Masters can materialize a body within the spectrum of Man's vision. This type of manifestation is one of the most convincing and satisfactory ways of appearing and appealing to Man at a crucial stage of Earth history and civilization.

This he can understand, even if it is revelationary and awes his

UFO PROPHECY

limited senses : even if it may shock his entire system for some while afterwards. It should be affirmed here, too, that each aspect has a specific set of functions coming into play with increasing intensity to impress minds of men today.

Aspect Four is where a minute part of an Interplanetary Master will reincarnate into the reincarnatory cycle of Earth. This aspect is rarely aware of its higher potentials until made fully cognisant for a Divinely decreed purpose. *The promised Second Coming of Christ would be one such valid reason.*

Privileged people on our planet are becoming—or have become—aware of alterations in patterns of individual thought, behaviour and radiation power, suddenly realising with startling clarity of mind their rightful place in a huge jigsaw puzzle closely enmeshed into the UFO enigma. They should not boast of this change, but be quietly grateful it is effected.

With all great books of knowledge, particularly when essential truths have been deliberately omitted by power-wielding factions in past ages, the Holy Bible should be read with more than the human complement of two eyes. The inner eye of reason, the invisible yet important ' third eye ' that glows to prick Man's insatiable curiosity and excite his detecting abilities, must come into play here.

One can have eyes and not discern correctly, ears that hearken yet not construe with understanding, a mind that is clogged by materializm and false values, unreceptive influences. Dare we believe the following to be true ? This is what Thomas told me :

At the commencement of the Piscean Age, a Saturnian spacecraft travelled very slowly for three days through the atmosphere of Terra, while three sages followed it at camel speed. At the court of Herod the photons (units of light measurement) were revolved around the craft, resulting in its invisibility.

When it reached its predetermined destination, it hovered or ' stood over ' the crib at Bethlehem. But had a star, a powerful sun, moved within the ionosphere layer, one thing and one disastrous thing only could possibly have taken place. That is, total and complete annihilation of all life on Earth as sun and planet converged !

Yet this was avoided. How and why ? This was no ordinary birth. It was predestined as part of a Divine Plan. If a star, or a comet of sufficient proportions, had come within thousands of miles of Terra, a flip or physical shifting of the axis—with inevitable loss of life as

UFO PROPHECY

INTERPLANETARY EXISTENCE 'PRICELESS PEARL'

water masses moved over land masses—would be the least that could be anticipated.

It is no assumption when it is stated categorically that the Star of Bethlehem was in fact an extraterrestrial space vehicle. This information has been received by a considerable number of Earth contactees from Interplanetary Masters or Gurus. Logic adds weight of credence to the stipulation.

To the Pharisees the founder of Christianity stated: ' You are of this world. I am not of this world.' At the Garden of Gethsemane, knowing full well the details of His transition, He prayed for his disciples and said: ' As they are not of this world, neither am I of this world.'

In Chapter 22 of Revelation, verse 16, Christ gives the secret of where He as a Master originated: ' I am the root and the offspring of David ' (reincarnation) ' and the radiant, the Morning Star ' (the morning star is the planet Venus).

This statement in no way contradicts His claim to being the Second Person of the Trinity, for the Christ overshadowed the Venusian Master Jesus as is explained in Chapter 17 of John, verses 1-5. The Christ overshadows all Masters or Angels (as the Bible describes Masters resident upon other planets), for they are at-one with the Christ within themselves.

The Aspect Three of certain Interplanetary Masters materialized bodies upon several instantly recalled occasions, in the work that is available to all: namely, the angels who visited the shepherds, those at the sepulchre, the Angel Gabriel who informed Zacharias that his sixty-year-old wife Elizabeth would give birth to a son and that his name would be John.

After Herod had decapitated John, Jesus took disciples Peter, James and John up to a mountain. Then, out of the heavens came ' a shining cloud '—or what Man now calls a UFO. After Elijah and Moses, who had arrived in the spacecraft, had conversed with the Messiah, they returned to the planet from which they came—Mars.

The disciples did not understand this, for Elijah had been seen by his disciple Elisha being taken up into the heavens in a fiery chariot; or what we today recognize by that unfortunate and very terrestrial name, flying saucer. He prophesied that he would return to Earth to prepare the way for the Messiah.

' Why then say the scribes that Elijah must first come ? ' they asked. The reply came, ' I tell you that Elijah has already been and they did not recognize him. On the contrary, they did with him what they pleased; and in the same way the Son of Man will be treated by them.'

The disciples then fully realised that He spoke to them about John the Baptist. (Matthew Chapter 17 verses 1-13). John the Baptist was the Aspect Four of the Master Elijah, as were the twelve disciples; and as were the majority of the prophets of the Old Testament.

Daniel in Chapter 3 describes the events that took place when the Aspect Fours (Shadrak, Meshak and Abednego) were thrown, bound, into an excessively hot fire by the orders of Nebukadnezzar. The soldiers who cast them into the flames were killed by the heat, while Shadrak, Meshak and Abednego were walking at their leisure in the middle of the furnace.

They were able to do so, for the Aspect Three of an Interplanetary Master had placed a force screen—similar to that which surrounds an interplanetary space vehicle—around the trio. They were thus protected. 'And the appearance of the fourth is like the Son of a God.' (Chapter 3 verse 25).

In the case of Paul, on the road to Damascus he—even though prior to the event engaged in persecuting the Christians—was suddenly made clairvoyant, for his companions were not aware of the Aspect One of the Way shower (Christ) in vision, but were in sound. (Acts, Chapter 9).

Initially, when Christianity was practised it made a logical philosophy, because reincarnation was taught. This is a vital truth of which most Earth people are ignorant by reason of it having been obscured and omitted from the teachings.

Interplanetary Masters have confirmed that reincarnation was banned as a Christian teaching in 150 AD by the leaders of the Church of Constantinople, due to their weakness of power. They knew that if the original teachings were released, Man would work full hard at transmuting all internal dross and worthless traits, as he gracefully accepted everything that came his way as his due.

By Man passing his tests and finding the narrow gateway on the journey of 'taking up his own cross,' he would become ever more conscious of the Divine spark of God or the Christ King within him. Eventually he would require no leaders, not even a book to teach him, being led to Truth instead by his only Leader, the Eternal Spirit of Creation and Universal Intelligence.

As the leaders of the church were not strong enough to live the

INTERPLANETARY EXISTENCE 'PRICELESS PEARL'

exacting precepts of the Way shower, during their lifetime, although they fully intended the original Bibles to be released after their death, the limitation of consciousness was so immense by this suppression that Man never earned the right to rediscover them.

Now, at this vexed and troubled stage, this historic juncture in Earth affairs, the Masters come once again to remind Man to use his own faculties to the utmost. They give a crumb here, a crumb there; and it is up to us to take a bite at the bread of life!

Man is at long last beginning to think for himself once more, tuning-in to the wavelength of the Universal Spirit and turning away from things material and corrupt. He has been Earthbound too long and his conscience and consciousness are being impacted by clarion calls he cannot ignore. Time is desperately short to make amends.

Signs foretold with beautiful simplicity in the Book of Matthew are occurring now. The time to reach the prized destination is very brief indeed. When the Messiah returns in a flying saucer or ' a cloud, in great power and glory and the angels of heaven ' with Him (in modern terms, Interplanetary Masters in UFOs), may prove all too short a period for Man's necessary readjustment, for falterers and unbelievers still unthinking and unseeing as they rebuke teachings of Bible and UFOs alike.

' Even while they were looking, He ascended and a cloud carried Him up from their view. And as they were gazing intently into the heaven at His departure, two men in white robes suddenly stood beside them (Aspect Threes) ' who said, " Men of Galilee, why do you stand gazing up into heaven ? This Jesus, who has ascended from you to the heaven, will even return in the same way as you have seen Him depart to the heaven." ' (Acts Chapter 1, verses 9-11).

Yes, the true interpretation of Biblical extracts of revealing quality are worth noting and studying in solving the overall UFO mystery. We never cease to learn if we diligently apply minds and one-tenth used brains to new thought that transcends wasteful pipe-dreams and forlorn hopes of past centuries unillumined by truth.

Why should a sincere belief in the Bible, greatest book ever compiled, crucify one as ' a religious crank ' when it comes to Ufology ? Agreed, there are too many pseudo-religious fanatics obsessed by false inferences drawn blindly from sections of Holy Writ.

Because of their loud and offensively imperious tones, volumes of their wrath, self-righteousness and indignation, they can be heard the proverbial mile away. Unfortunately, they cannot be spotted at the same distance, so many have joined us on Cradle Hill and made the UFO subject a thing of ridicule.

Cheerless Holy Joes and Jills depress me. What a pity their mental and spiritual energies are dissipated and misdirected, aiding destructive rather than constructive thought, simply due to lack of sure love which is the keystone of Christian teaching! I would sooner believe persons who have sold or given away their worldly possessions; people who now live and work in vital areas such as Warminster for very special reasons . . .

Thomas described to me 'the journey to perfection' involved in processes of reincarnation. As a Christian teaching, it was banned by a weak Church 1,818 years ago, after the last of the apostles had died and their memories were forgotten. The original motive was to guard against the people, as a whole, being able to think for and also govern themselves.

'Once again, as in all Earth history, it was a case of one wanting more power than his brother—and meaning to make right his mistakes at a later date. That date never arrived,' explained Thomas. 'That seeing, they may see and not perceive, and hearing, they may hear and not comprehend; otherwise they would turn back (to the knowledge of their former incarnations), where their sins would be forgiven them as one reads in Mark Chapter V, verses 11 and 12.

'How? Simply by "burning up" their karma, by taking up their own cross—that is, transmuting the weaknesses that incurred the negative sowing. The esoteric interpretations of these words are understood when reincarnation and the Law of Karma are more fully realised.

'It is written that "he who lives by the sword shall die by the sword." This is not necessarily the case in the same incarnation: but in a future life metal could destroy the body, such as in a car accident or similar incident. This "reaping" is then registered in the Akashic Records of the superconscious mind or soul of Man.

'Not one jot, not one tittle of the law, is left unreaped. But by transmuting the weaknesses that were expressed during the sowing, the harder path of learning the lessons of life is unnecessary. Some of the emotional and mental weaknesses of Man are:

'Hatred, jealousy, fear, sadizm, revenge, lust, power, greed, miserliness, covetousness, egotizm, possessiveness, vanity, selfishness,

INTERPLANETARY EXISTENCE 'PRICELESS PEARL'

dishonesty, envy, impatience, intolerance, condemnation, pride, apathy, laziness, superiority, inferiority, reaction, worry, depression, worship of mammon, and lack of the qualities of love, humility, faith, hope, charity, understanding and trust. These are the principal weaknesses Man must learn to overcome for the sake of redemption.

'Only those who can be completely honest with themselves can gain control over emotion with mind, which in time leads to heightened consciousness. By this constant reminder, it enables us to dig out the soft soil and dross within, until our house can be built upon the rock of our superconscious faculties, which will then be unaffected by the turmoil that the process of evolution brings.

'Mastery has to be earnt to attain at-one-ment with the Christ within. To succeed in this, it is wise to learn the metaphysical secret of drawing down within the subtler bodies " the Presence of Light." This white spiritual energy is drawn from the Holy Spirit or Divine spark of God in Man, which is part of the Absolute, the highest Aspect of God.

'Constant practice of this exercise assists the aspirant to reach " the pearl of great price," the bliss of Interplanetary Existence,' he added. Thomas and other professed disciples and incarnated beings stressed the futility of ' casting pearls before swine ' when I lecture.

Some will listen and benefit; the majority, if I keep to this theme, will shut their ears against truth, fearing it, hating it and its implications. The hidden meanings of Holy Writ and the parables of Christ are understood in depth only when one has mastered emotional hazards and brought an enlightened mind to bear on one-hundred per cent correct interpretation.

The important aspect of ' twin souls, male and female ' has been mentioned. This is the true basis of the Adam and Eve legend in physical form, for those well advanced along the trail of spiritual truth. ' He who made them in the beginning made them male and female.

'What therefore God hath joined together, let not Man put asunder.' We use a similar phrase in Holy Matrimony, yet it denotes little without implementation of actual historical and religious significance. Matthew c. 7, v. 14, gives a vital clue to achievement of Mastery:

'How narrow the gate and difficult the path that leads to life (the New World, the Kingdom of Heaven, Interplanetary Existence), and they are few who find it.' Another clue is in Revelation c. 7, v. 14:

' And they are those who have gone through great tribulation and washed their robes (subtler bodies, astral and mental) and made them white (the highest spiritual vibration) in the blood of the Lamb (final terrestrial path of the Cross, of strengthening all weaknesses under the guidance of a Master as depicted by the Way shower or Christ King). They shall cry no more and God shall wipe all tears away from their eyes.'

Thomas and his counterparts assured me it would be well, at this present critical stage in Earth history, for all people on Earth to mark strongly and consider most carefully these things . . . So much depends on proper awareness, now. To those who think I am falling apart at my mental seams, joining the very cranks I condemn, I would swear to this :—

I made every endeavour to 'trip' these chelas up, to catch them out in what they said and did, to expose them as charlatans and not vessels of truth. I was blunt, pugnacious even, in my questioning and verbal battering for the smallest chink in their armour, the least loophole in what they said. They came through with flying colours . . . But my final assessment comes later.

UFO PROPHECY

CHAPTER TWENTY-ONE

What do Unique UFO Experiences Foretell?

Verbal messages and vocal vibrations from the distant past may still be lingering in our atmosphere, lying dormant in low-pressure pockets, waiting to be 'picked up' and recorded by electrical receivers such as radio sets . . . This is a stunning possibility that challenges science.

The main difficulty, if such an eventuality is more than thinkable, would be to attune correctly to matching frequencies and wavelengths necessary to reproduce the original spoken words. Capturing the 'dead' past in the 'live' present presents certain technical problems.

Brigadier Tony Arengo-Jones, commandant of the School of Infantry at Warminster in 1966-67, brought forth a minor revelation at the annual luncheon in the officers' mess for tenant farmers who lease War Department land in the Warminster area. He told an amusing yet amazing true story concerning a recent military exercise around Imber Ranges, on Salisbury Plain.

It was nothing to do with the machinations of UFOs, of course; yet may explain one of the reasons why alien spaceships haunt the Warminster district, proving that exceptional magnetic properties exist there. Brigadier Arengo-Jones confided that the troops on the battle exercise, in tanks, lighter armoured vehicles, personnel carriers and other fighting vehicles, were working on a specific radio frequency.

The operators of Army radio sets, transmitters and receivers, set their instrument dials accordingly, 'netting' on the given wavelength. However, there was a great deal of unexpected interference from an unknown factor in the ether throughout the exercise. This upset the mock battle campaign.

It seemed that the Royal Navy was in radio opposition to the Army troops so far as signal communication goes. The military operators were picking up strange nautical messages on their receivers. The signalling seamen's 'intruders' occasionally came over at maximum strength and blotted out important transmissions.

UFO PROPHECY

It soon became clear that these R.N. signals, exceptionally strong considering the distance from points of origin, were being generated by wireless transmitters on board warships patrolling in the English Channel off Portsmouth, some seventy to eighty miles away from the Army battle area.

Crystal clear and obviously working on the same wavelength as Army sets, naval messages from ships' officers and telegraphists confused the poor military operators, also senior officers in charge of the battle exercise soldiers.

After all, tank crews cannot ' open up a six and four-inch broadside from the larboard bow ' on an ' enemy ' sloop or frigate in the middle of Salisbury Plain ! The ' trespassing ' naval signals and orders had more than a nuisance value effect on the success of the Army battle rehearsal.

Condemnation of the ' infernal impertinence ' the Royal Navy was showing in daring to use the same wavelength as the Army, on the same night and without a ' by your leave,' was expressed by officers and baffled troops alike, although couched in extremely strong Service language . . . The air was blue—and not simply with electrical interference !

Natural indignation and the sabotaging of the troops' exercise led to inquiries being instituted at top level, afterwards. The Navy denied blame, pointing out there was no battle exercise in territorial waters of the English Channel on that particular night. Furnished records proved this true.

When highlights of Naval transmissions were presented, however, reports of various ships' positions and manoeuvres, etc., duly given by military witnesses on signalling message pads, mild consternation dawned. Yes—something was definitely amiss—and the Army complaints were justified to a certain extent.

Incredible as it may seem, it developed that the Navy had indeed been responsible for relaying the radio calls while on a patrol exercise —but theirs took place five months earlier ! The generated nautical signals had ' infiltrated ' inland on to the Wiltshire downs around Warminster and Salisbury Plain, there lying dormant.

Subsequently, still ' alive ' and capable of being ' tapped ' and captured by radio receivers, the signals were picked up in low-lying pockets of ground around Imber Village and over a fairly wide area . . . If these electrical impulses, remaining static in areas of plain and still

UFO PROPHECY

WHAT DO UNIQUE UFO EXPERIENCES FORETELL?

preserving original messages relayed five months previously, in their entirety, could be re-employed after a long period and lead to confusion, who can tell whether other 'messages' of greater antiquity persist in these or similar areas?

If they do, it is conceivable that words broadcast hundreds or even thousands of years ago are capable of being harnessed today, if precise instruments and special frequencies are permitted to 'snare' them for future enlightenment, perhaps. Stranger things have been known to happen, on the UFO front!

It has already been stressed that, in pursuing a subject of such importance and urgency as UFO materialization and significance, the ego must be dwarfed and the serious investigator careful always to remember he is a relative nonentity in the Universal scheme of things, although bearing great responsibility as a custodian of truth.

Certain happenings can leave a deep impress on the consciousness, only a new-found inner strength at vital periods preventing onset of complete exhaustion, mentally and physically. Only when personal experience hits home, bang on target, fiercely and forcibly, brooking no argument or protest, can one formulate firm ideas as to nature and import of a spectacular unknown.

Perhaps because of my extreme realism, my strictly practical approach to life and work, astonishing personal events of 1967 were designed deliberately to reshape my attitude—then on blatantly wrong lines—so drastically. One can be too mundane in searching studiously for truth, to a degree that proves extremely painful and almost humiliating when sharp realisation occurs.

Three personal incidents in the year 1967-68 burned my mind; events so astounding that—no matter how cynics laugh at and deride me—they convinced me there is profound purpose behind UFOs, which to me are no longer the mysterious force they constituted a year ago.

Before I attempt to describe them, let us recall the admonition and reproof mildly administered by Christ to his disciples on one occasion: 'Suffer little children to come unto me, for of such is the Kingdom of Heaven.' It is uncaring grownups who try and prejudice little minds in important formative years.

Here are two short stories from Warminster which illustrate this truism: A collection was made at a local school to help relieve the suffering of children in the Vietnam war. One boy brought along

UFO PROPHECY

two shillings and sixpence, given him as pocket money for the week. He asked the teacher what kind of Vietnamese children they were subscribing for—North or South?

Told 'The South,' he promptly handed over the half-crown piece. 'My father told me that if it was towards little children in the North, I must not give anything. They are heathens and do not deserve any help from anybody.' the boy said firmly. (One wonders whether God was 'listening-in' to that pathetic betrayal of Humanity in miniature...)

A Warminster father warned his five-year-old daughter, about to start school: 'You can sit next to any child you like at school, boy or girl, just so long as they are white like you are. You must not sit next to a black child. That is not right and proper.' Adults are blind!

These are true stories which show the narrow outlook of some people, the incredibly stupid, short-sighted and inhuman attitude to life and those who live it which, when unchecked, can poison the minds of the innocent young, who trust everyone they meet no matter what skin colour differences exist!

In modern times the UFO phenomena appeared in earnest in 1947, simultaneous with our entrance into the atomic age. Parallel to and contemporary with saucer observations in the past twenty-one years, there have occurred throughout our planet increasing numbers of inexplicable events bearing striking resemblance to biblical accounts of so-called 'angels' and their actions.

In spite of energetic and painstaking inquiry by Ufologists, none has succeeded in giving a complete explanation of these celestial chariots as an isolated phenomenon. Only when we draw them into a larger perspective—into the light of history, archaeology, parapsychology, philosophy, paranormal, para-physical and religious happenings —does a fully conceptive picture emerge.

It is one which certainly urges the inquirer to meditate when viewed against the backcloth of the present world situation and in the light of biblical tales and prophecies concerning the Last Days. It should now be patent that these flying mysteries are one of the predicted 'signs in the skies.'

One 'person' who entered my life, when I was on the point of finishing with Ufological research altogether through sheer frustration at lack of tangible evidence, came to me after I had been lecturing at Caxton Hall in London on Saturday, August 26th last year. When I

UFO PROPHECY

WHAT DO UNIQUE UFO EXPERIENCES FORETELL?

arrived home in the early hours of next morning, tired and unaware how my address had 'gone over' in the Tudor Room, I resolved to cease nocturnal observations from Cradle Hill.

Readers might adjudge me guilty of blasphemy if I say too much about my 'visitor' on this occasion. If a 'man' of the following description ever enters your life, forbid him not: Long hair flowing gently down to white-robed shoulders, parted in the centre from the crown and a rich copper beech red colour. Face and eyes—glorious eyes!—truly 'out of this world.' Violet blue, glowing lamps of eyes, beautiful and blazing a mute appeal: unlined skin a soft pink; great majesty and strength, a noble spirit, in the set of the high yet broad forehead, slightly jutting outward over finely chiselled features. He had no beard—and that puzzled me . . .

After initial shock, I simply could not bear to look for long at those marvellous eyes, knowing myself to be in the presence of a unique 'person.' Had he been the devil, I would have 'stared him out'— in the final glance before tearing myself from his captivating radiance, I noticed the brilliant light shining from and around him, illuminating the room more brightly than the largest chandelier in faceted reflections.

I was emotionally overcome, a rare experience in my life. Later, I learned that something I said at Caxton Hall saved one listener from committing suicide. This was heartening news. While speaking, at one period I was aware of an uncanny factor: many of the words and sentiments I used were not from my own mental reasoning at all. Crazy? Of course it is—but I am left wondering Who or What has been working through me, at times like these . . . Please do not misunderstand me: I am a nonentity, a nobody who may have stumbled on Divine truths, not of my own volition, a former disbeliever in God (an awful admission!) who can doubt no further.

There were two other bewildering personal experiences, of which I will relate just one: It was 11.7 p.m. on Friday April 5th this year. On Cradle Hill with me were: Lady Marjorie Stewart, of Manley, in New South Wales, Australia; her English friend Mrs. Jean Sydney; and Veronica Cadby, who has several times seen UFOs in the Keynsham area.

About forty-two minutes earlier, a radiant UFO swept gently towards us from the South, noiseless, very low in flight, casting a pinkish amber glow into the clear night sky. It veered towards Battlesbury, to the East of us, then dramatically 'blacked-out' after Lady

UFO PROPHECY

Stewart had taken several photographic shots of it, the obliging moon to her right and slightly behind her.

I sensed very strongly that it would reappear. It was 'one of those nights.' At 11.7 p.m. we noticed it gliding in duck-bobbing fashion towards the copse on our hill. It was much higher this time, but certainly no satellite of Earth, its pulsating halo giving it a silver-ringed magnificence. It was what happened after it vanished that churned us all up, emotionally . . .

Bright searchlight beams flickered from the heavens over the two copses, lighting them clear as day. Everything was bathed by their brilliance. Then what one can only describe as 'tremendous angel forms' appeared in the sky, radiant robes billowing above the trees, a peculiar shade of red and violet admixture predominant in the twin pattern of aerial-formed figures.

I have seen Northern Lights, fan-shaped and usually whitish-blue, on the distant horizon: but these phenomena were immediately above us, over the trees, near and 'localised' to our vision. It was awe-inspiring, obviously a spiritual emanation extraordinary and *par excellence*. We were all shaken as we mentally and physically 'soaked in' the majesty of it all—and for a brief while I wondered whether the Second Coming was about to materialize.

I repeat: It was 'one of those nights'—the greatest visual and soul stirring experience I have ever known, even on Cradle Hill, that mound of mounting mysteries. The shafts of downbeating light gave the impression of a huge cathedral organ, fluted pipes illumined, so that one half expected to hear melodious strains cascading in rivulets, then swelling into floods of harmony, from the heavens.

The vivid glow of the twin robed figures persisted for several minutes, while we stood in dumbstruck wonder and feasted our eyes upon a truly memorable phenomenon. Then the outlines faded, to leave two dull-red heart-shaped aeroforms that gradually faded also, one above each copse. The hour was not very late, yet apparently we were the only witnesses. No reports came in from the district. It could have been a traumatic impression only, purely psychic, apart from one indisputable fact: Not one of us saw these wonders, but four.

I shall be eternally ridiculed if I dare to mention my third indelible experience in an eventful year. Suffice to reiterate, sincerely: There is undoubtedly a powerful spiritual corollary to the UFO enigma

UFO PROPHECY

WHAT DO UNIQUE UFO EXPERIENCES FORETELL?

which may indeed prove to be the primary key that will unlock the whole treasure chest of aerial mysteries.

Although flying saucers are one of the predicted 'signs in the skies,' at the same time they are a link—a purely practical help—in a gigantic mission and operation on Earth. Contacts have lately been considerably intensified. They now take place globally as a necessary prelude to a forthcoming climax. Consider the following . . . Who might be giving this advice nowadays?

'There have always been sincere seekers to be found within the church, but they have never had any decisive influence on it. This state of affairs will shortly be over. It will be the real believers who will establish the church that is to come on Earth, but mark my words:

'The church will no longer be a house along the roadside where one goes on Sundays. The church will now be drawn into everyday life. Wherefore you may find yourselves, wherever you move about, you will always be in my church; for my spirit will saturate and change everything.

'Joy and happiness will radiate from it. There will be no sulking, no gloom—it will be all smiles and happiness. It will be life and joy—it will be a delight to live! I am tired of cassocks and ruffs. I want to see rolled-up sleeves and action!

'Who performs true worship? Those who sit with their hands folded and heads bowed and do nothing, or those who are ready to act and help? Churches and synagogues—let all of these belong to the past. All kinds of religion will now melt together into one in my coming, in true compassion and love.'

Always victors are those attuned to guiding dictums of the Spirit of Creation, whose finger is forever on the pulse of the Universe, from the blazing heart of star clusters in the vast firmament to the farthermost capillaries of light and life marking inhabited planets.

In spite of lamentable press distortions and inane descriptions of graceful spaceships, Ufology and Ufologists are terms now becoming respectable. No longer does the earnest research student have to skulk in isolated places, fearing the ridiculing pupil and iris of the public eye. That alone is a big consolation and step forward.

Man must not live in awe of the great unknown throughout his three score years and ten. Caution is a necessary safeguard; unreasoning fear is unwarranted and constitutes a barrier against closer understanding between worlds at a vexing period in our history.

UFO PROPHECY

Man must learn—and quickly—to look upon the advent of a more tangible approach to us in near future years as a beautiful, timely experience, for Earth time as we know it could well be in short supply as space friends warn. They come at a highly critical stage of our development, not bent on arresting it where it is already proceeding along the right lines and positive vibrations, yet dedicated to putting affairs on Earth, and in the Earth, in order. This can only be effected by them.

We shall shortly be immersed in the bright light of pure understanding that shows what the signs in the sky and stirrings in the human heart are all about at this present time, as preludes of the Golden New Age and radically changed dimensional status Man must undergo in the next decade at most.

' Man has reached a stage from where he cannot actually progress further. He has reached a point where his science has outrun his spirit. Man is today able to exterminate himself and all other life on this planet. Not only that: he has reached so far that he is able to interfere, harmfully, in the Universe.

' He can interfere with the galaxy to which he belongs. This must not happen, for thereby he would interfere in such a way that it would disturb life on other planets, in other stages of the heirarchy. This the Law simply forbids, and for that reason that which has been prophesied through many years is being fulfilled.

' Man's sciences have reached far, his knowledge is multifarious, today so great that Man is capable of doing things he cannot spiritually control. So he cannot be permitted to continue at the level on which he is moving: he has to be elevated spiritually, so that he may continue walking in knowledge he already has, plus knowledge he will acquire in future.

' This is a message of joy, a new birth of Man's spirit. Hereafter, every single person will be grateful for life, conscious of what it stands for and by whom it has been given, adapting himself and herself accordingly, voluntarily and obediently.'

That is a message from Outer Space. Truth can be boldly emblazoned in the heart of each one of us; shining through physical exteriors from love-dispensing interiors. Discovering the true meaning of religion, and practical application in spreading happiness to others in life, means that the cheerful distributor finds inward peace, contentment, joy of the spirit.

UFO PROPHECY

WHAT DO UNIQUE UFO EXPERIENCES FORETELL?

These ultimate qualities count more than any material treasures. Man carries his own 'riches' within him, once he learns how to excavate them properly. UFOs may be teaching him this and other more valuable truths, soon . . . Here are some other comments from space people:

'The most dangerous thing for you today is the owning of forces which can contaminate the whole Earth. These forces do not only strike inwards towards you, but also outwards towards us. Therefore the state of affairs has reached a peak so acute that the end of Earth time is near. What is shortly to happen to and on Earth will change everything. This change will be final and total.'

And: 'Mankind faces a war. His knowledge is now so manifold that slaughter is brought to perfection. If Mankind were not given a helping hand, spiritually and physically, all Mankind and all living things on Earth would be lost . . . A human body renews itself on the way of life.

'Cells are created and cells die. The blood is renewed and thus one creates within one's-self a new body which, however, ages. Why? Simply because one has not understood the way of life and laws of life. For this reason, the cells one creates on his way through life are influenced by the actions one commits, including those in the animal kingdom.

'Things are first created in the thoughts: later in reality. When forces of will and thought become so enormous, and Man thoroughly masters those forces, he can execute actions and deeds solely through those forces, things that Man of today cannot understand.'

Personal vibrations radiate outwardly. These are individual aura forces. If many people harbour worried thoughts, their collective aura affects the aura of their planet. Thus danger signs around a planet can be seen by more enlightened space travellers. The healthy aura and the unhealthy, neurotic aura of a whole globe, can be seen by them. On this 'second sun' theme I can expound barest details. It is worth thinking about.

Imagine that the mental, moral and spiritual thoughts of Man on Earth are reflected as a sun's rays into space. Wrongful thoughts, if persisting among a majority of people, change the aura of the planet itself and can adversely affect the sun. If, for instance, many people are desperately anxious over threats of nuclear extinction, their radiating patterns alter the planetary aura, flashing out 'danger' signals to watchers farther afield in the Universe.

As a sick individual gives warning signs in shape, texture and colour of his aura, so does an unhealthy planet. This explains more in relation to the macrocosm and microcosm referred to in an earlier chapter. The main sun can in turn influence mental and spiritual attitudes of Man, just as the collective pattern forming the 'second sun' can shoot warning signals or mute calls for help into Outer Space.

You have seen old pictures and paintings, Nativity scenes and so forth, angels depicted as wearing haloes around heads and shoulders. Sometimes a flat, gold and circular disc surmounts the halo. In modern terms transcribed from ancient truths, the halo is equivalent to the human aura.

The disc is the physical expression of the invisible reality—the individual 'second sun' which is so important as a Universal characteristic. Emanations from this second sun are most important and figure conspicuously in Cosmic consciousness we shall soon be mastering as an integral part of future existence in the New Order.

In essence, around every human there is an electromagnetic force field. Earth scientists know about this, and that electric impulses flow through the human body. The force field of the individual is simply his aura, which can be measured and registered.

The frequency of the aura is an exact reflection and guarantor of the spiritual qualities of the man in question. Very soon, according to my information, flying saucers will come in great numbers, all around the Earth demonstrating their capability of flight, appearing and disappearing, confusing many—but heralding 'a sign in the sky' everyone will see, if they have not already done so . . .

UFO PROPHECY

Conclusions

By no stretch of the imagination, elastic though it may be, is Man on Earth a complete and fully enlightened being, an acme of human perfection, his weaknesses self-recognized and transmuted. His aimless wandering and inner yearning are in urgent need of absolute direction, sensible control, wise guidance: and awareness.

A ship without a rudder and compass to keep it unswervingly on course is an unseaworthy vessel, a danger to others. Journeying into troubled waters of life pocked with unseen perils, Man is safe in any 'shipwreck' if comforted beyond doubt that rescuers are close at hand to prevent his sinking.

Yet he must never shirk individual responsibility, learning to seek positive flows and ignore negative currents. The latter are static and get him nowhere, impediments to smooth passage in travel. Without confidence in his own abilities and assurances that help is always nearby, he cannot survive submerged icebergs lurking around every jutting rock and knifing reef.

A man who makes of his life an island, cut off from civilizing influences, guarantees that it lacks purpose, substance and continuity. It has pale perception and shadowy perspective. It is an unlit canvas in the still darkened mind of the artist. It falls woefully short of maximum potential—glowing colours that can be richly exciting, stimulating to his own senses and warming frozen hearts around him.

It is therefore deficient, warped, inadequate, unbalanced, robbed of essential ingredients, propped up and vainly sustained only by vague hopes of fulfilment embraced by an average life expectancy of three score years and ten. There must be more to life than this!

This brief physical existence, this narrow bridge, is a totally false basis on which to entertain the lively traffic of contributions he can surely offer to society. Given opportunity and encouragement to overcome inherent handicaps, putting his own house in order first, he is then able to help others, constructively, to build or rebuild theirs.

Under present circumstances and conditions in a materialistic world, the personal dilemma has arisen that so few years are grossly insufficient to seek earnest knowledge of what dwells in an unfathomable sphere beyond death. What has to be accomplished before the stage is reached where, truly, death has no sting?

Many have yet to learn that reincarnation does not of necessity clash with formal doctrines, religious or scientific beliefs, despite apparent separating chasms. The human frame is but a shell, its demise equivalent to flaking free an old, outmoded sheath or skin, when taking on new form and dimension.

It is a physical vessel to be used and abandoned in due course and season, serving a temporary purpose only towards soul perfection. The soul is the living and permanent jewel, improving its texture and triumphing over ignorance and adversity the more the 'wearer' or 'container' reduces his ego in sincere searching for ultimate truths.

Genuine measures of deep concern for fellow travellers redeem many 'lost' souls. One does not have to be a philosopher or master psychologist to appreciate that inhumanity of Man towards Man applies as much today, in a relatively civilized and affluent society, as it did in the Middle Ages.

Sensitive to the needs of the less fortunate on lower rungs of the evolutionary ladder, rational elements in the community know that only full knowledge of Universal Truth in all its beneficial and transcendental aspects can satisfy the questing soul; can supply missing, vital fragments of a jigsaw puzzle that Man represents in an Earth-bound concept.

Amassing of scientific or religious data in the storehouse of the mind does not present clear insight to final answers. There must be correct balance of both, plus the elusive 'X' quality that binds both together, making everyone a scientist and theologian in the highest and most rewarding sense. Until Man discovers this for himself, with startling clarity of vision that nothing short of intense self-examination in depth can achieve, he continues to feel insecure, devoid of other than superficial or artificial meaning, uncertain of precious values in life and their significance, oddly cheated by his own ineptitudes and unsure of his future destiny in the overall pattern of creation.

In all sectors of this Planet of Strengthening, especially at this momentous time, the consciousness of Man is changing slowly but surely. It had to happen, in face of the governmental and racialistic pandering to power-mad obsessions for building better and bigger megaton missiles of death-dealing devilment and destruction. War

UFO PROPHECY

CONCLUSIONS

and Man have gone hand-in-glove for far too long in this present civilization.

Is it not feasible that members of more enlightened societies from other planets, perhaps far outside the boundary of our own Solar System, are combining on a mission to Earth at a worrying, fretful, fearfilled phase of our evolution? Their bounden duty is to assist during the ushering in of a New Age. It is of equal probability that they are concerned over their own self-preservation if we are in danger of precipitating unretractable folly in nuclear experimentations of inflammable dimensions, aggravating the inner core damage.

The balance of Nature throughout a sizeable proportion of inhabited planets in the Universe, maybe in distant galaxies even, might be upset in calamitous depth by our ignorance of fault lines and zones in our substrata, suspect sky territory in our atmosphere proper, protective belts that girdle Earth, defects in the central gravity core of our planet, allied to changes in magnetic fields and frequency resulting from any malfunctioning.

If one adds the terminology of 'a holy crusade' to 'a combined mission of mercy' from other planetary dwellers, who have millenia ago passed through troublesome throes of nuclear technology and safe harnessing of unpredictable power, we can assume it has literal and physical urgency geared to higher mechanizms of Divinely inspired overtones.

Personally, on evidence accumulating from humble Warminster research alone, I am confident that the Old Order of things must be swept away in favour of a New Order, studded with promises of golden years stretching into eternity and unfettered by the three main retrogressive influences of War, Disease and Hunger that stifle the growth of the global soul . . .

What does the end of the world mean, in actual fact? Should we heed the plain and blunt warnings of flying friends about absolute physical collapse being the necessary prelude to the Glorious Rebirth of Earth civilization? Or should we cling to belief that the 'coming with a sword' is purely symbolical, that the 'changeover' will be in the heart and mind of Man on Earth?

The coming of Christ will usher in the Golden Age: the defects of the inner core will either be completely remedied, or allowed to accentuate to total disruption point after His coming, perhaps the whole balance of the Solar System and Sun radically changed: and Man,

UFO PROPHECY

conscious at last of his Divine purpose in life, shocked into sudden realisation by the advent of more and more UFOs appearing in the skies and landing in near future years, will turn as an obedient child to his Supreme Teacher and none other when the final curtain drops on the last act of iniquity . . .

There are changes on the 'outside' taking place which will become ever more visible and meaningful to the masses ; that much is fairly certain. But it is from the 'inside' of Man that Inspiration must come, eventually, prompted ' as lightning strikes from the East ' by the Second Advent of the Living Son of God. We dare not fail Him again !

Although still a realist, basically, I am aware that the vibrationary pattern of my life has been altered by external media of persuasion. Without hesitation, I affirm that the spiritual corollary to physical and practical reasons for the coming of the UFOs strongly exists. My candid opinion, after very careful thought and assessment of happenings on the Warminster front, used so frequently by flying friends from other aerial continents, is :—

Changes must be enormous to be 'total and absolute.' We would be well advised, therefore, to effect great changes for the better within ourselves to make sure the pendulum of our future evolutionary clock swings to our advantage . . . Time is a relative quantity, but will have a special effect in our transition into fourth dimensional status. The space-time continuum means far more than we imagine in our un-tutored simplicity. Vibrational qualities of sound and colour are factors whose future importance will quickly dawn, too, on our receptive faculties, I am given to understand. The nine-tenths of untapped mental energy we shall be permitted to employ, granted we measure up to expectations at and before the Coming, will bring exciting new vistas to the fore.

At this present stage of UFO investigation, bearing in mind highly unusual and unexpected ancillary offshoots of spiritual experience that have sometimes been demonstrated in physical form. I would simply recommend that we cannot go very far wrong if we abide by the timeless principles of :

True love and concern for others ; appreciation that Something far more compelling than the human ego carries us through life ; and dedicated separation of the gold from the dross within each one of us, with conquering of weaknesses. UFOs and crews are not making meaningless joyrides in our atmosphere. Majority evidence is against

CONCLUSIONS

any prospects of physical and forceful invasion and take-over. They come in ineffable peace, hoping to find matching attitudes and emotions from Earth brothers when the Great Day comes.

Preparations cannot be engineered too soon! By the end of 1974, at latest, my humble guess is that many amazing things will have come to pass... And, if some readers imagine that I must have had a spiritual brainstorm to bring forth these conclusions, may I solemnly assure them that I am just as great a realist as ever, as my reporting work shows to many satisfied editors. It is the horizon of my personal vision which has widened in recent months—and, condemned and reviled though I may be in certain quarters, I stick to these conclusions, come what may!

For the moment, I would meekly ask harsh critics to wait until the end of 1974 before flaying the hide off my reputation, as a journalist and as an individual. Surely that is fair enough? Let us wait and see...

* * * *

Going back to David Holton, of Crockerton, near Warminster, who is a registered homoeopathic practitioner, surgical chiropodist and medical herbalist... He believes the UFO manifestations are attributable to etheric energies.

He says that the release of these energies from the soil, and more particularly from the soil of the tumuli, plague pits, graveyards and battlefields around Warminster, is the cause of strange occurrences which have mystified people all over the world.

'Energy cannot be destroyed, only changed from one form to another, and this process going on in soil receiving the mortal remains of Man from the time he first appeared on this planet has resulted in an enormous build-up of subtle energies which are released periodically for good or ill.

'This is very similar to a radioactive mineral slowly breaking down and giving off harmful radiation in the process. The energies released from the atoms of our mortal forms are modified by disease processes in life and by the activities of such subtle etheric forces as mind at work through our entire being during life.'

He maintains that UFOs, or a large majority of them, are not material objects but etheric emanations appreciated by extra-sensory perception.

UFO PROPHECY

Therefore, they do not register their presence on any radar screens. Asked to account for noises reported by some witnesses of unusual objects in the sky, he said one can hear at the ESP level as well as see.

'Are the Warminster "things" back?' asked a headline on the front page of the *Wiltshire Times and News* dated Friday, July 5th of 1968. It recounted that three saucer-shaped objects were watched for an hour by two women at Great Cheverell, near Devizes, 'like nothing we have ever seen before.'

Housewives Mabel Wilshin and Constance Clements were out with a dog at 10.15 p.m. Mrs. Wilshin said: 'We then saw these three saucer-shaped objects in the sky. They were very dark against the sky and then something like a ball appeared. It was even blacker and seemed to move back into the sky. Two of the other objects disappeared, leaving one big one which after a time appeared to divide in two. Another seemed to come out of it and appeared much lighter. There was not a cloud in the sky. They appeared to the N.W. of the village and not very high. We watched them until 11.15 p.m.'

Mrs. Clements said the outlines were far too sharp and definite for the objects to be clouds. 'I called my husband out to have a look when we got back to the house.'

Mr. George Clements, of Stanley Terrace, Devizes, said he saw them quite clearly, but by then they were drifting away. They did not appear to be much higher than a tree. He would very much like to know what they were. Perhaps the content of this book will help enlighten the trio of witnesses.

Mrs. Wilshin lives at the Homestead, Great Cheverell.

UFO PROPHECY

Above: "The Thing." UFO over Warminster - Photo taken by Gordon Faulkner

Below: Cradle Hill, October 1, 1967. UFO beginning to move right after hovering. Seen by over 30 witnesses - Bob Strong.

NORDIC LOOKING ALIENS GIVE HITLER PLANS FOR A TIME TRAVEL DEVICE!

THIS IS BY FAR THE MOST SHOCKING AND POTENTIALLY TROUBLING BOOK WE HAVE EVER PUBLISHED.
IT COULD VERY WELL CHANGE THE FUTURE— AND THE TRUTH IS—IT MIGHT HAVE ALREADY!

Here is disturbing evidence that Hitler had a top secret brigade of Nazi engineers working in deep underground laboratories – in conjunction with off world interstellar cosmonauts – to establish space flight and time travel, years before the start of America's rocketry program in which the U.S. sought the help of thousands of Nazi war criminals bought into this country under the auspicies of the tight lipped Project Paperclip. Information recently obtained by the authors indicates that the UFO that crashed outside Roswell might have been part of this Nazi space/time travel program cleverly covered up by our military in order to look like the arrival of an out of control interplanetary vehicle. The top brass was ultimately looking to cover their tracks which showed that they were inappropriately working in tandem with war criminals, whom they had excused of all evil misdeeds, eventually giving them citizenship. This "wonder weapon" and time travel device was named Die Glocke or "The Bell," and it is probably being seen and flown to this day; some even manned by Aryan- looking occupants (possibly Ets).

Devices like "The Bell" may have been used to bend both space and time and give the Nazis the unthinkable power to explore the past freely and even to CONTROL THE FUTURE. Are we plummeting headlong toward a world under fascist domination – a nightmare in which sadistic, jackbooted thugs are waiting for us to "catch up" in time with our own predestined subjugation to open worldwide rule by the Nazis, possibly hiding out on the surface of the moon or at "secret cities" at the Poles? Do they lie in wait for us as the clock on our freedom runs down?

The shocking facts can be read in NAZI UFO TIME TRAVELERS / Just $20 + $5 S/H

── **WANT TO READ MORE?** ──

☐ **THE OMEGA FILES: SECRET NAZI UFO BASES REVEALED!**

Did Hitler's henchmen escape from Germany and set up secret bases at the South Pole and deep in the Amazon? Are they operating from these top secret quarters to establish a Fourth Reich and take over the world? – **$21.95**

☐ **UFOS NAZI SECRET WEAPONS**

Banned in 22 countries the author was imprisoned for over 20 years because he spoke out on this controversial topic. Did the SS have its own arsenal of super secret weapons which they planned to unleash? Here are pages of drawings showing these devices along with German plans of operation. – **$24.00**

☐ **THE SECRET SPACE PROGRAM**

Do we already have bases on the Moon? Who is responsible? Tesla? Nazis? Secret Societies? NWO? Something pretty damn strange is happening under our very eyes! – **$24.00**

FREE AUDIO CD OF THE MYSTERIOUS INTELLIGENCE OPERATIVE COMMANDER X TALKING ON THE NAZI UFO SPACE PROGRAM WHEN ORDERING TWO OR MORE TITLES FROM THIS AD. Special – All 4 books this advt $79.95 + $8 S/H

TIMOTHY G BECKLEY, BOX 753, NEW BRUNSWICK, NJ 08903

ALL TITLES AVAILABLE ON AMAZON.COM — PRINT AND KINDLE EDITIONS.

ARE ANCIENT ALIENS THE CUSTODIANS OF EARTH?
HERE ARE NEW LINKS TO THE SPACE GODS

They have been with us since the dawn of civilization, an intricate part of our religious and cultural belief systems. They have guided us, prodded us and perhaps even tried to control us. Some say they are the custodians of the planet, that they are here to show us the path to enlightenment. Others see them as being more nefarious in their intentions. Here at your fingertips are insightful works that reveal the secrets of the ages.

☐ **LEGACY OF THE SKY PEOPLE** Is there an ET origin for Adam and Eve? The Garden of Eden? Noah's Ark? As early as the 1960s, Britain's 8th Earl of Clancarty, Brinsley Le Poer Trench, made an astounding revelation that life on earth had originated on the planet Mars and the first voyagers here had been the Biblical couple. Thus the roots of the various Biblical stories taught to this day. With added material by Nick Redfern, Tim Beckley and Sean Casteel, questions include: Why the CIA and the military show an unprecedented interest in the remains of what many claim to be Noah's Ark that came to rest on Mount Ararat? Is there a new race of humans being formed in these uncertain times? According to the Earl of Clancarty, some of us are rapidly reacquiring the telepathy and psychic abilities we were originally created with. **$20.00 + $5 S/H**

☐ **ALIEN SPACE GODS OF ANCIENT GREECE AND ROME** Was the Mediterranean region of our planet visited by a race of "Super Beings" in ancient times? Was the Oracle of Delphi a conduit for prophetic messages from outer space – perhaps the first telepathic channeler? Researcher W.R. Drake asks: Did giants from space establish a UFO base atop the picturesque Mount Olympus? – Were they the gods and goddesses of "Mythology" idolized and given names such as Apollo, Hades, Athena, Hermes, Zeus, Artemis and Hestia? – Did the powerful deities of Greece help save Athens from being invaded by the mighty armies of Atlantis in 10,000 BC? —Is there reason to believe that the Greeks and Trojans were inspired to fight for the beauteous Helen, surely a space queen? – 318 pages, **$22.00 + $5 S/H**

☐ **THE ARK OF THE COVENANT AND OTHER SECRET WEAPONS OF THE ANCIENTS** Was the Ark of the Covenant a nuclear device capable of killing large segments of the population? Did "God" give it supernatural powers? Was it responsible for the collapse of the Walls of Jericho thus allowing the Israelites to take control of the city? Was Moses able to speak directly to the Lord through the two angels positioned on the Ark's top? David Medina offers proof the ancients possessed "secret technology" that made them exceptional worriers. But how did they develop such devices on their own? Centuries ago "wonder weapons" could be found in many lands, laying waste to man and property. – **$20.00 + $5 S/H**

SUPER SPECIAL – ALL 3 TITLES $52.00 + $8 S/H
ORDER FROM: TIMOTHY G BECKLEY, BOX 753, NEW BRUNSWICK, NJ 08903

Write us for a free catalog of books and other interesting items that are sure to thrill you.

Timothy Beckley
P.O. Box 753
New Brunswick, NJ 08903

You can also send us an email at:
mrufo8@hotmail.com

Visit our website: www.conspiracyjournal.com

Also check out our YouTube Channel...Over 100 Videos, Movies and Interviews.

Mr UFOs Secret Files

https://www.youtube.com/user/MRUFO1100